TEENAGE MUTANT NINJA TURTLES

SINS OF THE FATHERS · VOL. 4

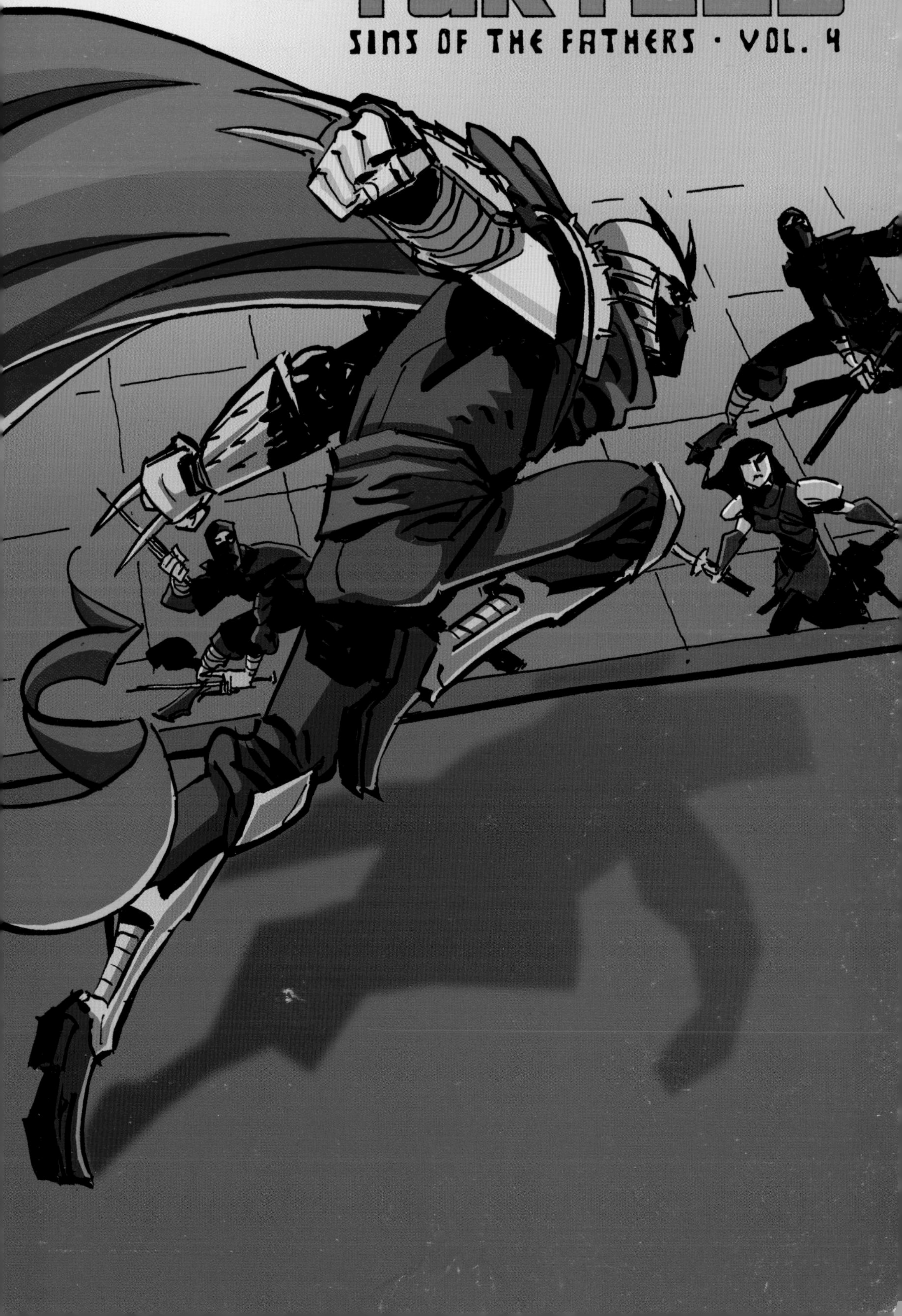

Story by Kevin Eastman & Tom Waltz • Script by Tom Waltz   Art by Andy Kuhn

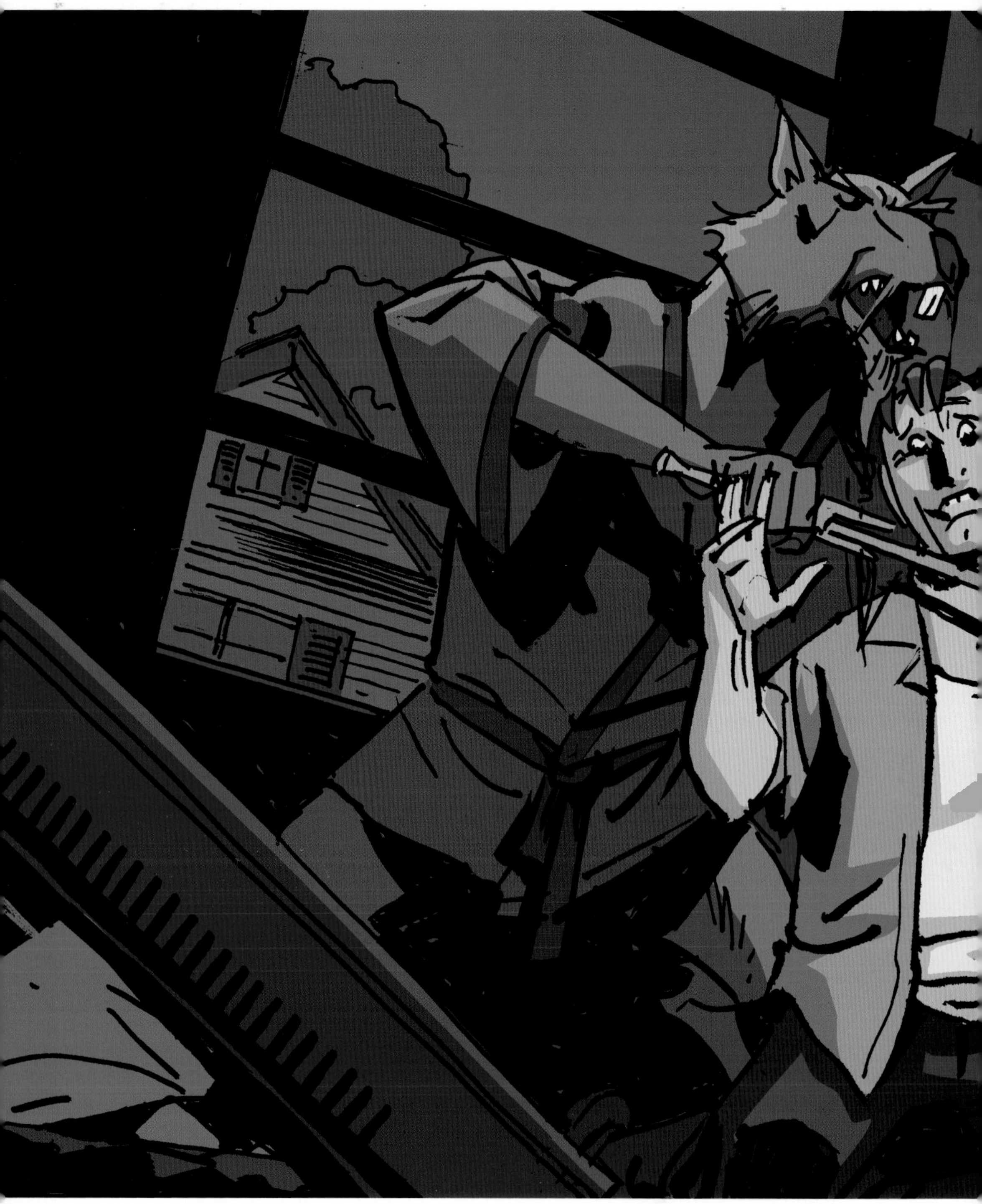

Special thanks to Joan Hilty, Linda Lee, and Kat van Dam for their invaluable assistance.

nickelodeon

IDW founded by Ted Adams, Alex Garner, Kris Oprisko, and Robbie Robbins

ISBN: 978-1-61377-568-4

16 15 14 13   2 3 4 5

IDW

Ted Adams, CEO & Publisher
Greg Goldstein, President & COO
Robbie Robbins, EVP/Sr. Graphic Artist
Chris Ryall, Chief Creative Officer/Editor-in-Chief
Matthew Ruzicka, CPA, Chief Financial Officer
Alan Payne, VP of Sales
Dirk Wood, VP of Marketing
Lorelei Bunjes, VP of Digital Services

Become our fan on Facebook **facebook.com/idwpublishing**
Follow us on Twitter **@idwpublishing**
Check us out on YouTube **youtube.com/idwpublishing**
www.IDWPUBLISHING.com

Originally published as TEENAGE MUTANT NINJA TURTLES Issues #13-16.

Colors by Ronda Pattison • Letters by Shawn Lee

Series Edits by Bobby Curnow

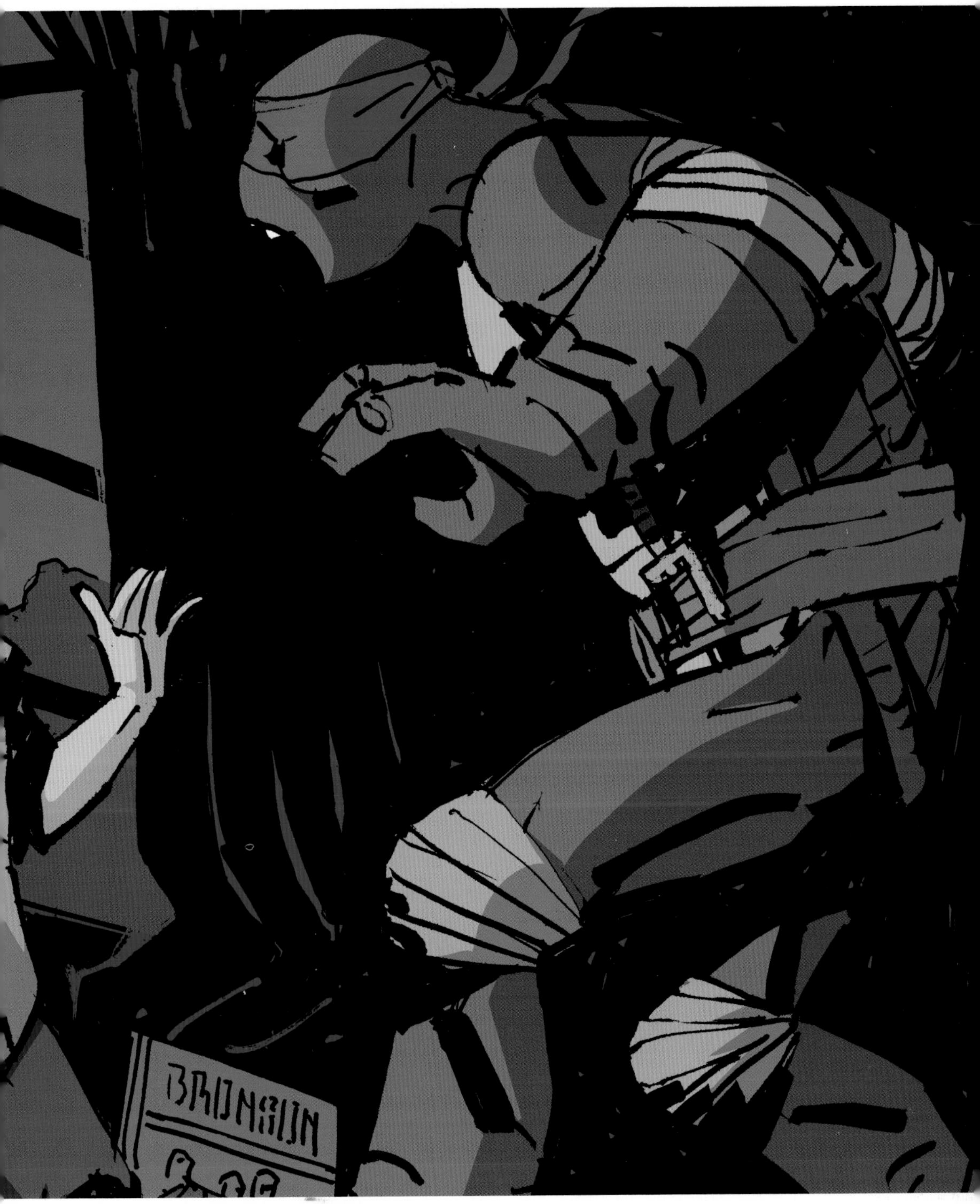

Collection Edits by Justin Eisinger & Alonzo Simon

Collection Design by Tom B. Long • Cover by Andy Kuhn

Based on characters created by Peter Laird and Kevin Eastman

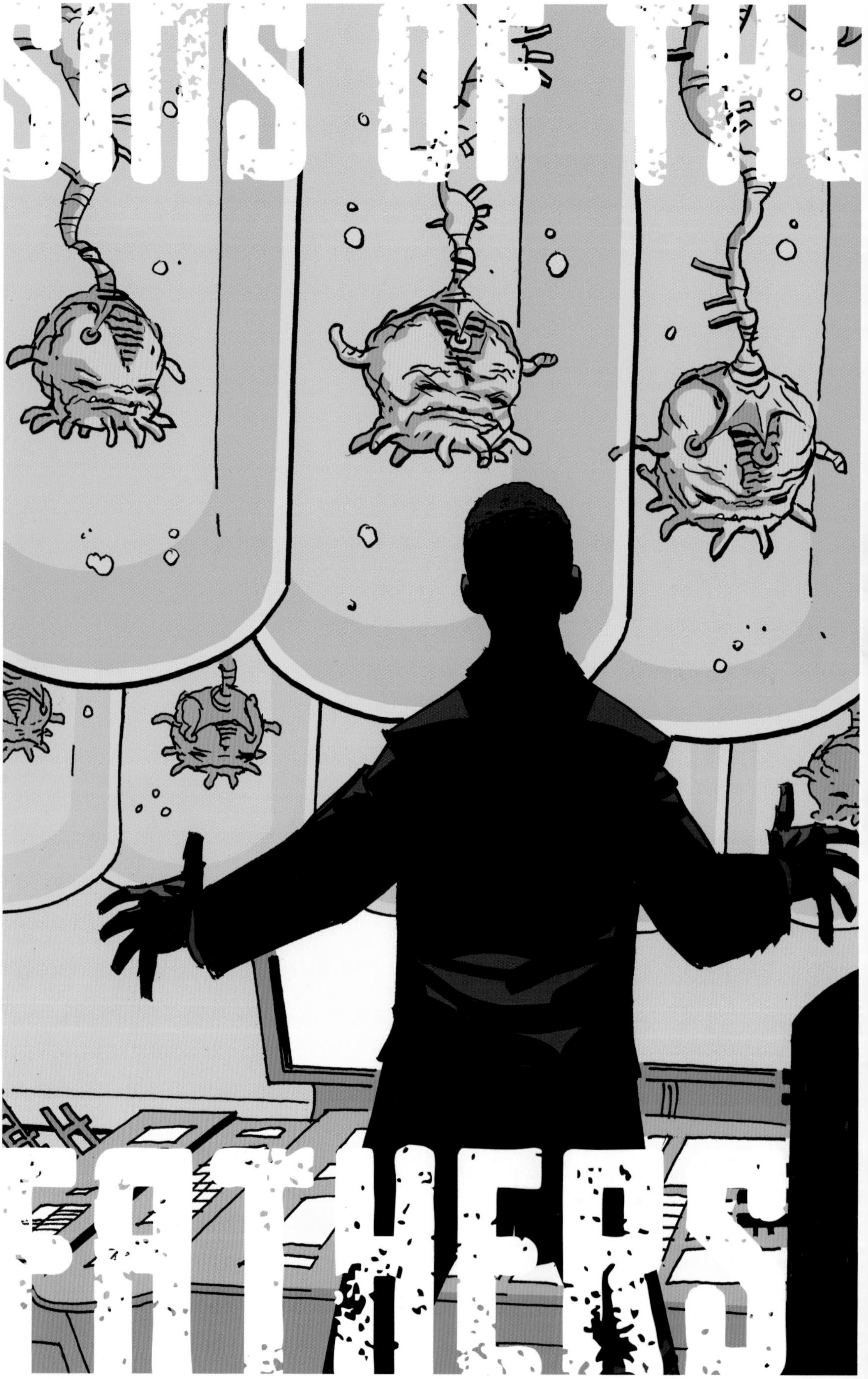
SONS OF THE
FATHERS

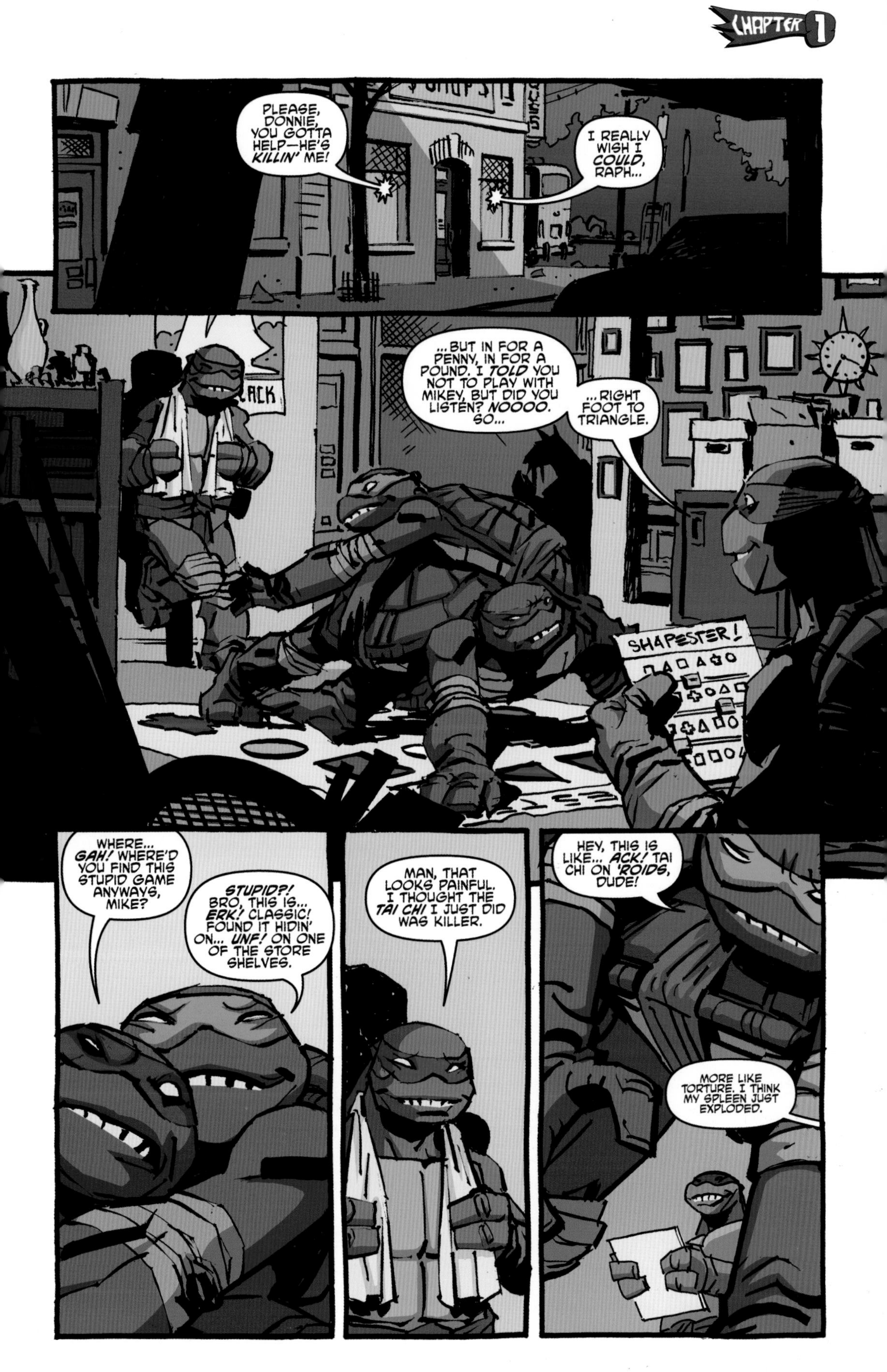
CHAPTER 1
PLEASE, DONNIE, YOU GOTTA HELP—HE'S KILLIN' ME!
I REALLY WISH I COULD, RAPH...
...BUT IN FOR A PENNY, IN FOR A POUND. I TOLD YOU NOT TO PLAY WITH MIKEY, BUT DID YOU LISTEN? NOOOO. SO...
...RIGHT FOOT TO TRIANGLE.
SHAPESTER!
WHERE... GAH! WHERE'D YOU FIND THIS STUPID GAME ANYWAYS, MIKE?
STUPID?! BRO, THIS IS... ERK! CLASSIC! FOUND IT HIDIN' ON... UNF! ON ONE OF THE STORE SHELVES.
MAN, THAT LOOKS PAINFUL. I THOUGHT THE TAI CHI I JUST DID WAS KILLER.
HEY, THIS IS LIKE... ACK! TAI CHI ON 'ROIDS, DUDE!
MORE LIKE TORTURE. I THINK MY SPLEEN JUST EXPLODED.

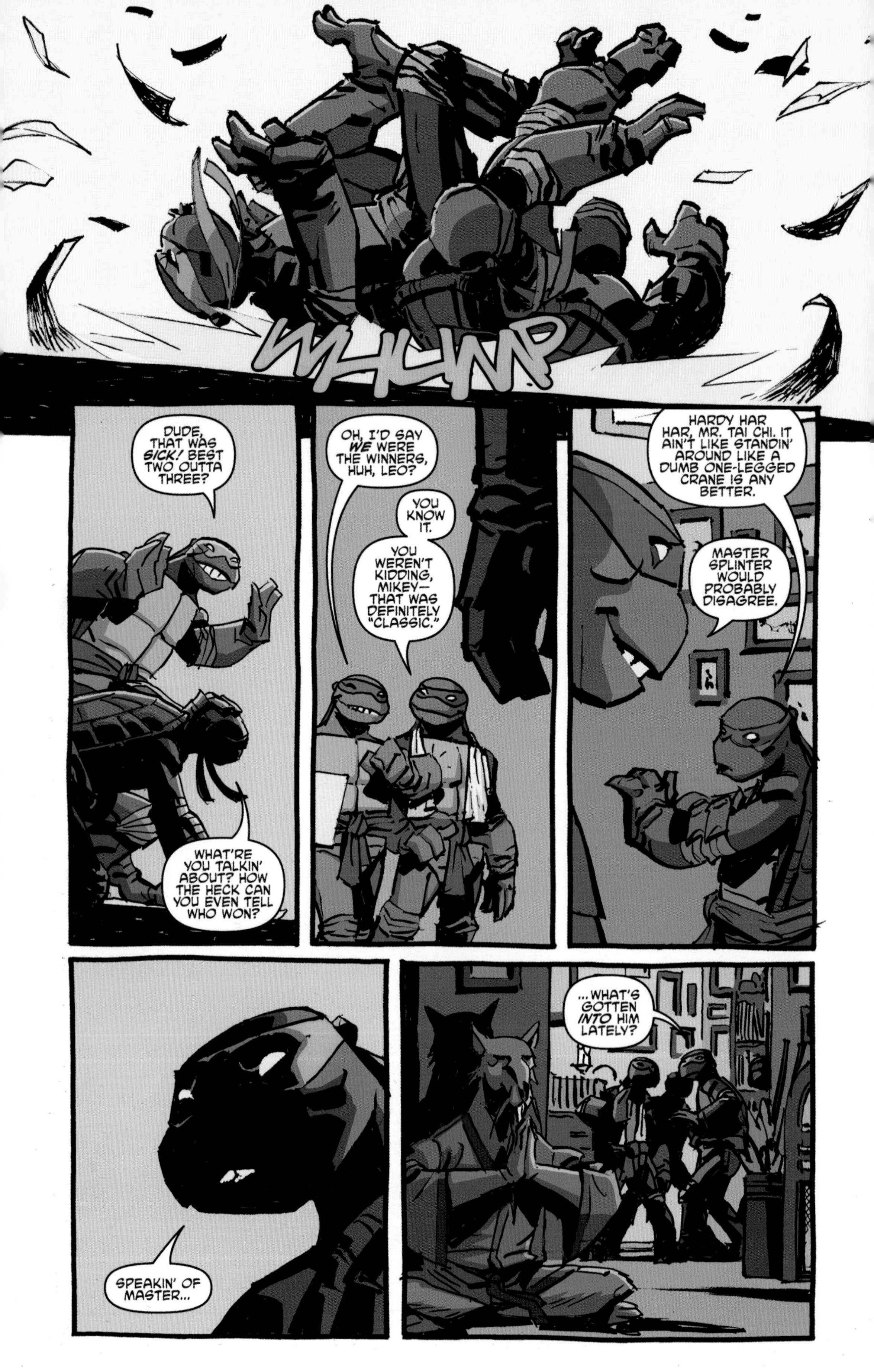

WHUMP
DUDE, THAT WAS *SICK!* BEST TWO OUTTA THREE?
WHAT'RE YOU TALKIN' ABOUT? HOW THE HECK CAN YOU EVEN TELL WHO WON?
OH, I'D SAY *WE* WERE THE WINNERS, HUH, LEO?
YOU KNOW IT.
YOU WEREN'T KIDDING, MIKEY— THAT WAS DEFINITELY "CLASSIC."
HARDY HAR HAR, MR. TAI CHI. IT AIN'T LIKE STANDIN' AROUND LIKE A DUMB ONE-LEGGED CRANE IS ANY BETTER.
MASTER SPLINTER WOULD PROBABLY DISAGREE.
SPEAKIN' OF MASTER...
...WHAT'S GOTTEN *INTO* HIM LATELY?

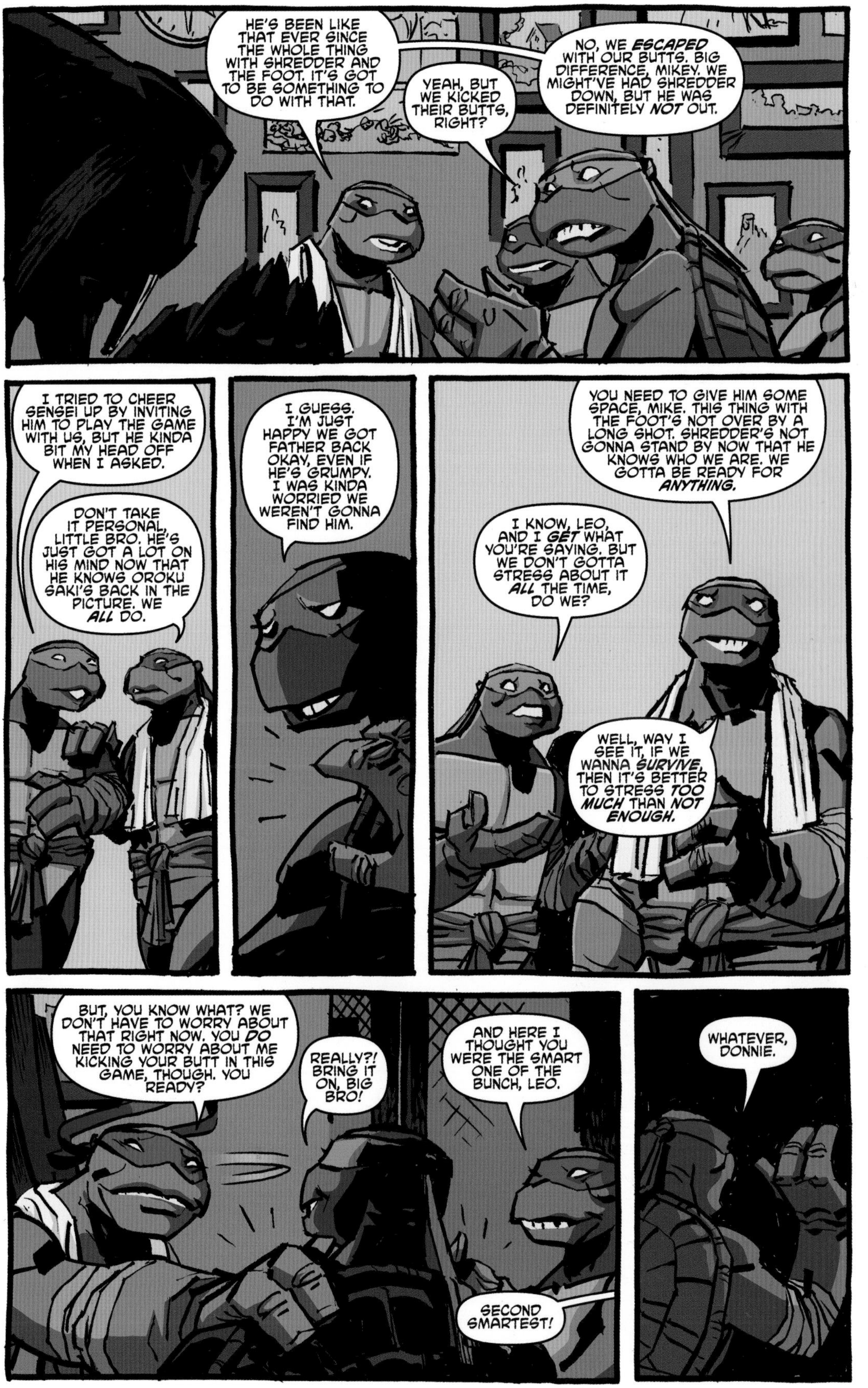
HE'S BEEN LIKE THAT EVER SINCE THE WHOLE THING WITH SHREDDER AND THE FOOT. IT'S GOT TO BE SOMETHING TO DO WITH THAT.
YEAH, BUT WE KICKED THEIR BUTTS, RIGHT?
NO, WE ESCAPED WITH OUR BUTTS. BIG DIFFERENCE, MIKEY. WE MIGHT'VE HAD SHREDDER DOWN, BUT HE WAS DEFINITELY NOT OUT.
I TRIED TO CHEER SENSEI UP BY INVITING HIM TO PLAY THE GAME WITH US, BUT HE KINDA BIT MY HEAD OFF WHEN I ASKED.
DON'T TAKE IT PERSONAL, LITTLE BRO. HE'S JUST GOT A LOT ON HIS MIND NOW THAT HE KNOWS OROKU SAKI'S BACK IN THE PICTURE. WE ALL DO.
I GUESS. I'M JUST HAPPY WE GOT FATHER BACK OKAY, EVEN IF HE'S GRUMPY. I WAS KINDA WORRIED WE WEREN'T GONNA FIND HIM.
YOU NEED TO GIVE HIM SOME SPACE, MIKE. THIS THING WITH THE FOOT'S NOT OVER BY A LONG SHOT. SHREDDER'S NOT GONNA STAND BY NOW THAT HE KNOWS WHO WE ARE. WE GOTTA BE READY FOR ANYTHING.
I KNOW, LEO, AND I GET WHAT YOU'RE SAYING. BUT WE DON'T GOTTA STRESS ABOUT IT ALL THE TIME, DO WE?
WELL, WAY I SEE IT, IF WE WANNA SURVIVE, THEN IT'S BETTER TO STRESS TOO MUCH THAN NOT ENOUGH.
BUT, YOU KNOW WHAT? WE DON'T HAVE TO WORRY ABOUT THAT RIGHT NOW. YOU DO NEED TO WORRY ABOUT ME KICKING YOUR BUTT IN THIS GAME, THOUGH. YOU READY?
REALLY?! BRING IT ON, BIG BRO!
AND HERE I THOUGHT YOU WERE THE SMART ONE OF THE BUNCH, LEO.
SECOND SMARTEST!
WHATEVER, DONNIE.

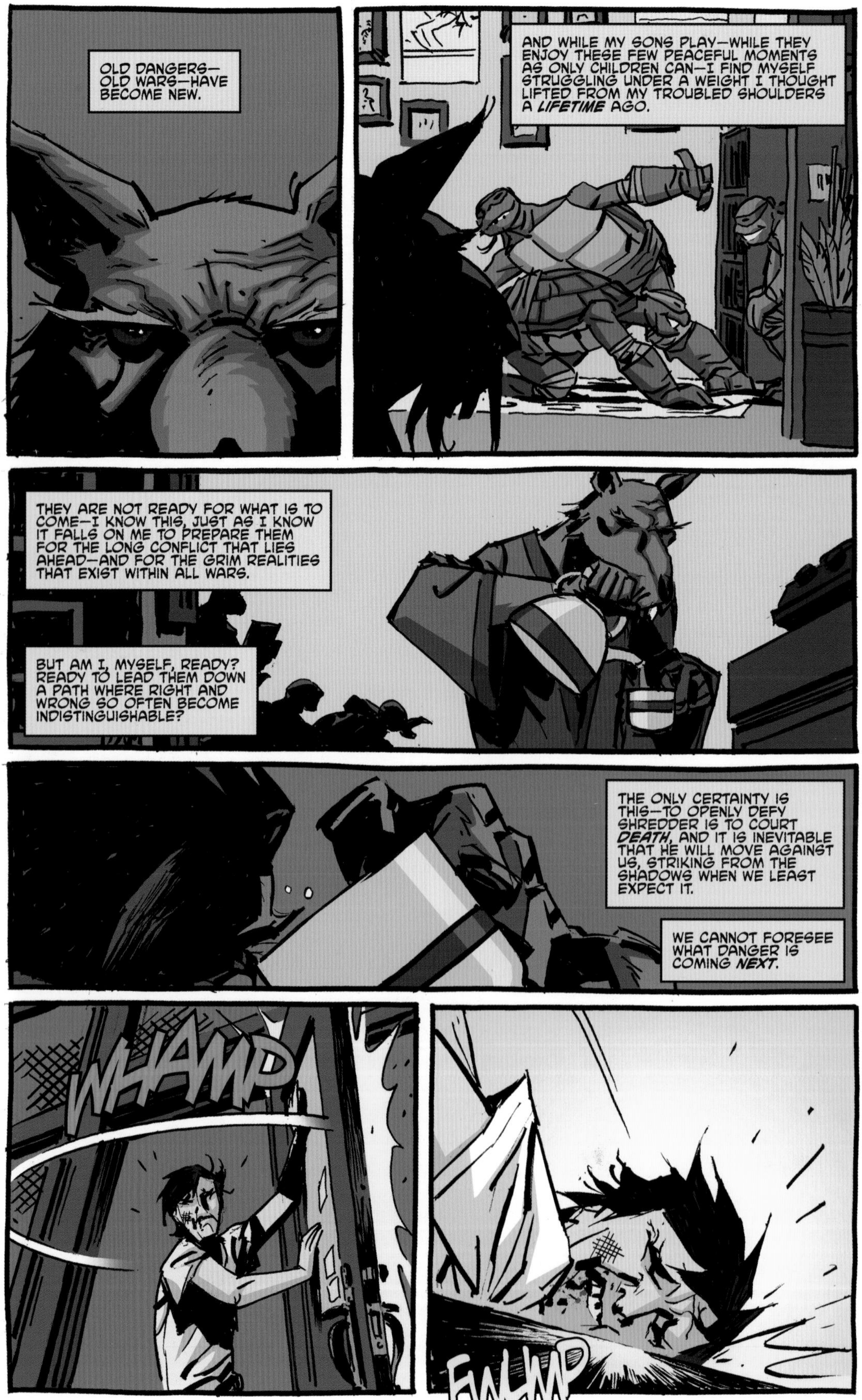
OLD DANGERS—OLD WARS—HAVE BECOME NEW.
AND WHILE MY SONS PLAY—WHILE THEY ENJOY THESE FEW PEACEFUL MOMENTS AS ONLY CHILDREN CAN—I FIND MYSELF STRUGGLING UNDER A WEIGHT I THOUGHT LIFTED FROM MY TROUBLED SHOULDERS A *LIFETIME* AGO.
THEY ARE NOT READY FOR WHAT IS TO COME—I KNOW THIS, JUST AS I KNOW IT FALLS ON ME TO PREPARE THEM FOR THE LONG CONFLICT THAT LIES AHEAD—AND FOR THE GRIM REALITIES THAT EXIST WITHIN ALL WARS.
BUT AM I, MYSELF, READY? READY TO LEAD THEM DOWN A PATH WHERE RIGHT AND WRONG SO OFTEN BECOME INDISTINGUISHABLE?
THE ONLY CERTAINTY IS THIS—TO OPENLY DEFY SHREDDER IS TO COURT *DEATH*, AND IT IS INEVITABLE THAT HE WILL MOVE AGAINST US, STRIKING FROM THE SHADOWS WHEN WE LEAST EXPECT IT.
WE CANNOT FORESEE WHAT DANGER IS COMING *NEXT*.
WHAMP
FWUMP

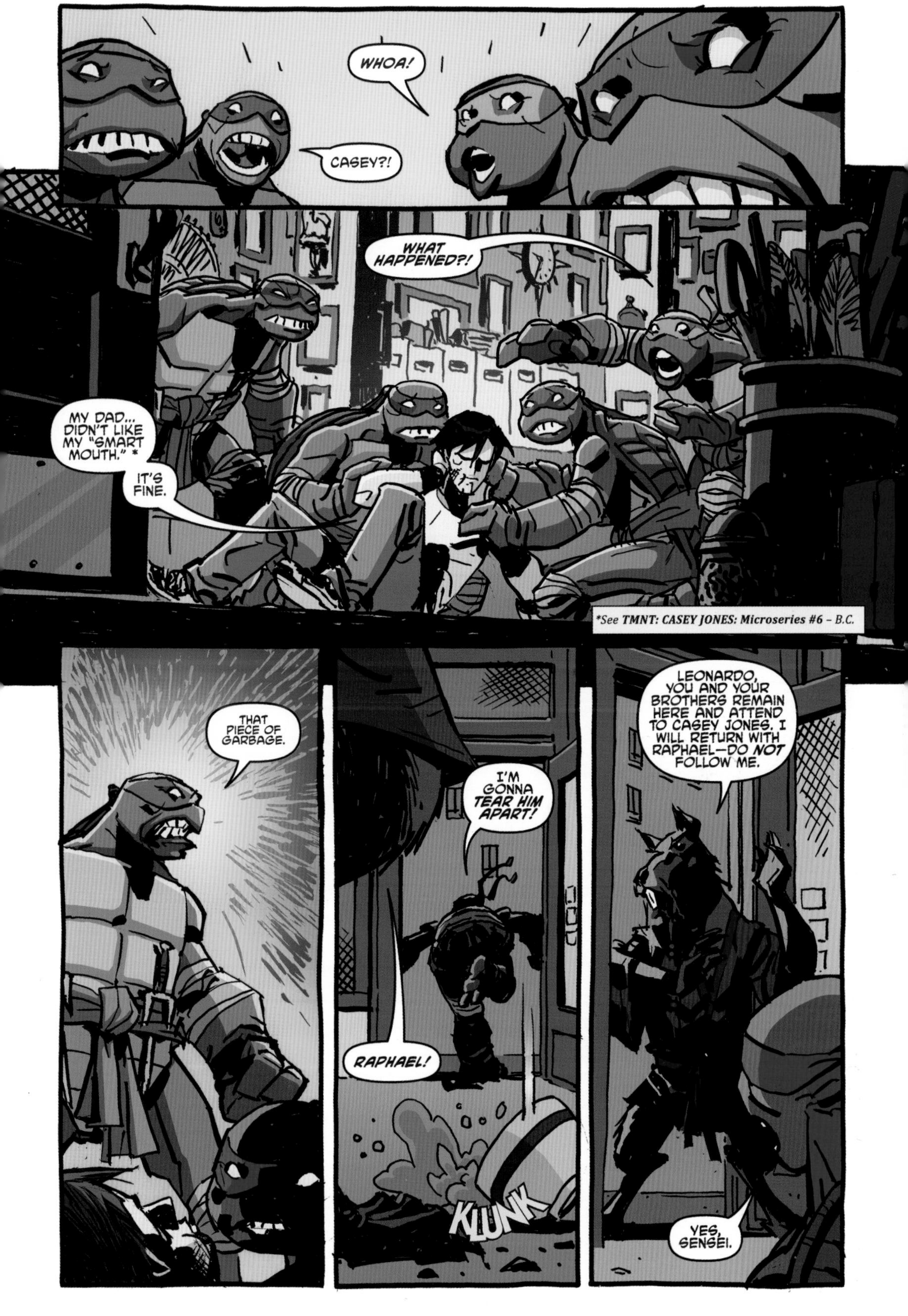
WHOA!
CASEY?!
WHAT HAPPENED?!
MY DAD... DIDN'T LIKE MY "SMART MOUTH." *
IT'S FINE.
*See TMNT: CASEY JONES: Microseries #6 – B.C.
THAT PIECE OF GARBAGE.
I'M GONNA TEAR HIM APART!
RAPHAEL!
KLUNK
LEONARDO, YOU AND YOUR BROTHERS REMAIN HERE AND ATTEND TO CASEY JONES. I WILL RETURN WITH RAPHAEL—DO NOT FOLLOW ME.
YES, SENSEI.

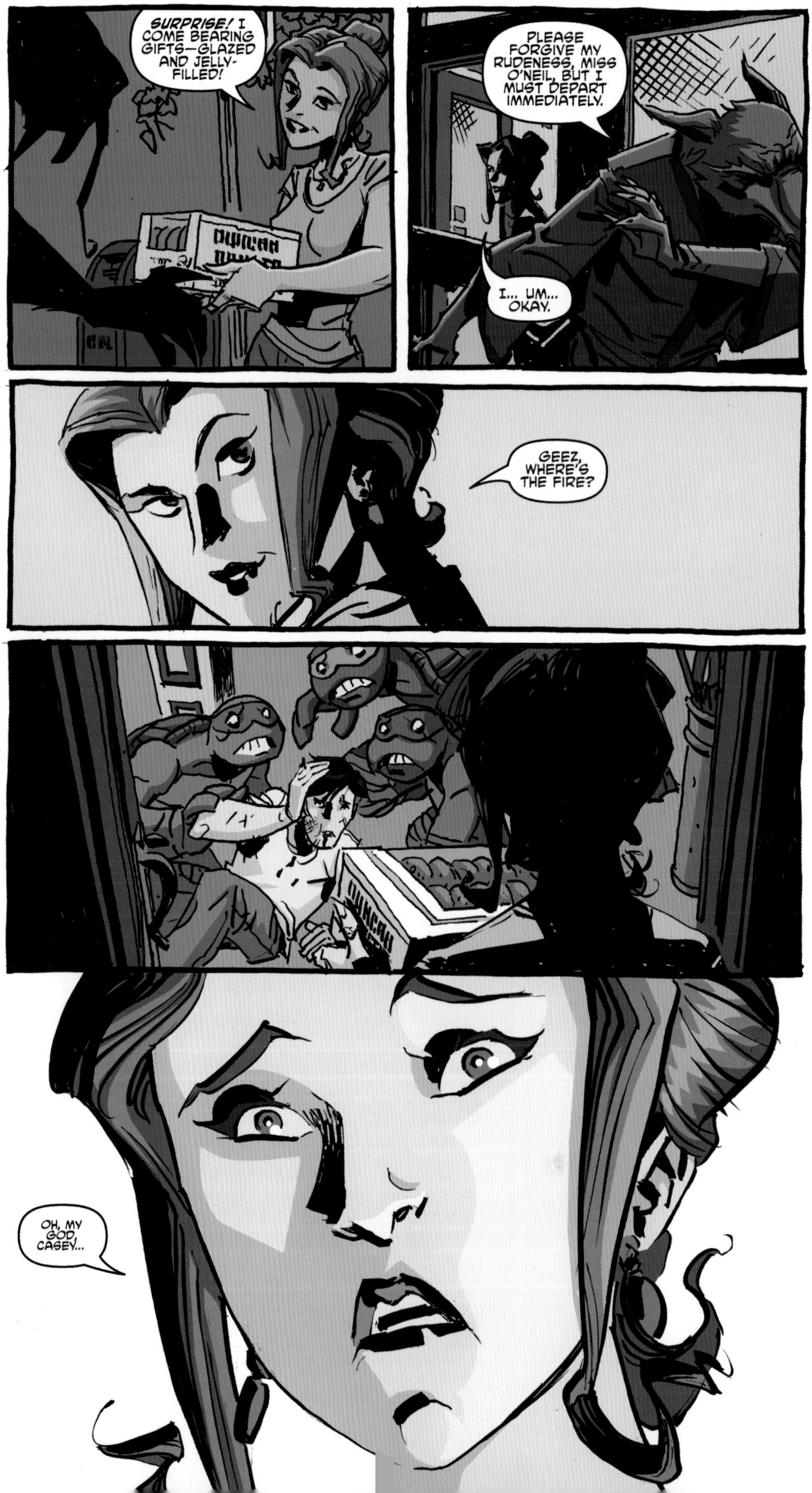
SURPRISE! I COME BEARING GIFTS—GLAZED AND JELLY-FILLED!
PLEASE FORGIVE MY RUDENESS, MISS O'NEIL, BUT I MUST DEPART IMMEDIATELY.
I... UM... OKAY.
GEEZ, WHERE'S THE FIRE?
OH, MY GOD, CASEY...

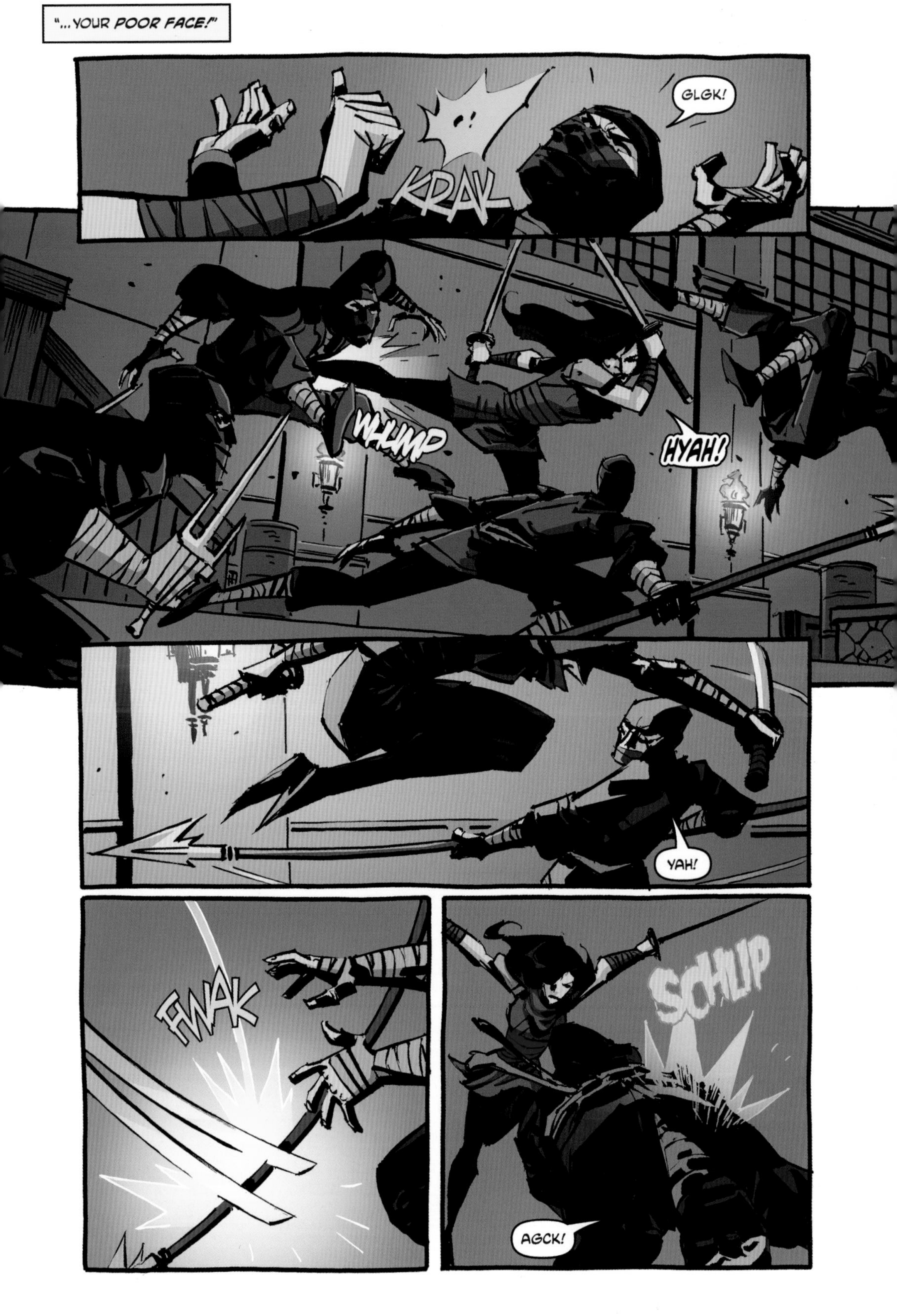
"...YOUR POOR FACE!"
KRAK
GLGK!
WHUMP
HYAH!
YAH!
FWAK
SCHLIP
AGCK!

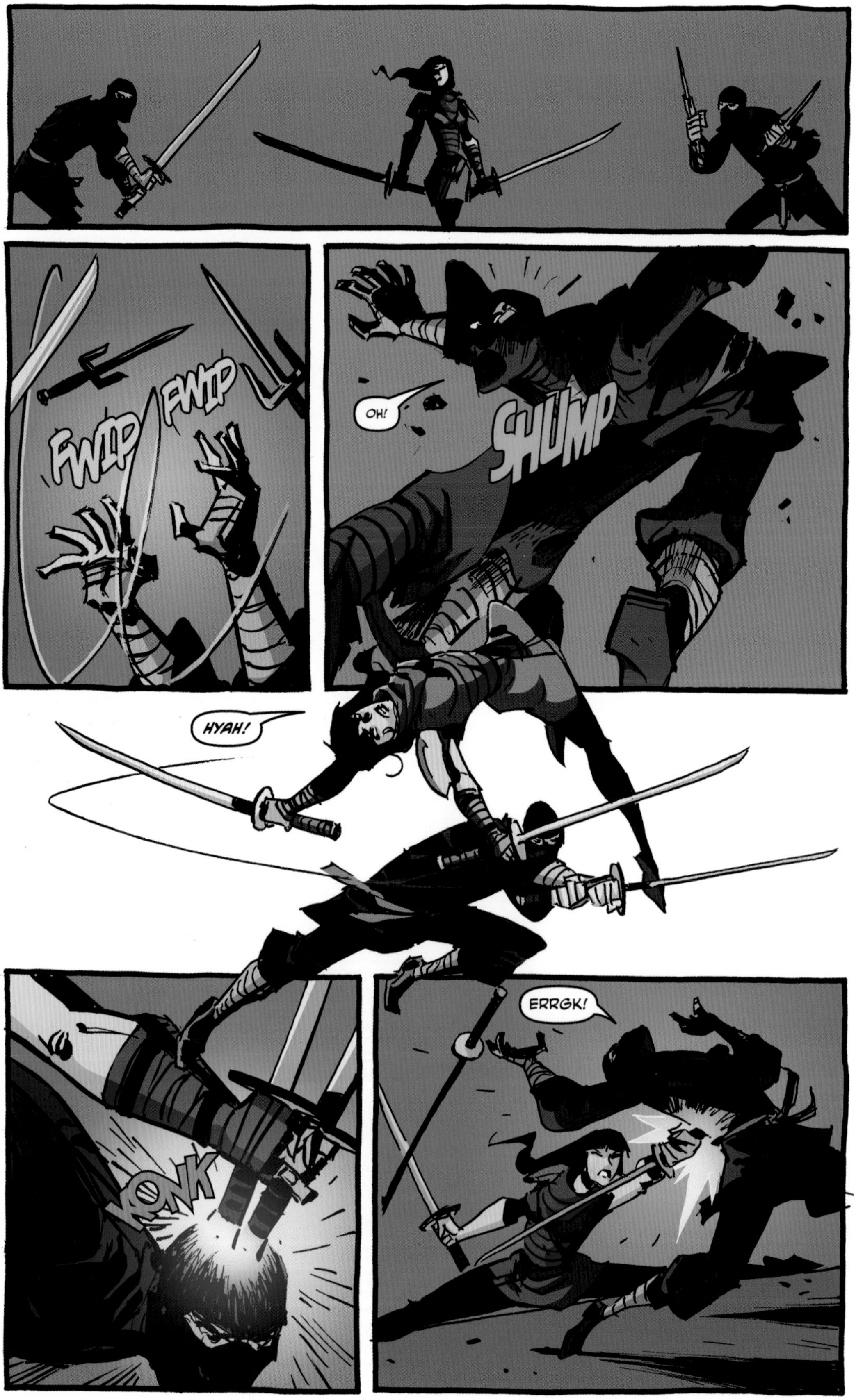
FWIP
FWIP
OH!
SHUMP
HYAH!
KONK
ERRGK!

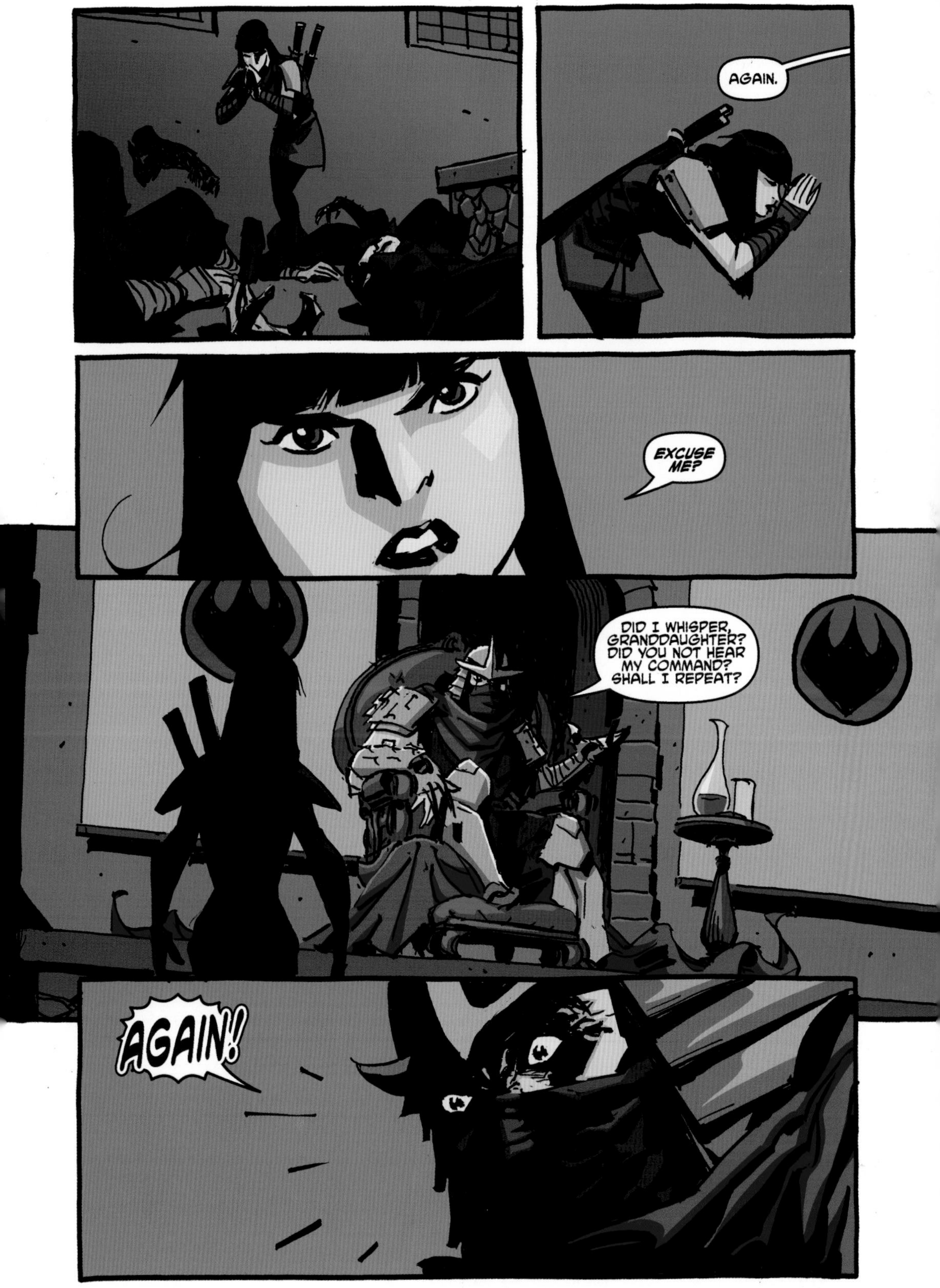
AGAIN.
EXCUSE ME?
DID I WHISPER, GRANDDAUGHTER? DID YOU NOT HEAR MY COMMAND? SHALL I REPEAT?
AGAIN!

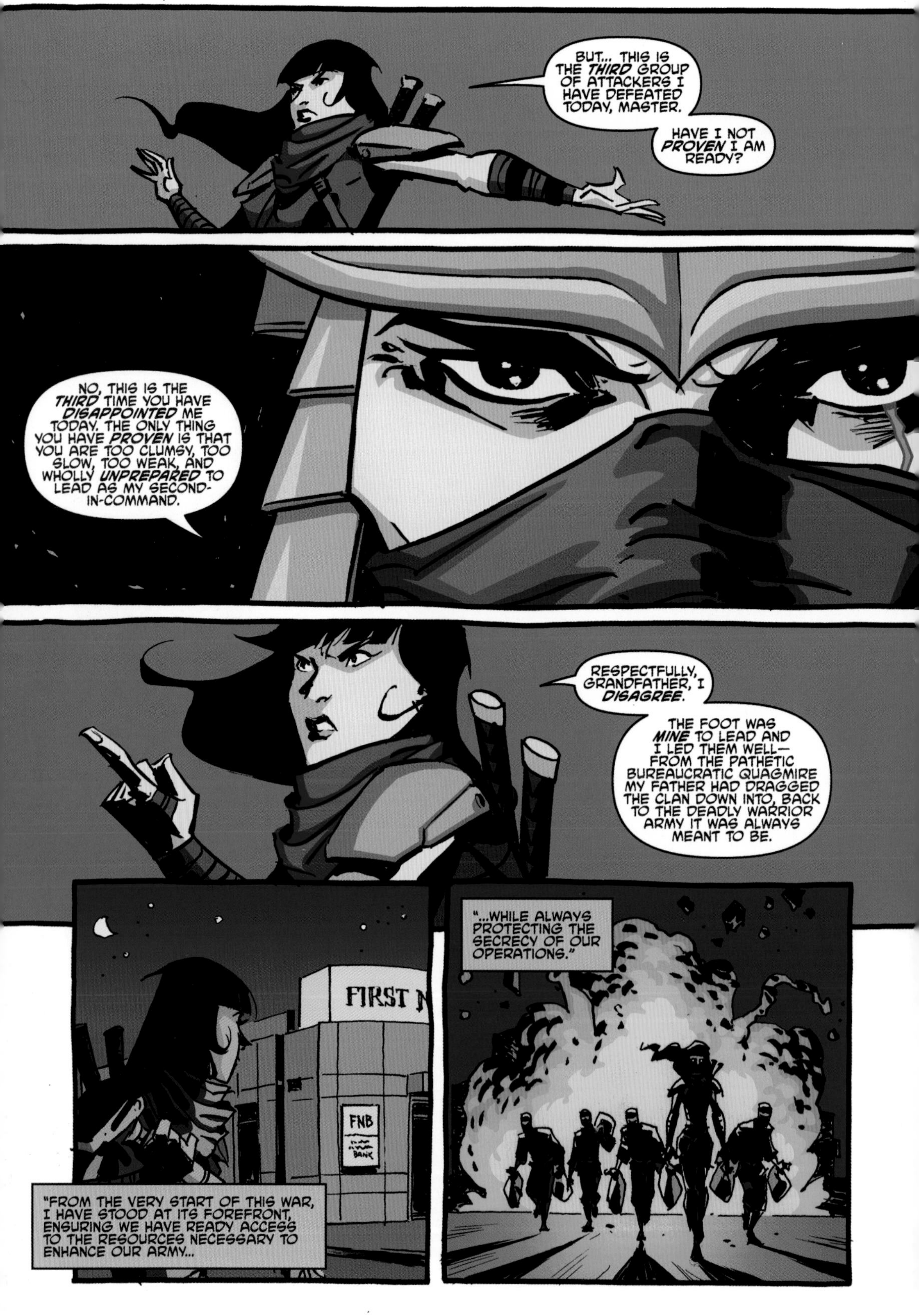
BUT... THIS IS THE THIRD GROUP OF ATTACKERS I HAVE DEFEATED TODAY, MASTER.
HAVE I NOT PROVEN I AM READY?
NO, THIS IS THE THIRD TIME YOU HAVE DISAPPOINTED ME TODAY. THE ONLY THING YOU HAVE PROVEN IS THAT YOU ARE TOO CLUMSY, TOO SLOW, TOO WEAK, AND WHOLLY UNPREPARED TO LEAD AS MY SECOND-IN-COMMAND.
RESPECTFULLY, GRANDFATHER, I DISAGREE.
THE FOOT WAS MINE TO LEAD AND I LED THEM WELL— FROM THE PATHETIC BUREAUCRATIC QUAGMIRE MY FATHER HAD DRAGGED THE CLAN DOWN INTO, BACK TO THE DEADLY WARRIOR ARMY IT WAS ALWAYS MEANT TO BE.
FIRST N
FNB
BANK
"FROM THE VERY START OF THIS WAR, I HAVE STOOD AT ITS FOREFRONT, ENSURING WE HAVE READY ACCESS TO THE RESOURCES NECESSARY TO ENHANCE OUR ARMY...
"...WHILE ALWAYS PROTECTING THE SECRECY OF OUR OPERATIONS."

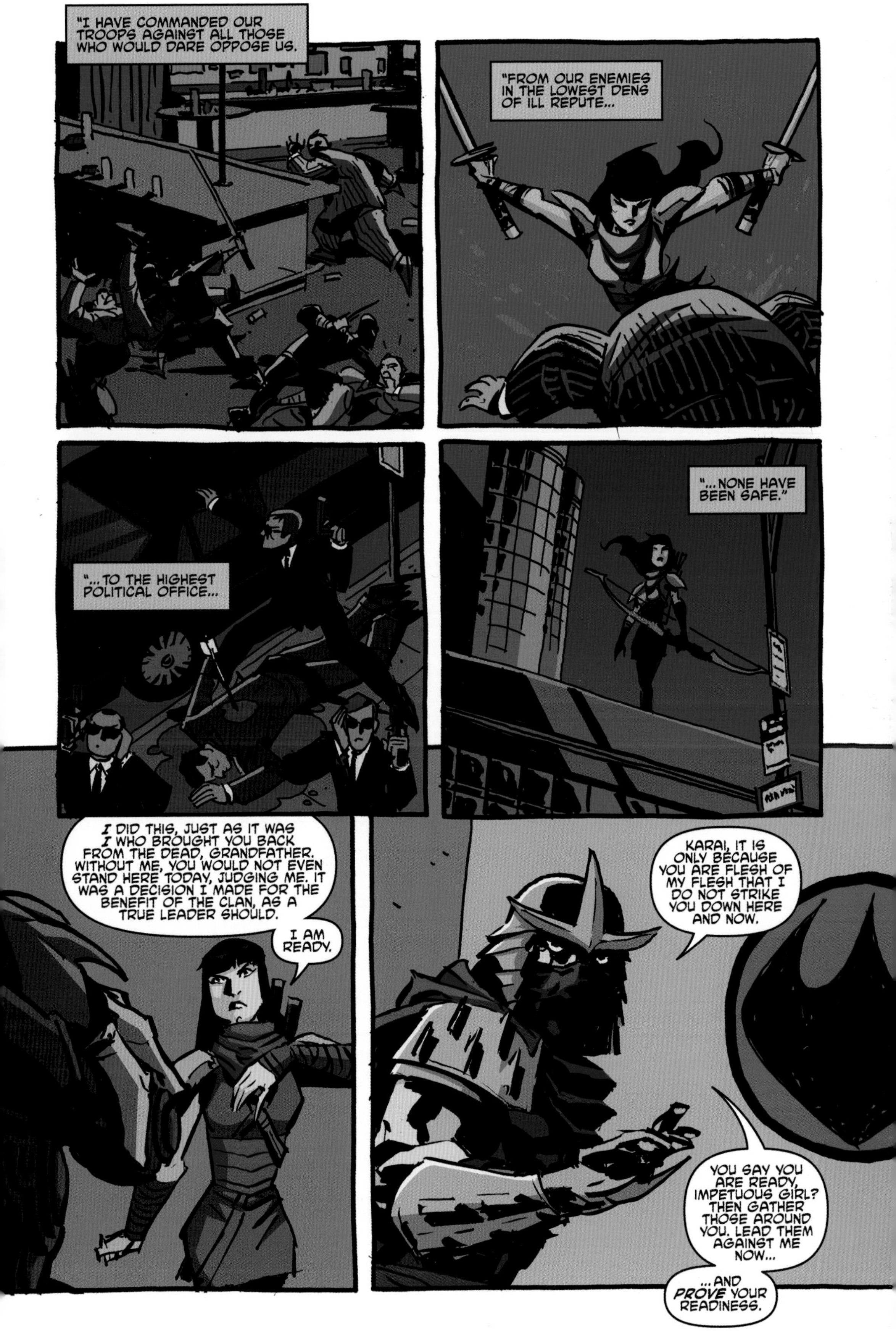
"I HAVE COMMANDED OUR TROOPS AGAINST ALL THOSE WHO WOULD DARE OPPOSE US.
"FROM OUR ENEMIES IN THE LOWEST DENS OF ILL REPUTE...
"...TO THE HIGHEST POLITICAL OFFICE...
"...NONE HAVE BEEN SAFE."
I DID THIS, JUST AS IT WAS I WHO BROUGHT YOU BACK FROM THE DEAD, GRANDFATHER. WITHOUT ME, YOU WOULD NOT EVEN STAND HERE TODAY, JUDGING ME. IT WAS A DECISION I MADE FOR THE BENEFIT OF THE CLAN, AS A TRUE LEADER SHOULD.
I AM READY.
KARAI, IT IS ONLY BECAUSE YOU ARE FLESH OF MY FLESH THAT I DO NOT STRIKE YOU DOWN HERE AND NOW.
YOU SAY YOU ARE READY, IMPETUOUS GIRL? THEN GATHER THOSE AROUND YOU. LEAD THEM AGAINST ME NOW...
...AND PROVE YOUR READINESS.

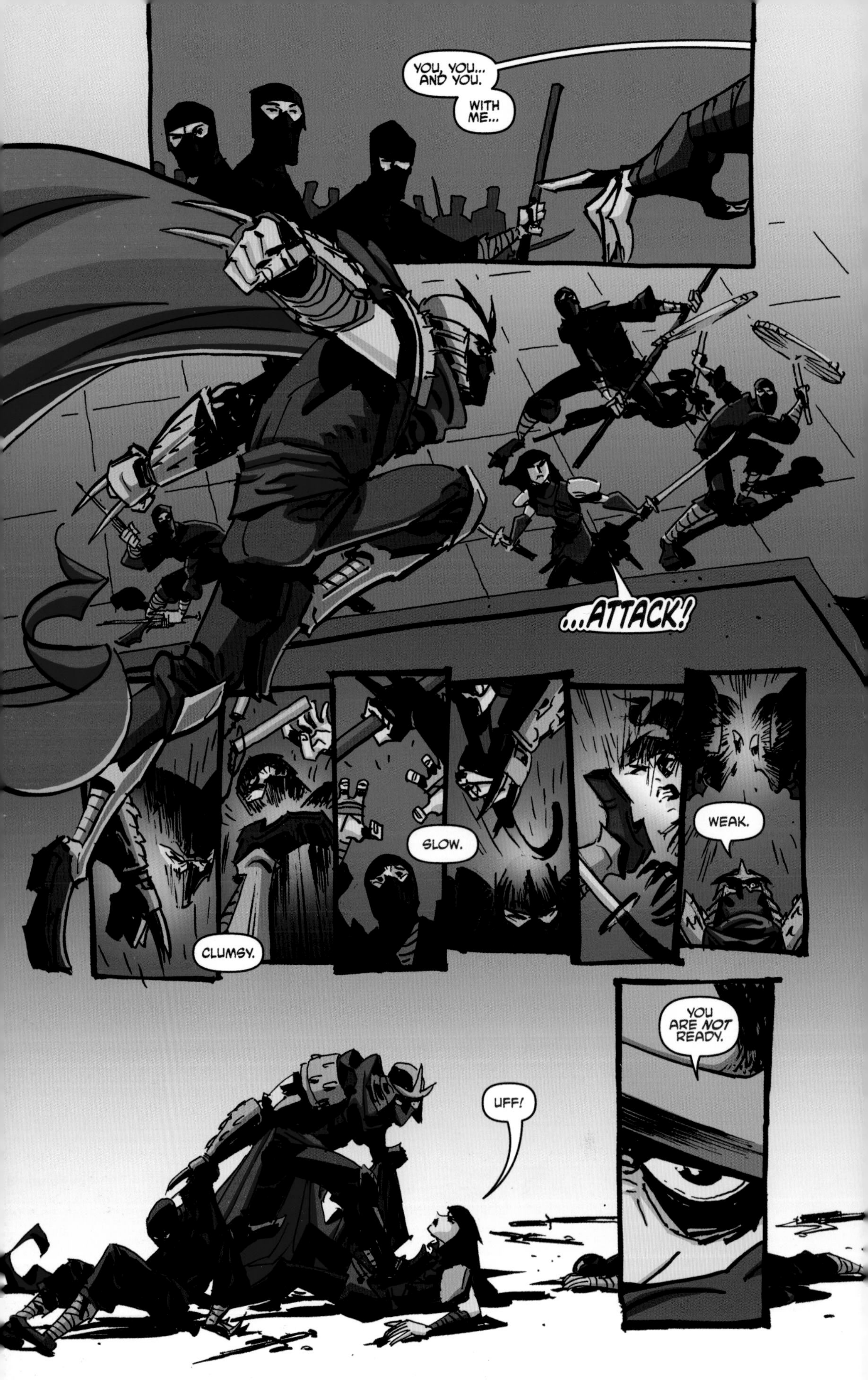

YOU, YOU... AND YOU.
WITH ME...
...ATTACK!
CLUMSY.
SLOW.
WEAK.
UFF!
YOU ARE NOT READY.

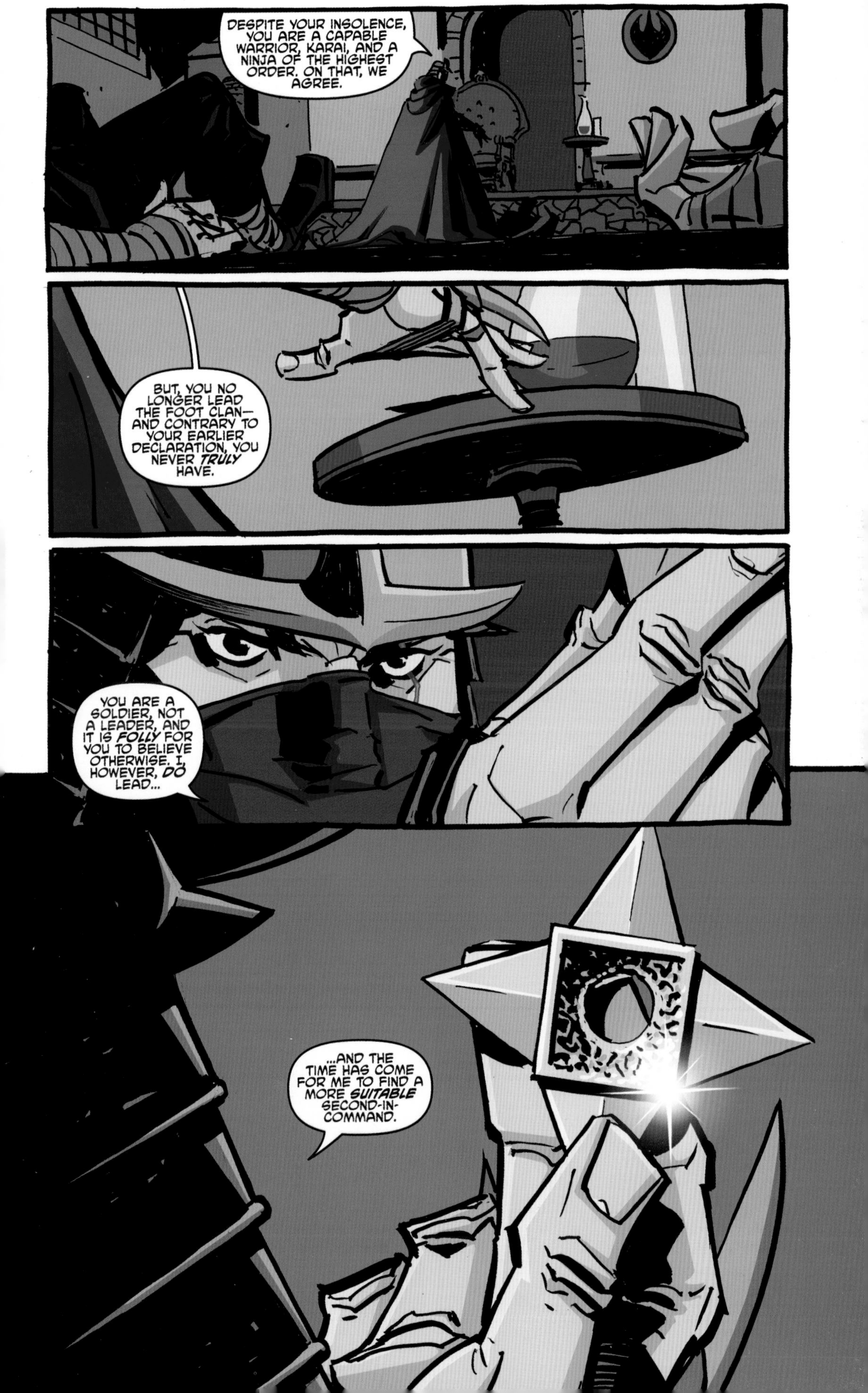
DESPITE YOUR INSOLENCE, YOU ARE A CAPABLE WARRIOR, KARAI, AND A NINJA OF THE HIGHEST ORDER. ON THAT, WE AGREE.
BUT, YOU NO LONGER LEAD THE FOOT CLAN— AND CONTRARY TO YOUR EARLIER DECLARATION, YOU NEVER *TRULY* HAVE.
YOU ARE A SOLDIER, NOT A LEADER, AND IT IS *FOLLY* FOR YOU TO BELIEVE OTHERWISE. I, HOWEVER, *DO* LEAD...
...AND THE TIME HAS COME FOR ME TO FIND A MORE *SUITABLE* SECOND-IN-COMMAND.

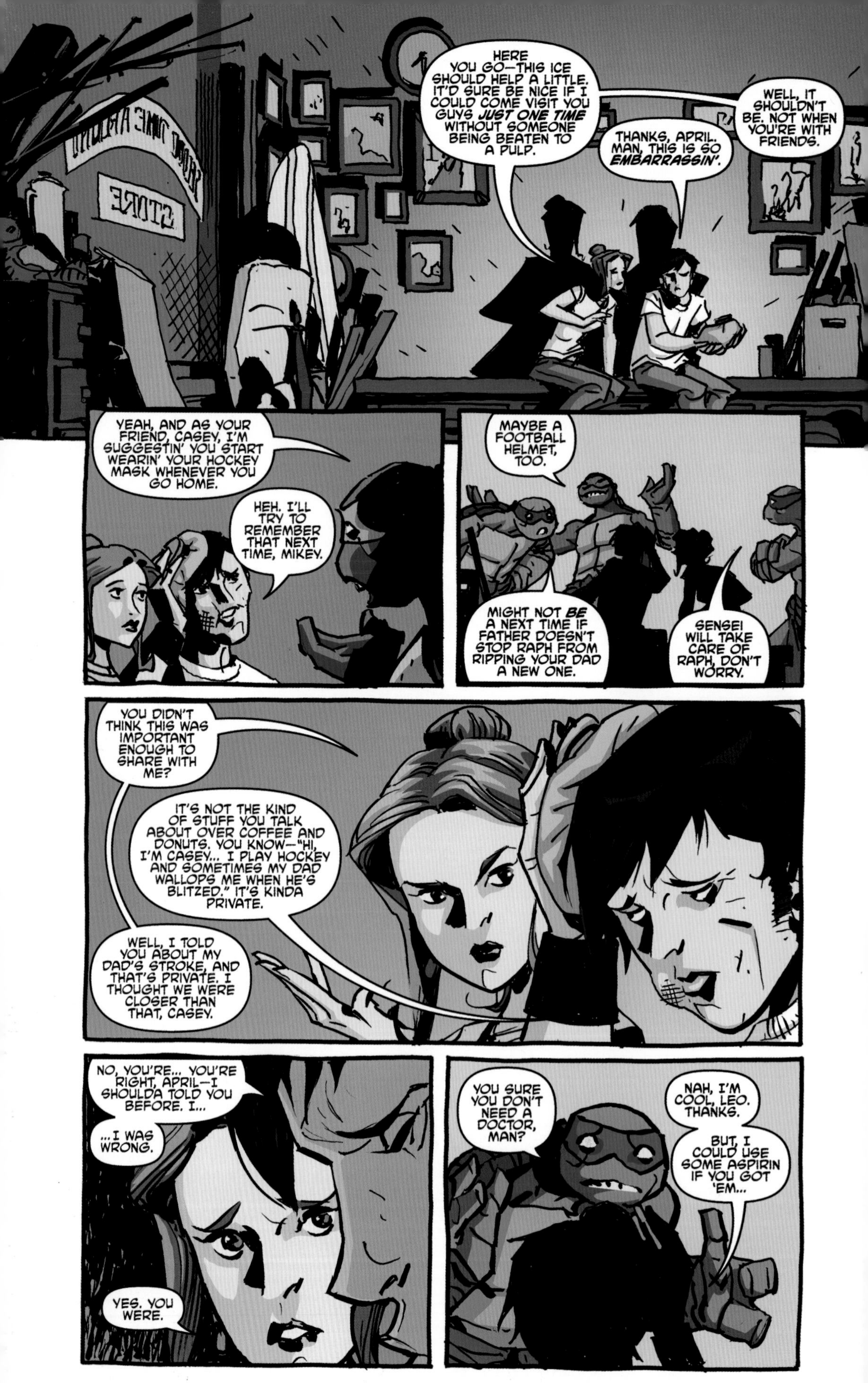
HERE YOU GO—THIS ICE SHOULD HELP A LITTLE. IT'D SURE BE NICE IF I COULD COME VISIT YOU GUYS JUST ONE TIME WITHOUT SOMEONE BEING BEATEN TO A PULP.
THANKS, APRIL. MAN, THIS IS SO EMBARRASSIN'.
WELL, IT SHOULDN'T BE. NOT WHEN YOU'RE WITH FRIENDS.
YEAH, AND AS YOUR FRIEND, CASEY, I'M SUGGESTIN' YOU START WEARIN' YOUR HOCKEY MASK WHENEVER YOU GO HOME.
HEH. I'LL TRY TO REMEMBER THAT NEXT TIME, MIKEY.
MAYBE A FOOTBALL HELMET, TOO.
MIGHT NOT BE A NEXT TIME IF FATHER DOESN'T STOP RAPH FROM RIPPING YOUR DAD A NEW ONE.
SENSEI WILL TAKE CARE OF RAPH, DON'T WORRY.
YOU DIDN'T THINK THIS WAS IMPORTANT ENOUGH TO SHARE WITH ME?
IT'S NOT THE KIND OF STUFF YOU TALK ABOUT OVER COFFEE AND DONUTS. YOU KNOW—"HI, I'M CASEY... I PLAY HOCKEY AND SOMETIMES MY DAD WALLOPS ME WHEN HE'S BLITZED." IT'S KINDA PRIVATE.
WELL, I TOLD YOU ABOUT MY DAD'S STROKE, AND THAT'S PRIVATE. I THOUGHT WE WERE CLOSER THAN THAT, CASEY.
NO, YOU'RE... YOU'RE RIGHT, APRIL—I SHOULDA TOLD YOU BEFORE. I...
...I WAS WRONG.
YES. YOU WERE.
YOU SURE YOU DON'T NEED A DOCTOR, MAN?
NAH, I'M COOL, LEO. THANKS.
BUT, I COULD USE SOME ASPIRIN IF YOU GOT 'EM...

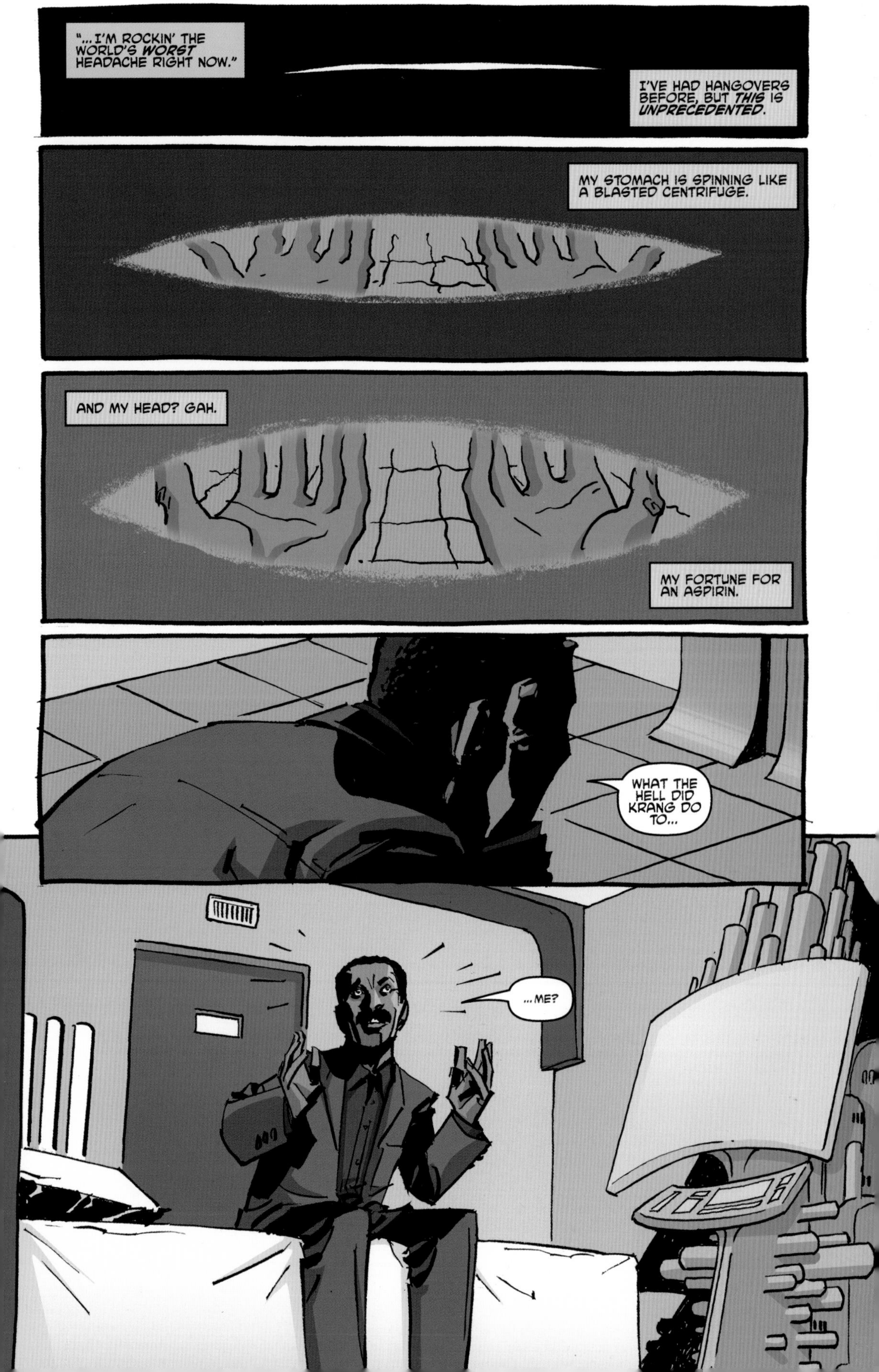
"...I'M ROCKIN' THE WORLD'S *WORST* HEADACHE RIGHT NOW."
I'VE HAD HANGOVERS BEFORE, BUT *THIS* IS *UNPRECEDENTED*.
MY STOMACH IS SPINNING LIKE A BLASTED CENTRIFUGE.
AND MY HEAD? GAH.
MY FORTUNE FOR AN ASPIRIN.
WHAT THE HELL DID KRANG DO TO...
...ME?

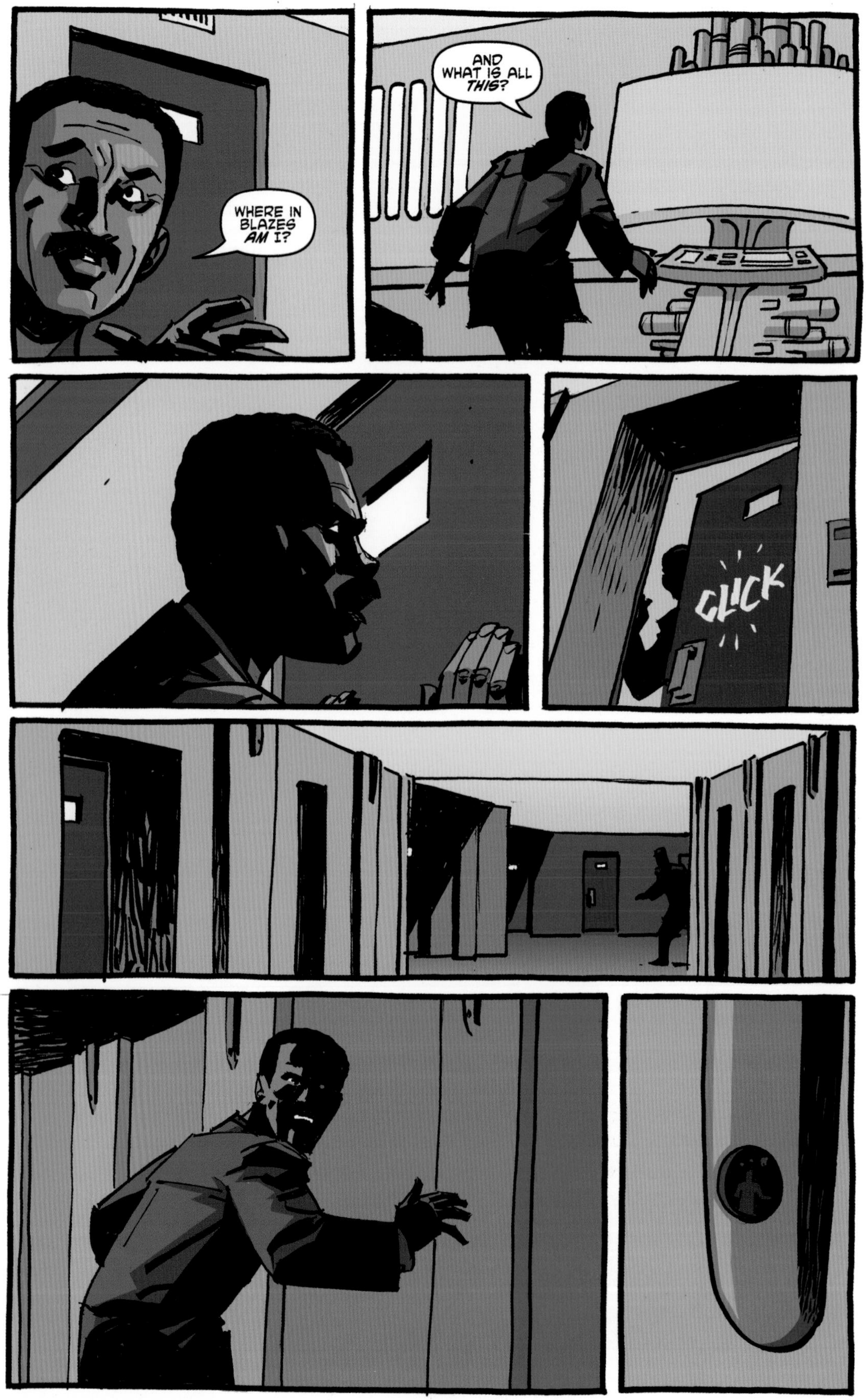
WHERE IN BLAZES AM I?
AND WHAT IS ALL THIS?
CLICK

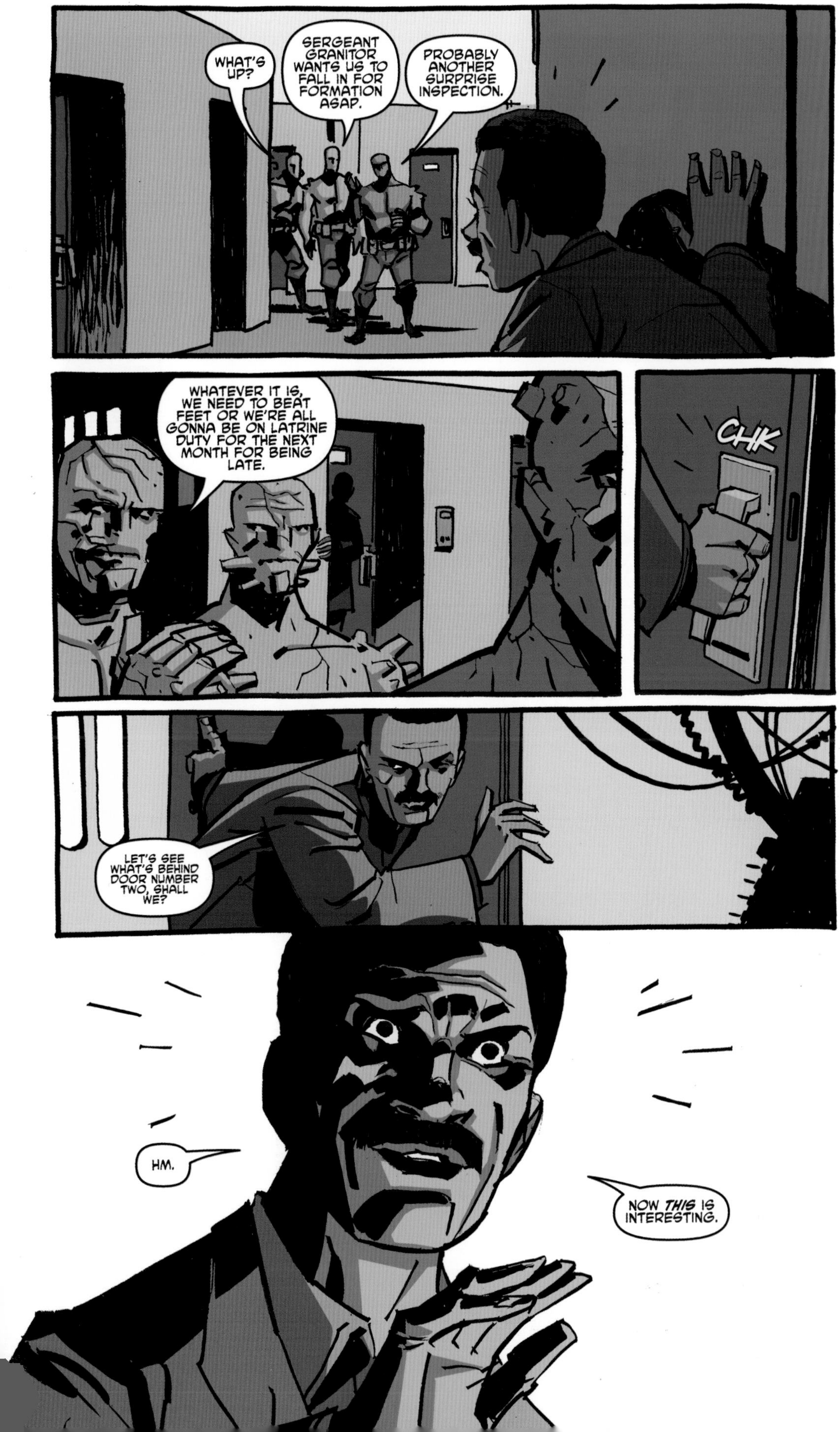
WHAT'S UP?
SERGEANT GRANITOR WANTS US TO FALL IN FOR FORMATION ASAP.
PROBABLY ANOTHER SURPRISE INSPECTION.
WHATEVER IT IS, WE NEED TO BEAT FEET OR WE'RE ALL GONNA BE ON LATRINE DUTY FOR THE NEXT MONTH FOR BEING LATE.
CHK
LET'S SEE WHAT'S BEHIND DOOR NUMBER TWO, SHALL WE?
HM.
NOW *THIS* IS INTERESTING.

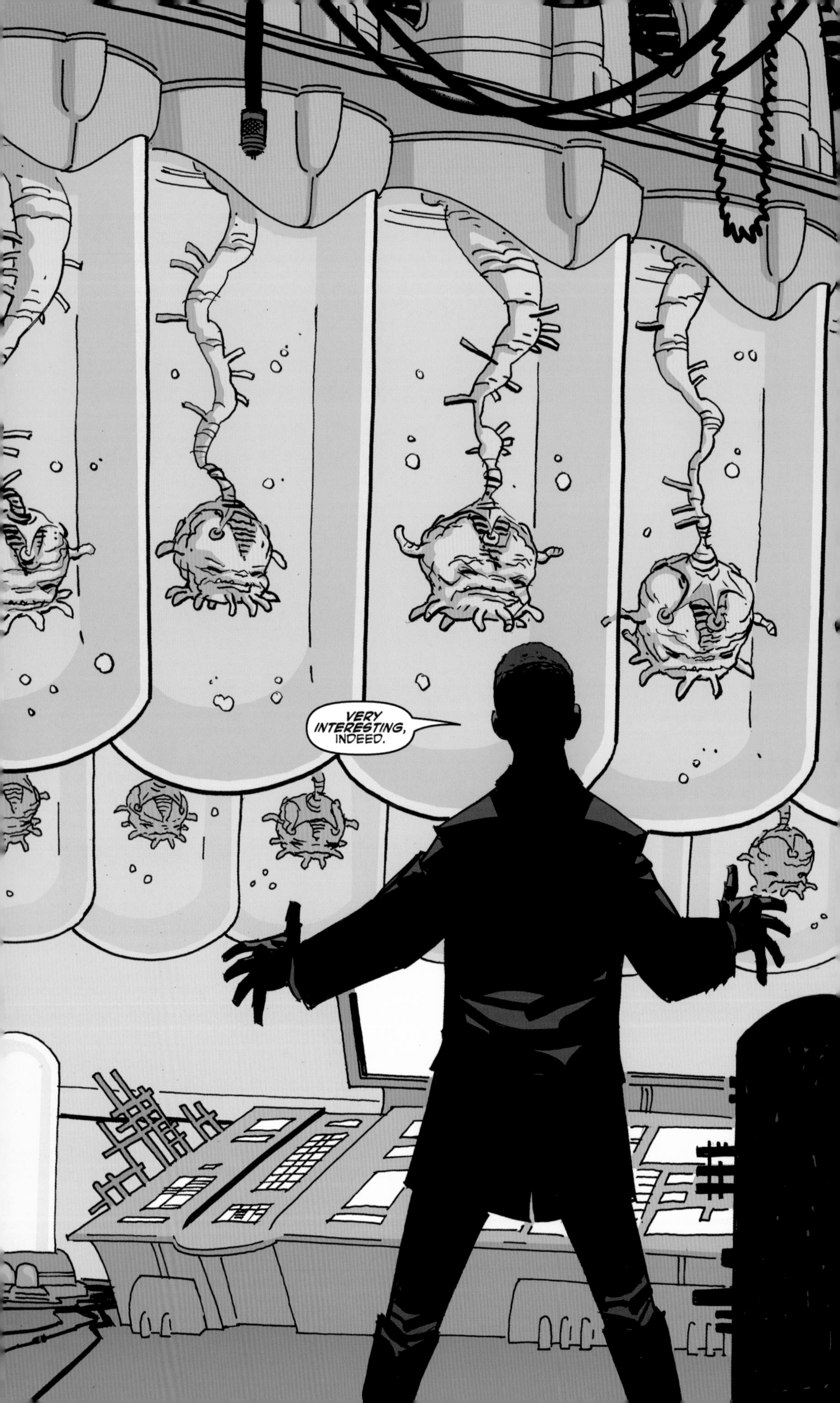
VERY INTERESTING, INDEED.

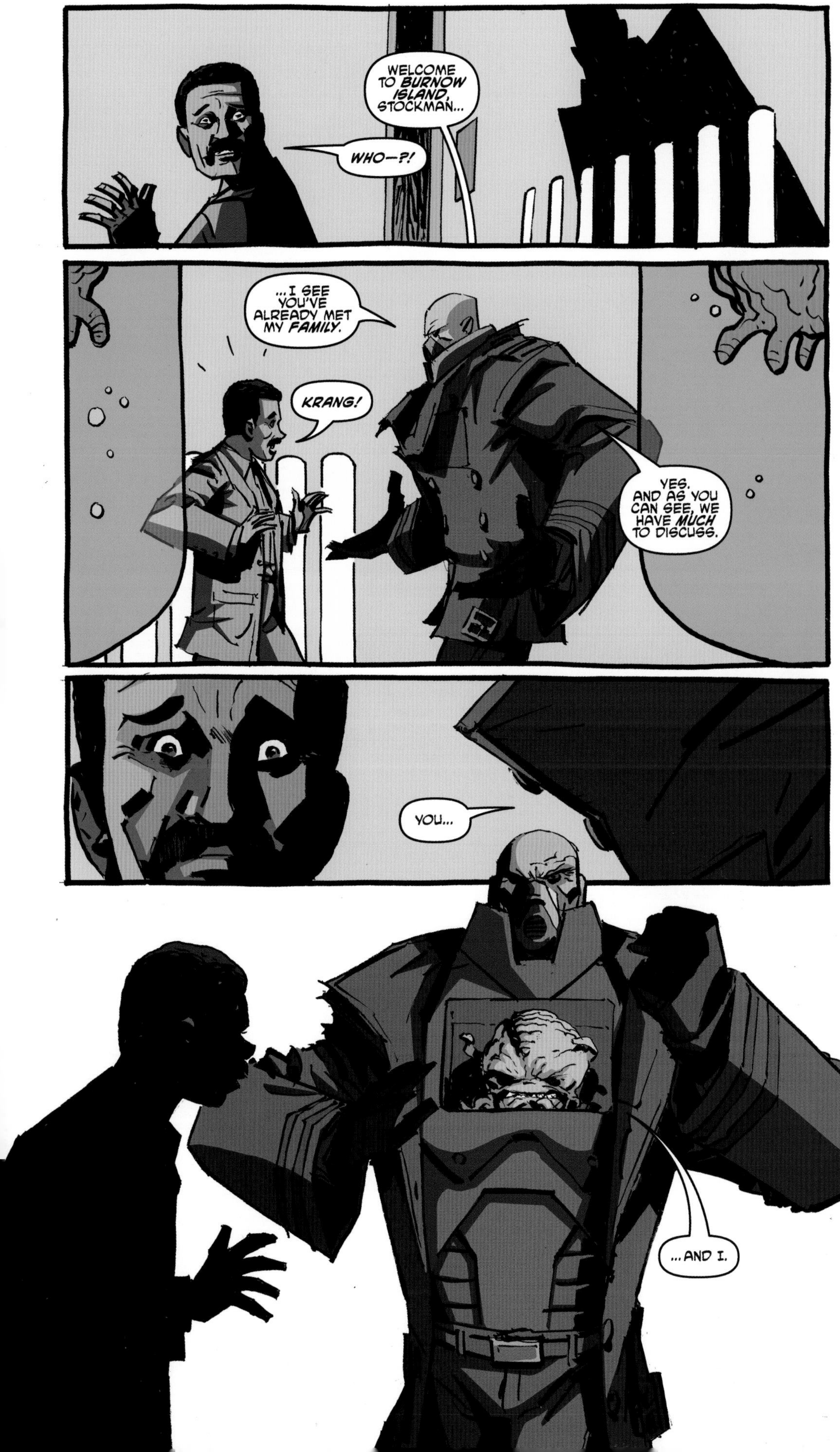
WELCOME TO BURNOW ISLAND, STOCKMAN...
WHO--?!
...I SEE YOU'VE ALREADY MET MY FAMILY.
KRANG!
YES. AND AS YOU CAN SEE, WE HAVE MUCH TO DISCUSS.
YOU...
...AND I.

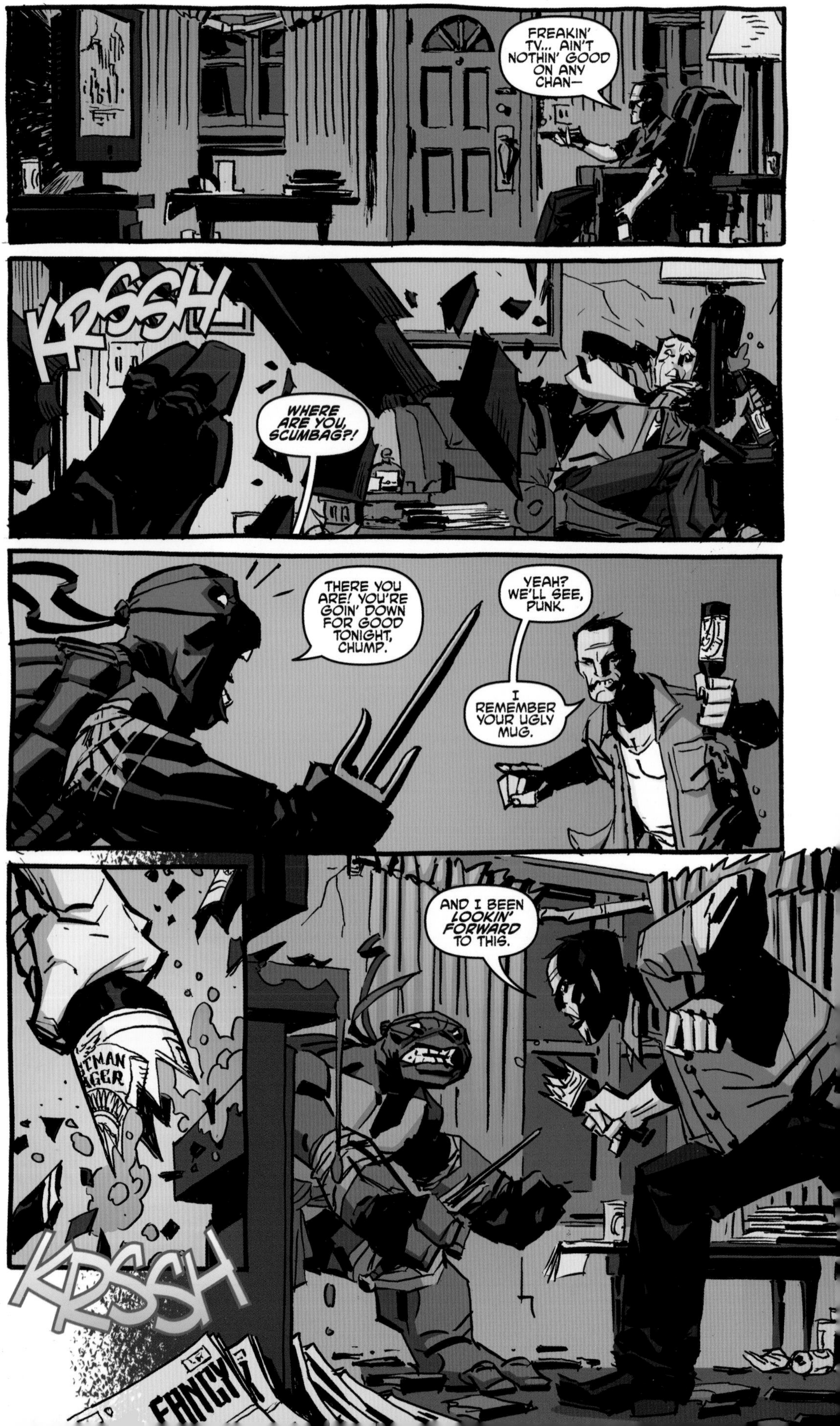

FREAKIN' TV... AIN'T NOTHIN' GOOD ON ANY CHAN—
KRSSH
WHERE ARE YOU, SCUMBAG?!
THERE YOU ARE! YOU'RE GOIN' DOWN FOR GOOD TONIGHT, CHUMP.
YEAH? WE'LL SEE, PUNK.
I REMEMBER YOUR UGLY MUG.
AND I BEEN LOOKIN' FORWARD TO THIS.
KRSSH
FANCY

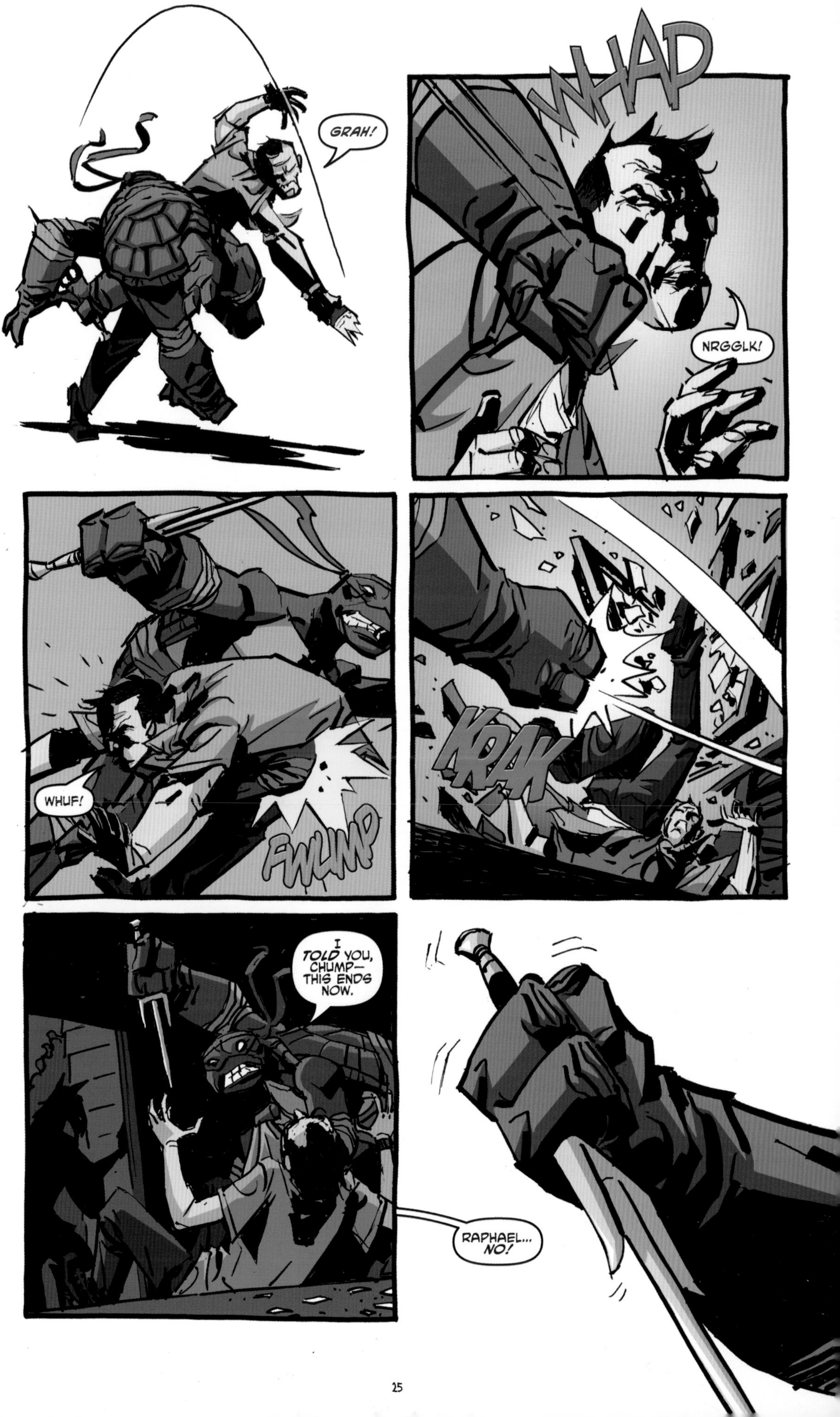
GRAH!
WHAP
NRGGLK!
WHUF!
FWUMP
KRAK
I TOLD YOU, CHUMP— THIS ENDS NOW.
RAPHAEL... NO!

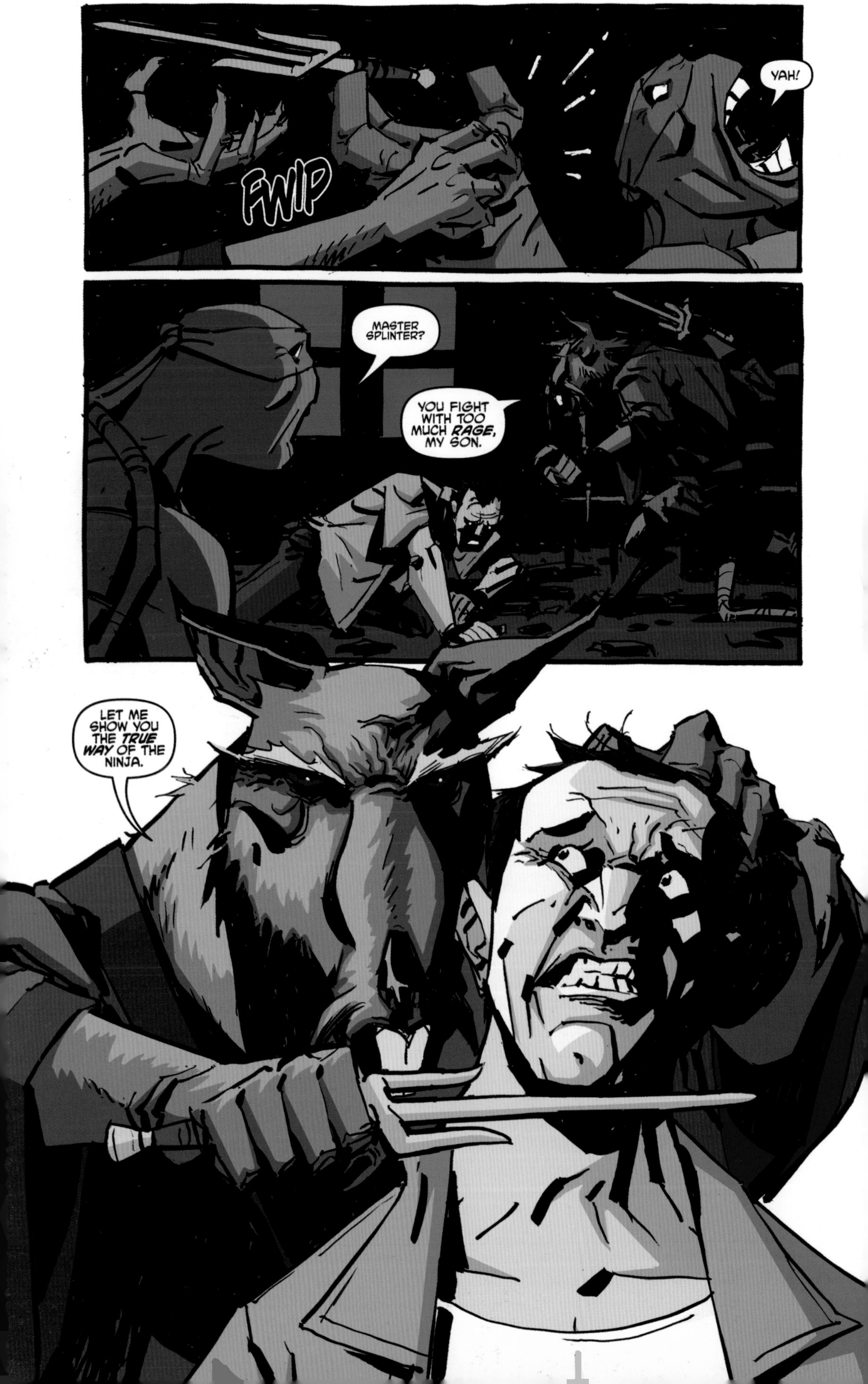
FWIP
YAH!
MASTER SPLINTER?
YOU FIGHT WITH TOO MUCH *RAGE*, MY SON.
LET ME SHOW YOU THE *TRUE WAY* OF THE NINJA.

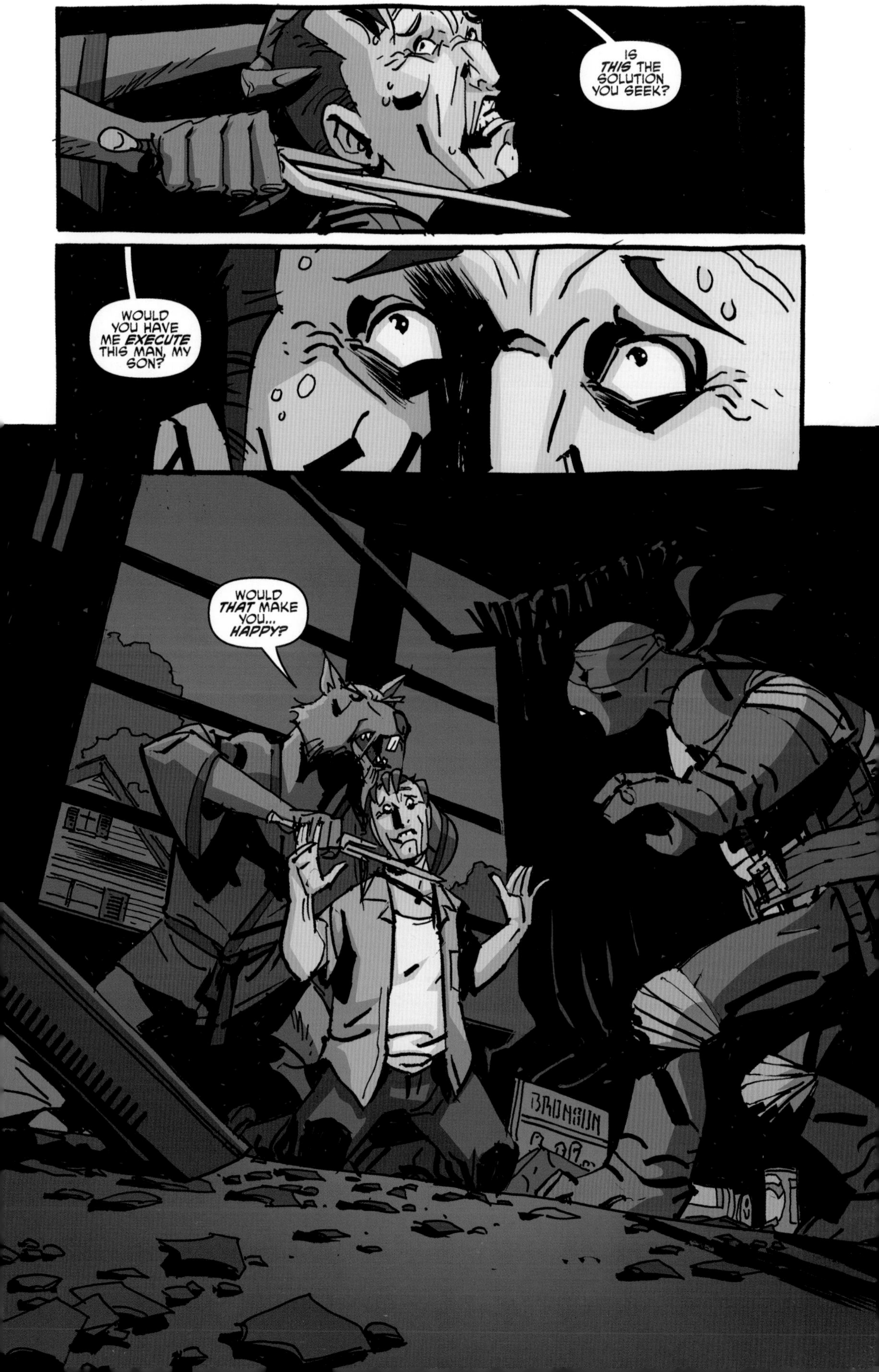
IS *THIS* THE SOLUTION YOU SEEK?
WOULD YOU HAVE ME *EXECUTE* THIS MAN, MY SON?
WOULD *THAT* MAKE YOU... *HAPPY*?
BRONSON

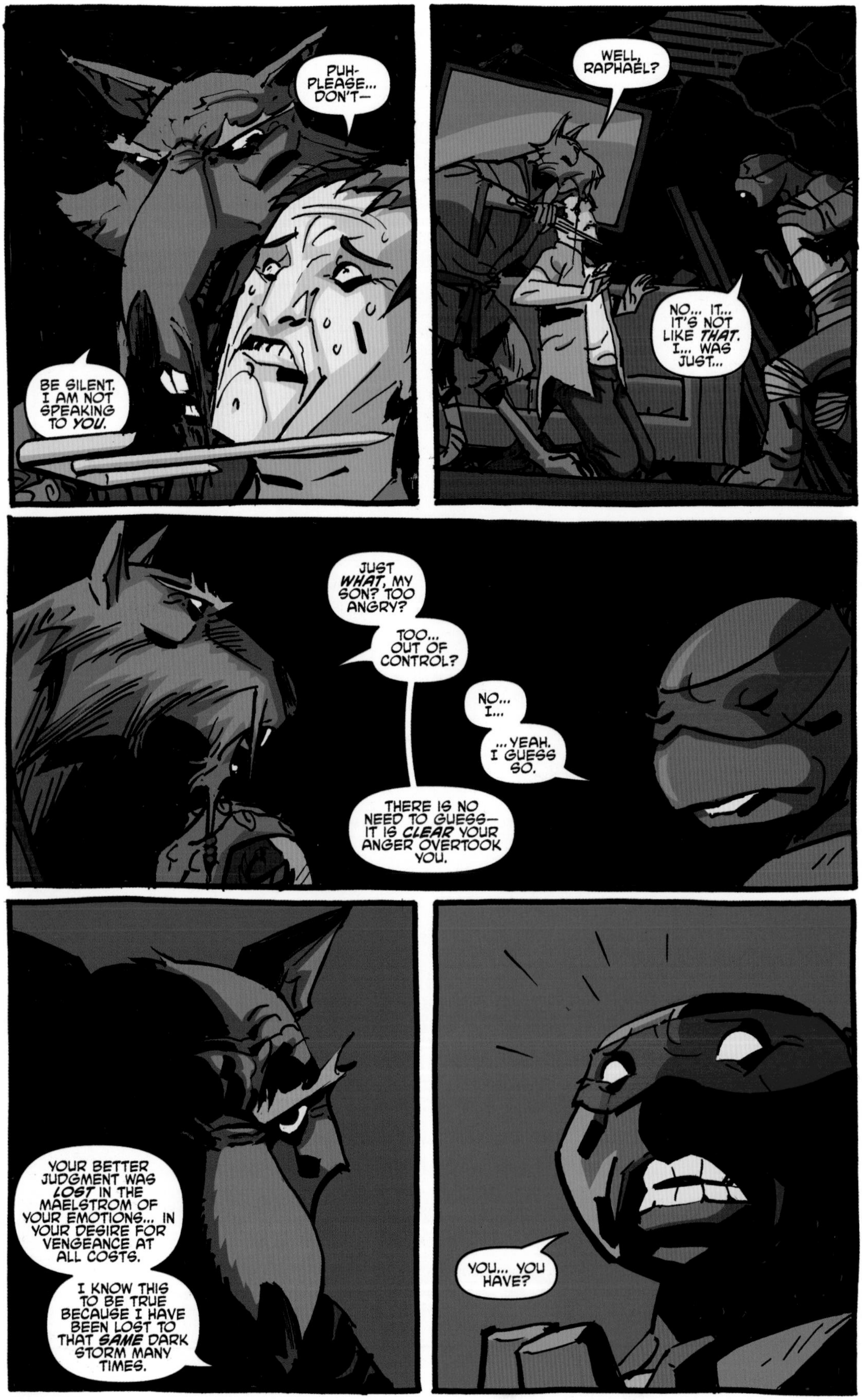
PUH-PLEASE... DON'T—
BE SILENT. I AM NOT SPEAKING TO *YOU*.
WELL, RAPHAEL?
NO... IT... IT'S NOT LIKE *THAT*. I... WAS JUST...
JUST *WHAT*, MY SON? TOO ANGRY?
TOO... OUT OF CONTROL?
NO... I...
...YEAH. I GUESS SO.
THERE IS NO NEED TO GUESS— IT IS *CLEAR* YOUR ANGER OVERTOOK YOU.
YOUR BETTER JUDGMENT WAS *LOST* IN THE MAELSTROM OF YOUR EMOTIONS... IN YOUR DESIRE FOR VENGEANCE AT ALL COSTS.
I KNOW THIS TO BE TRUE BECAUSE I HAVE BEEN LOST TO THAT *SAME* DARK STORM MANY TIMES.
YOU... YOU HAVE?

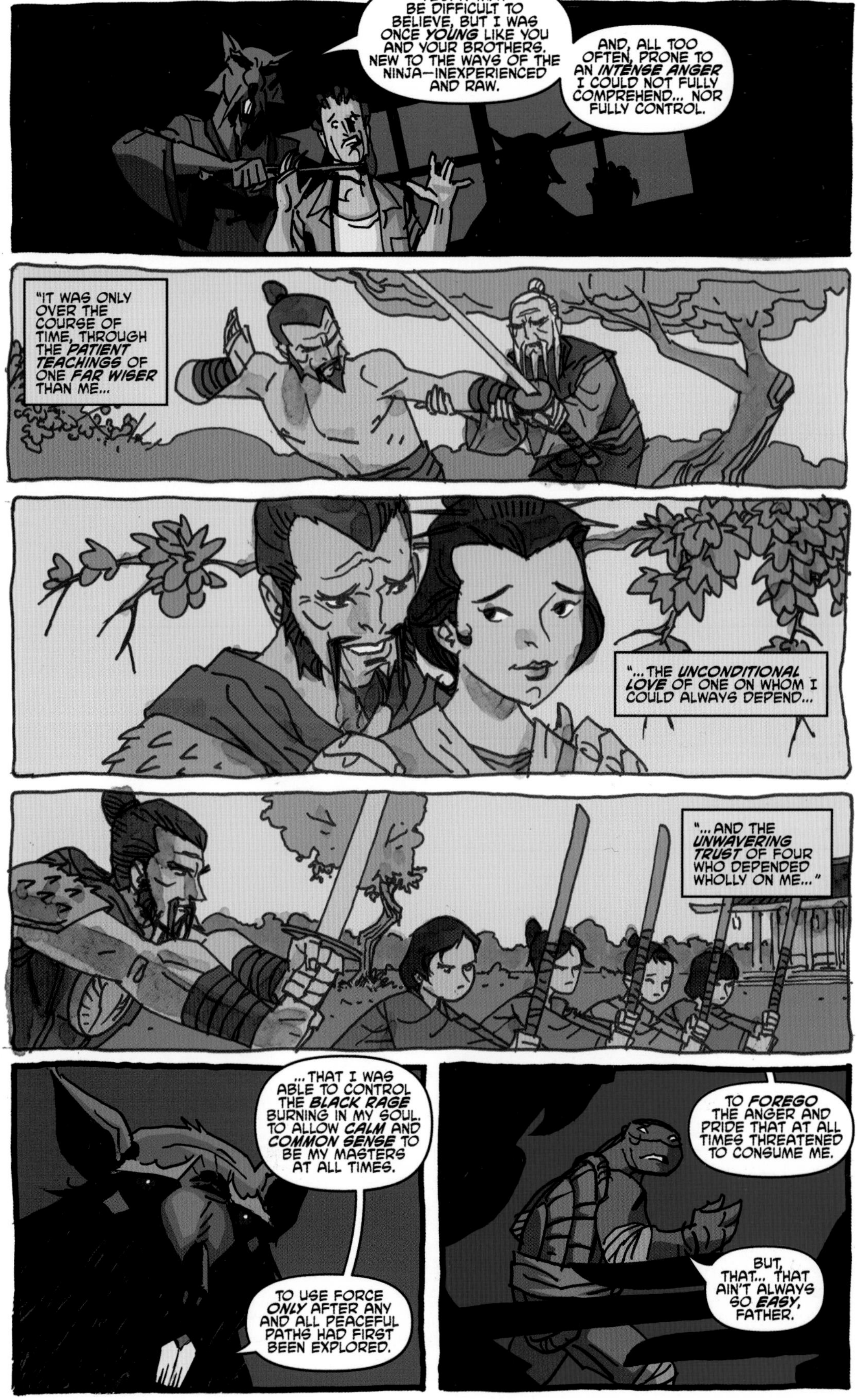
YES. IT MAY BE DIFFICULT TO BELIEVE, BUT I WAS ONCE YOUNG LIKE YOU AND YOUR BROTHERS. NEW TO THE WAYS OF THE NINJA—INEXPERIENCED AND RAW.
AND, ALL TOO OFTEN, PRONE TO AN INTENSE ANGER I COULD NOT FULLY COMPREHEND... NOR FULLY CONTROL.
"IT WAS ONLY OVER THE COURSE OF TIME, THROUGH THE PATIENT TEACHINGS OF ONE FAR WISER THAN ME...
"...THE UNCONDITIONAL LOVE OF ONE ON WHOM I COULD ALWAYS DEPEND...
"...AND THE UNWAVERING TRUST OF FOUR WHO DEPENDED WHOLLY ON ME..."
...THAT I WAS ABLE TO CONTROL THE BLACK RAGE BURNING IN MY SOUL. TO ALLOW CALM AND COMMON SENSE TO BE MY MASTERS AT ALL TIMES.
TO USE FORCE ONLY AFTER ANY AND ALL PEACEFUL PATHS HAD FIRST BEEN EXPLORED.
TO FOREGO THE ANGER AND PRIDE THAT AT ALL TIMES THREATENED TO CONSUME ME.
BUT, THAT... THAT AIN'T ALWAYS SO EASY, FATHER.

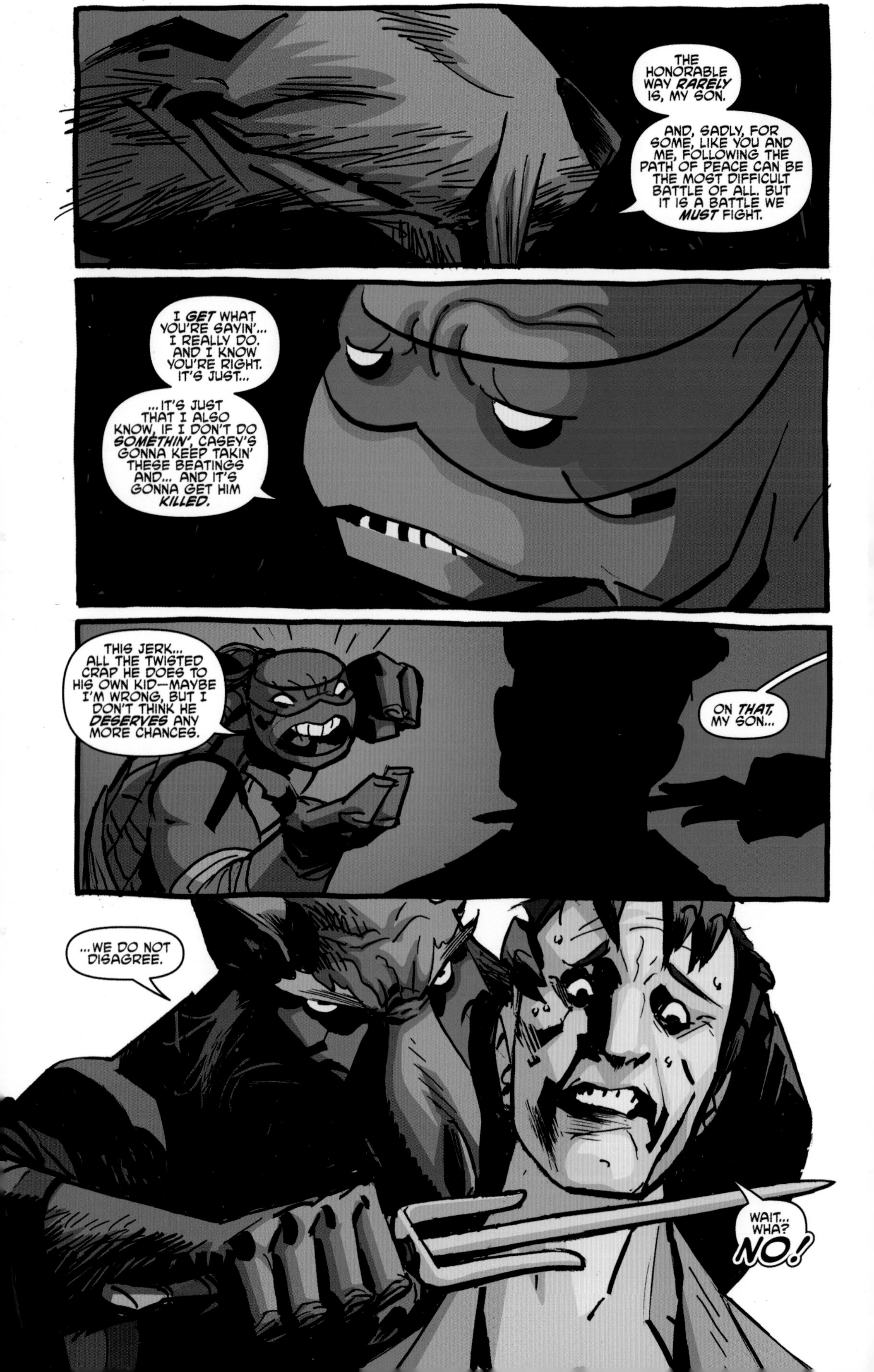
THE HONORABLE WAY *RARELY* IS, MY SON.
AND, SADLY, FOR SOME, LIKE YOU AND ME, FOLLOWING THE PATH OF PEACE CAN BE THE MOST DIFFICULT BATTLE OF ALL. BUT IT IS A BATTLE WE *MUST* FIGHT.
I *GET* WHAT YOU'RE SAYIN'... I REALLY DO. AND I KNOW YOU'RE RIGHT. IT'S JUST...
...IT'S JUST THAT I ALSO KNOW, IF I DON'T DO *SOMETHIN'*, CASEY'S GONNA KEEP TAKIN' THESE BEATINGS AND... AND IT'S GONNA GET HIM *KILLED.*
THIS JERK... ALL THE TWISTED CRAP HE DOES TO HIS OWN KID—MAYBE I'M WRONG, BUT I DON'T THINK HE *DESERVES* ANY MORE CHANCES.
ON *THAT,* MY SON...
...WE DO NOT DISAGREE.
WAIT... WHA? *NO!*

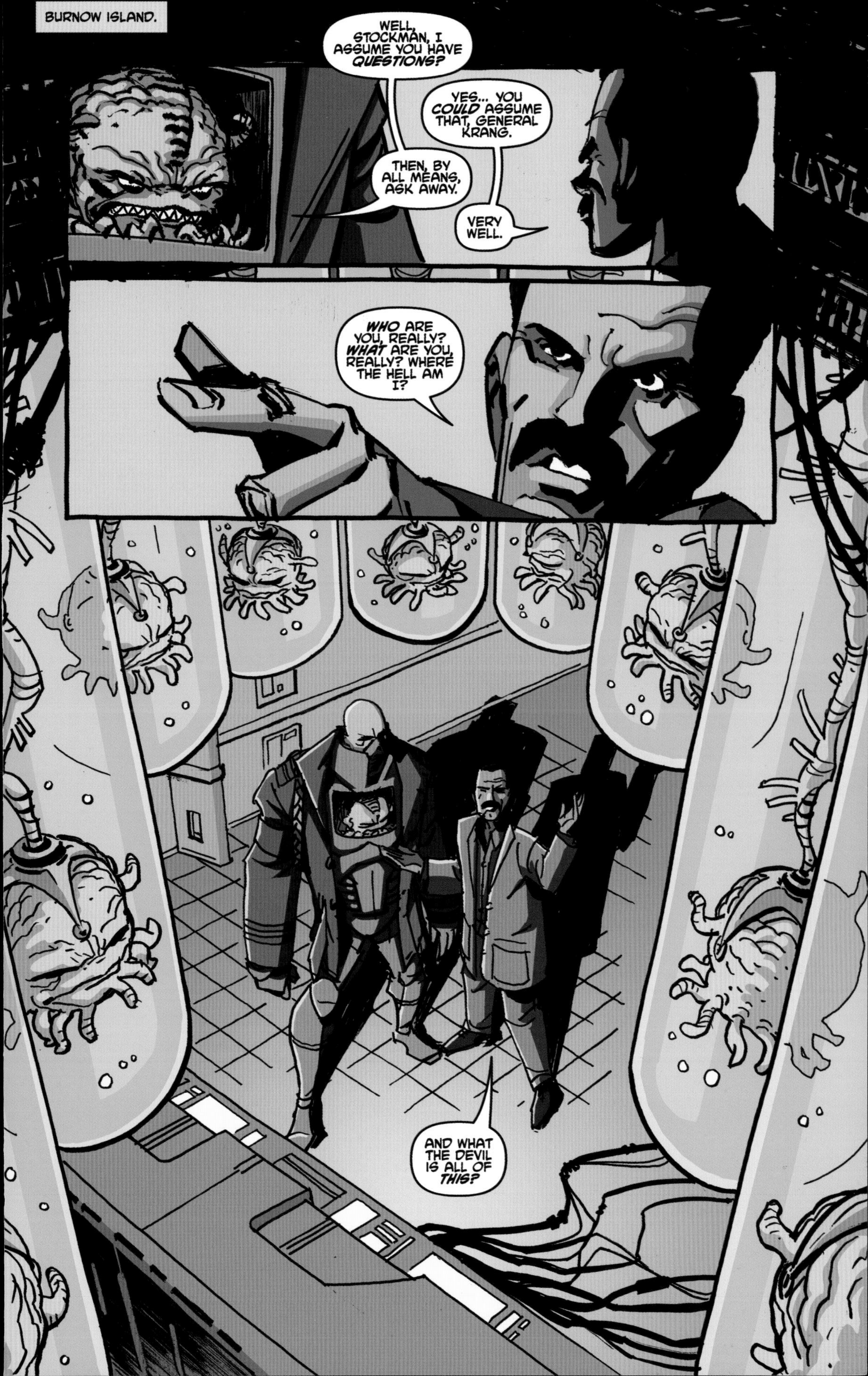
BURNOW ISLAND.
WELL, STOCKMAN, I ASSUME YOU HAVE QUESTIONS?
YES... YOU COULD ASSUME THAT, GENERAL KRANG.
THEN, BY ALL MEANS, ASK AWAY.
VERY WELL.
WHO ARE YOU, REALLY? WHAT ARE YOU, REALLY? WHERE THE HELL AM I?
AND WHAT THE DEVIL IS ALL OF THIS?

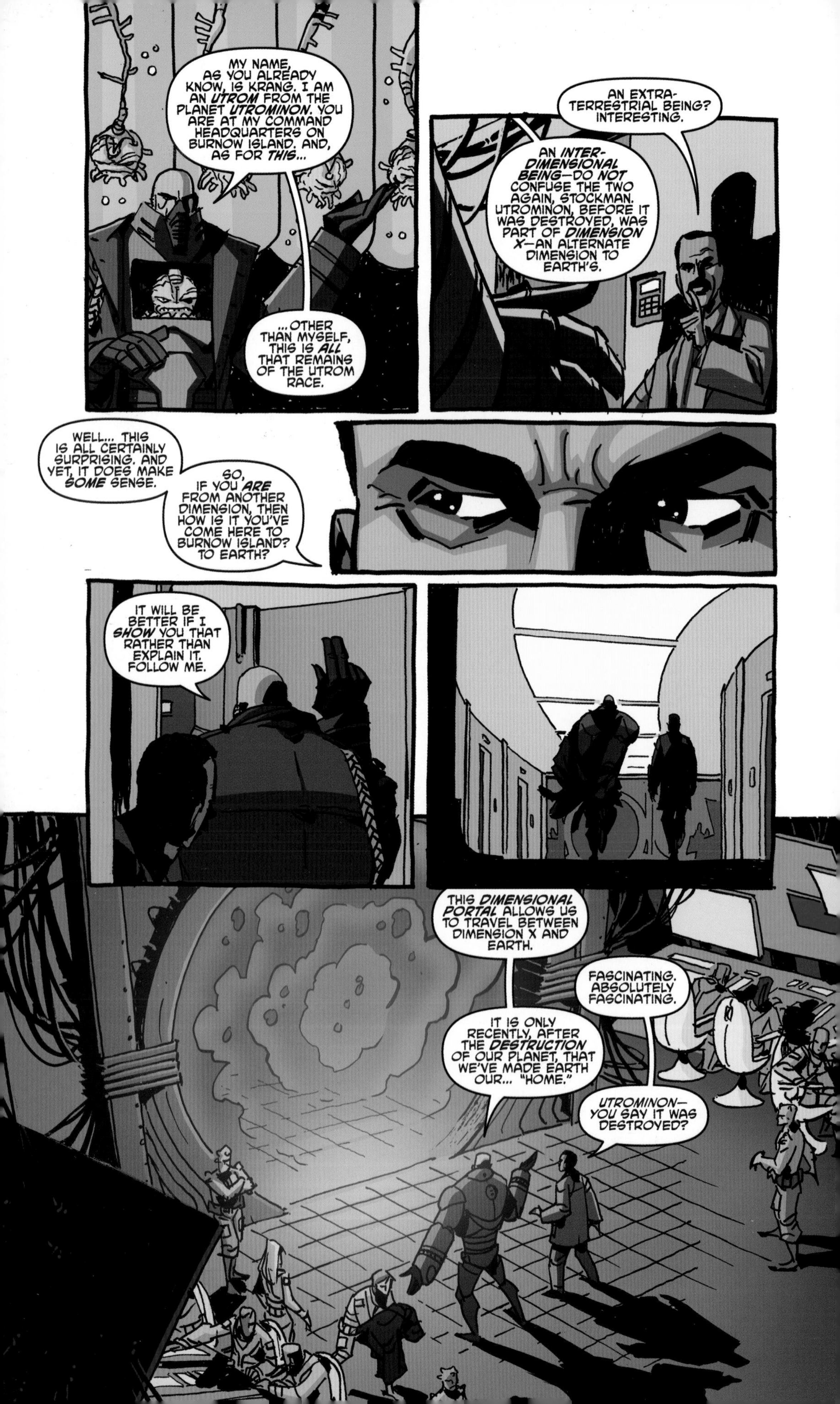
MY NAME, AS YOU ALREADY KNOW, IS KRANG. I AM AN *UTROM* FROM THE PLANET *UTROMINON*. YOU ARE AT MY COMMAND HEADQUARTERS ON BURNOW ISLAND. AND, AS FOR *THIS*...
...OTHER THAN MYSELF, THIS IS *ALL* THAT REMAINS OF THE UTROM RACE.
AN EXTRA-TERRESTRIAL BEING? INTERESTING.
AN *INTER-DIMENSIONAL BEING*—DO *NOT* CONFUSE THE TWO AGAIN, STOCKMAN. UTROMINON, BEFORE IT WAS DESTROYED, WAS PART OF *DIMENSION X*—AN ALTERNATE DIMENSION TO EARTH'S.
WELL... THIS IS ALL CERTAINLY SURPRISING. AND YET, IT DOES MAKE *SOME* SENSE.
SO, IF YOU *ARE* FROM ANOTHER DIMENSION, THEN HOW IS IT YOU'VE COME HERE TO BURNOW ISLAND? TO EARTH?
IT WILL BE BETTER IF I *SHOW* YOU THAT RATHER THAN EXPLAIN IT. FOLLOW ME.
THIS *DIMENSIONAL PORTAL* ALLOWS US TO TRAVEL BETWEEN DIMENSION X AND EARTH.
FASCINATING. ABSOLUTELY FASCINATING.
IT IS ONLY RECENTLY, AFTER THE *DESTRUCTION* OF OUR PLANET, THAT WE'VE MADE EARTH OUR... "HOME."
UTROMINON—YOU SAY IT WAS DESTROYED?

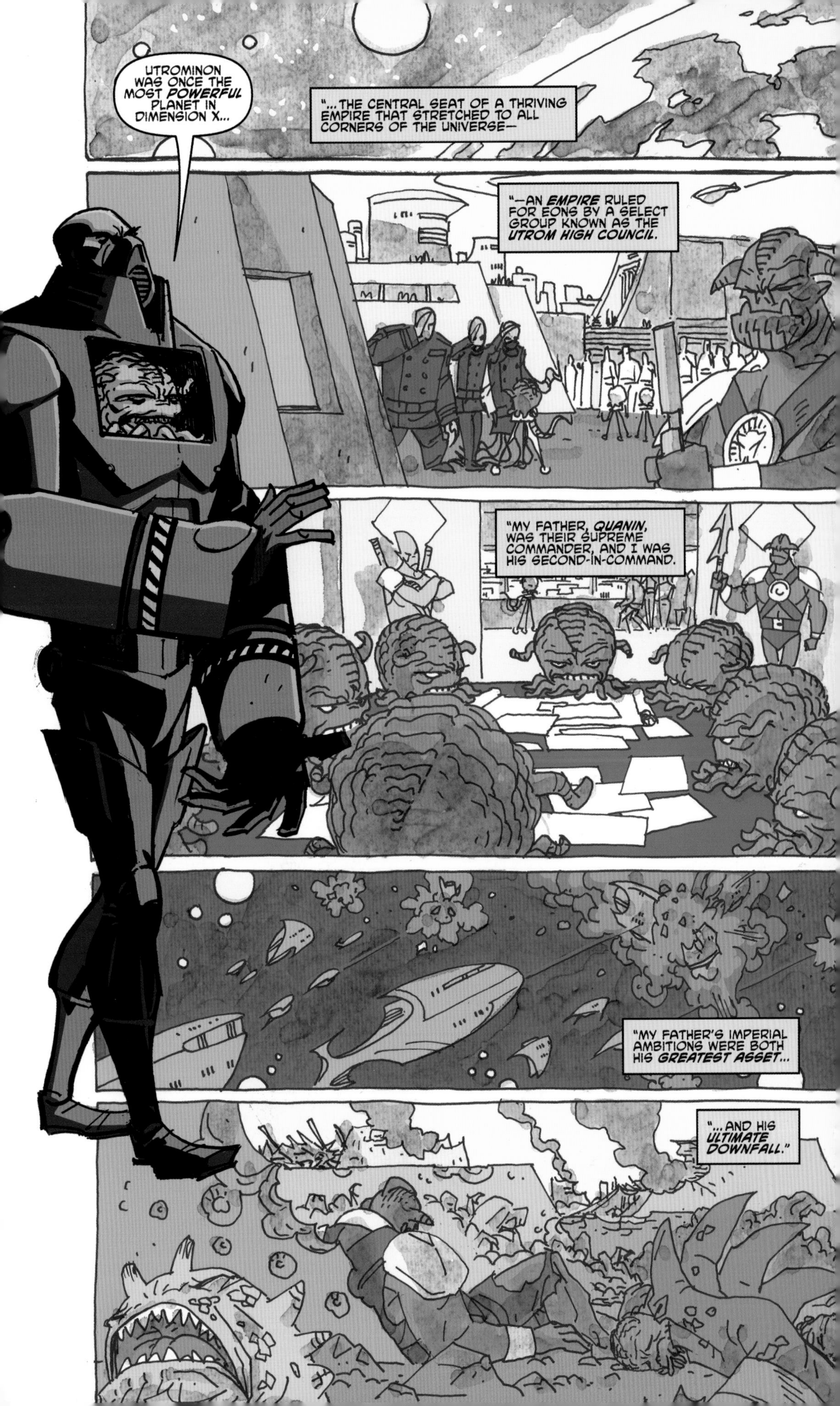

UTROMINON WAS ONCE THE MOST POWERFUL PLANET IN DIMENSION X...
"...THE CENTRAL SEAT OF A THRIVING EMPIRE THAT STRETCHED TO ALL CORNERS OF THE UNIVERSE—
"—AN EMPIRE RULED FOR EONS BY A SELECT GROUP KNOWN AS THE UTROM HIGH COUNCIL.
"MY FATHER, QUANIN, WAS THEIR SUPREME COMMANDER, AND I WAS HIS SECOND-IN-COMMAND.
"MY FATHER'S IMPERIAL AMBITIONS WERE BOTH HIS GREATEST ASSET...
"...AND HIS ULTIMATE DOWNFALL."

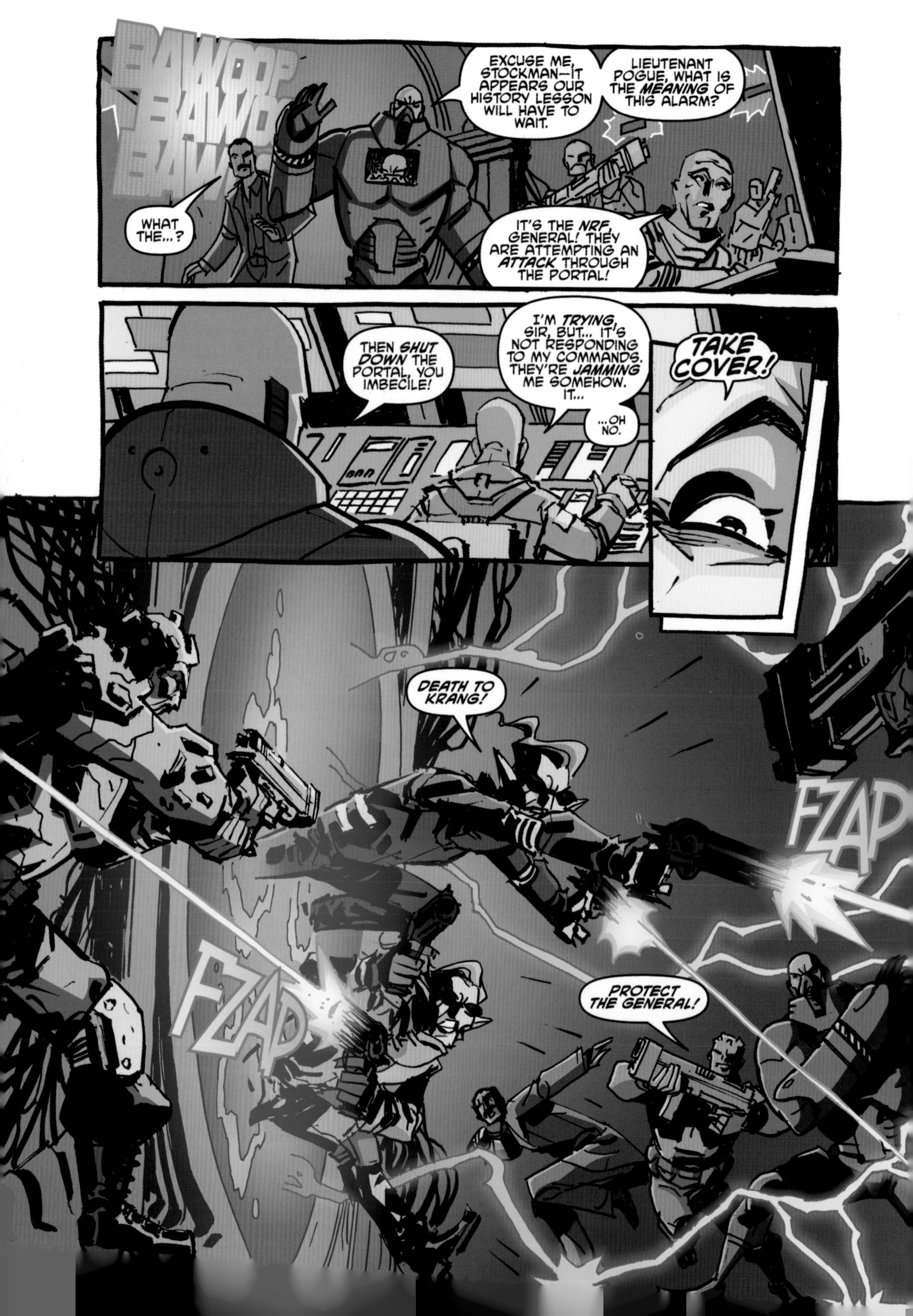
BAWOOP BAWOO BAW
EXCUSE ME, STOCKMAN--IT APPEARS OUR HISTORY LESSON WILL HAVE TO WAIT.
LIEUTENANT POGUE, WHAT IS THE MEANING OF THIS ALARM?
WHAT THE...?
IT'S THE NRF, GENERAL! THEY ARE ATTEMPTING AN ATTACK THROUGH THE PORTAL!
THEN SHUT DOWN THE PORTAL, YOU IMBECILE!
I'M TRYING, SIR, BUT... IT'S NOT RESPONDING TO MY COMMANDS. THEY'RE JAMMING ME SOMEHOW. IT...
...OH NO.
TAKE COVER!
DEATH TO KRANG!
FZAP
FZAP
PROTECT THE GENERAL!

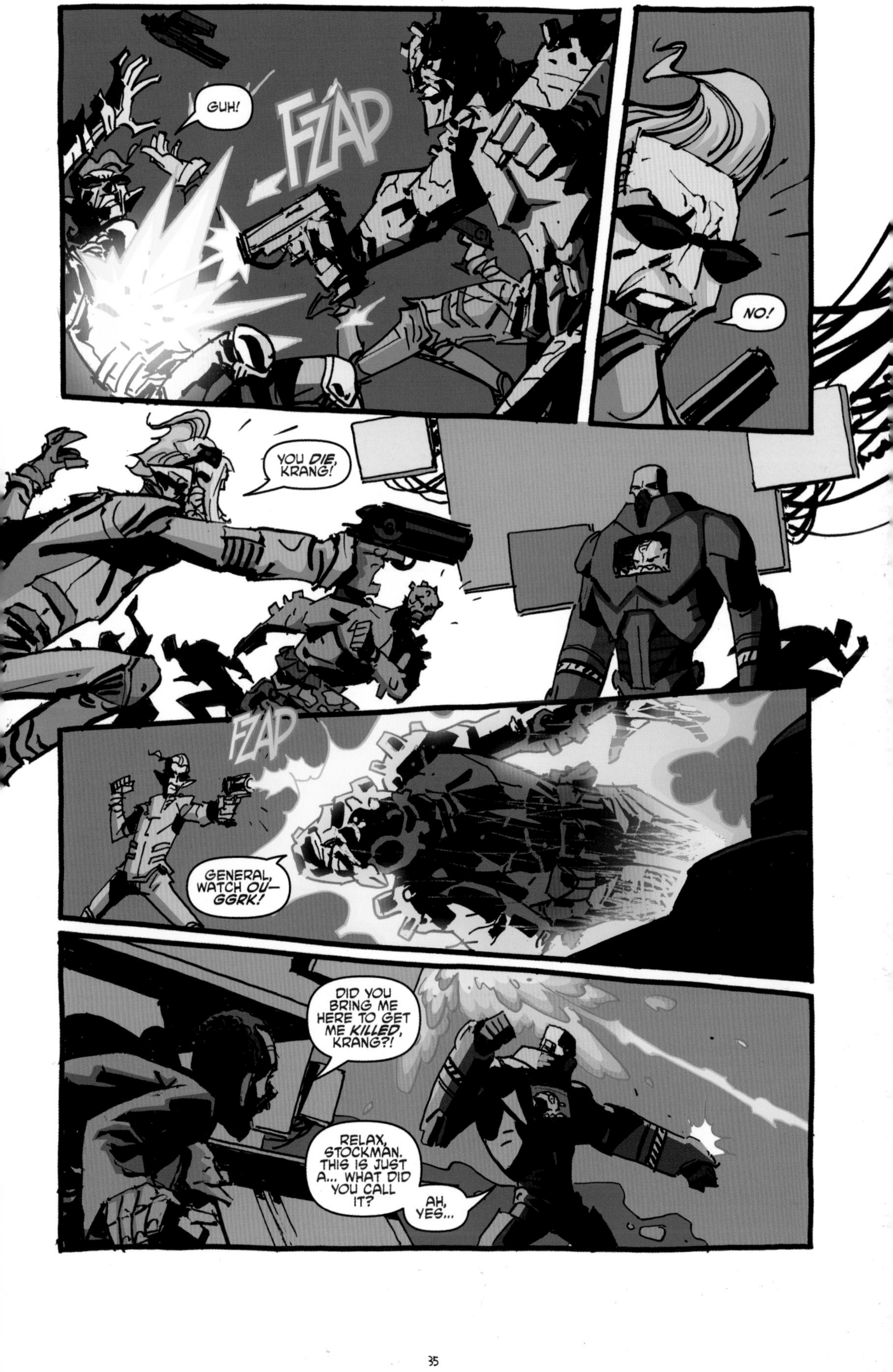
GUH!
FZAP
NO!
YOU DIE, KRANG!
FZAP
GENERAL, WATCH OU-GGRK!
DID YOU BRING ME HERE TO GET ME KILLED, KRANG?!
RELAX, STOCKMAN. THIS IS JUST A... WHAT DID YOU CALL IT?
AH, YES...

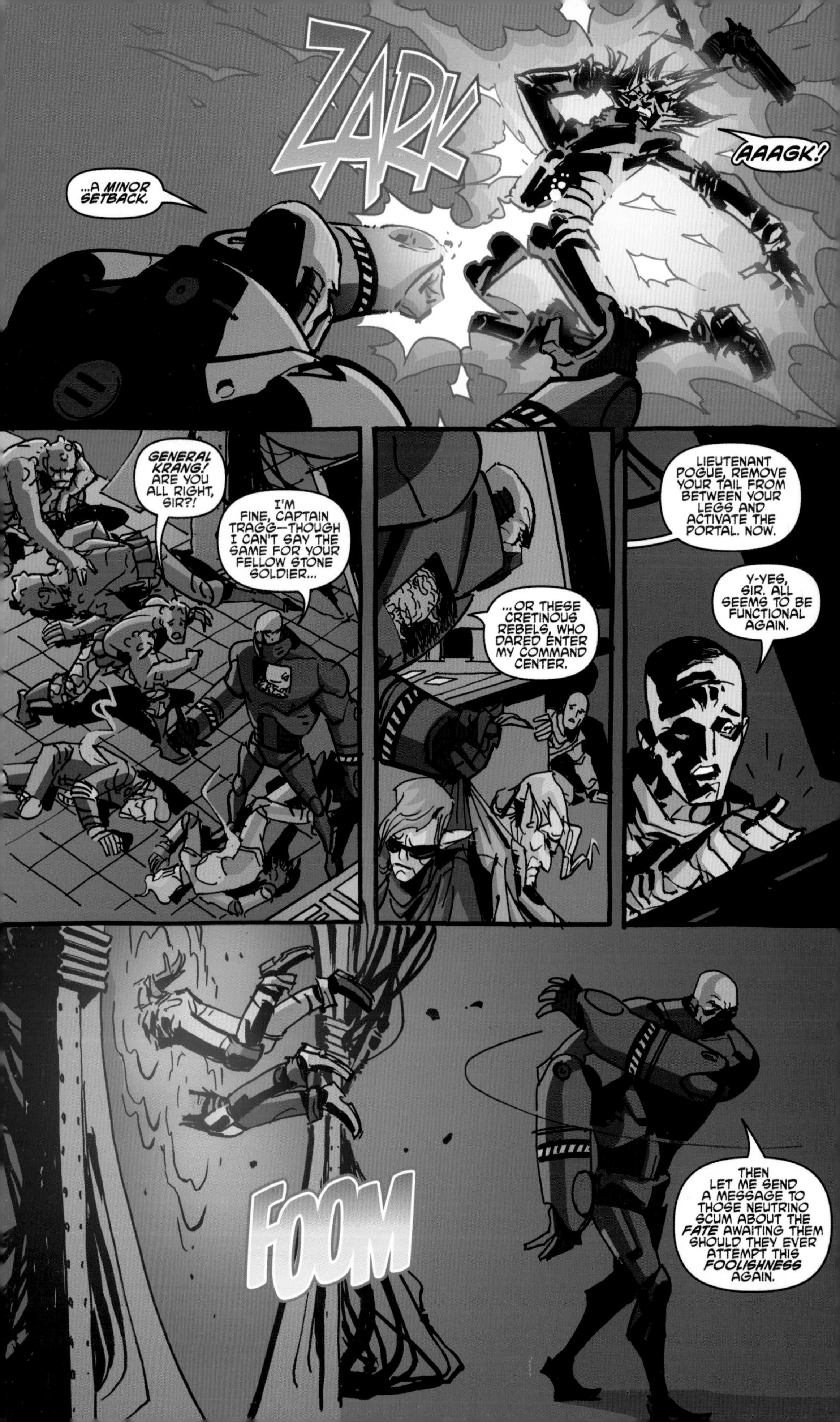
ZARK
AAAGK!
...A MINOR SETBACK.
GENERAL KRANG! ARE YOU ALL RIGHT, SIR?!
I'M FINE, CAPTAIN TRAGG—THOUGH I CAN'T SAY THE SAME FOR YOUR FELLOW STONE SOLDIER...
...OR THESE CRETINOUS REBELS, WHO DARED ENTER MY COMMAND CENTER.
LIEUTENANT POGUE, REMOVE YOUR TAIL FROM BETWEEN YOUR LEGS AND ACTIVATE THE PORTAL. NOW.
Y-YES, SIR. ALL SEEMS TO BE FUNCTIONAL AGAIN.
FOOM
THEN LET ME SEND A MESSAGE TO THOSE NEUTRINO SCUM ABOUT THE FATE AWAITING THEM SHOULD THEY EVER ATTEMPT THIS FOOLISHNESS AGAIN.

CAPTAIN TRAGG, I WANT POGUE AND THESE OTHER BUTTON PUSHERS WORKING ON A SOLUTION TO THIS PORTAL ATTACK *IMMEDIATELY.*

SERGEANT GRANITOR, YOU WILL DOUBLE THE GUARD CONTINGENT ON THE NEUTRINO SIDE OF THE PORTAL. HEADS WILL *ROLL* IF THERE IS ANOTHER BREACH!

AYE, AYE, SIR!

STOCKMAN—YOU FOLLOW ME.

I... UH... CERTAINLY, GENERAL.

WHAT... WHAT WAS ALL THAT ABOUT?

THAT WAS A PATHETIC ATTACK BY THE LOWLIFES OF A PLANET THAT WILL SOON BE UNDER MY CONTROL... IN *EVERY WAY* IMAGINABLE. THAT SAID, IT DOES *UNDERSCORE* MY REASON FOR BRINGING YOU HERE.

YES... I WAS A BIT *CURIOUS* ABOUT THAT.

THOUGH YOUR GENETIC WORK HAS BEEN AN UTTER *DISASTER,* YOU DO SEEM TO HAVE SOME *MECHANICAL* SKILL—YOUR MOUSERS WEREN'T *COMPLETELY* WORTHLESS. ONLY BECAUSE OF THIS, I'M ALLOWING YOU ANOTHER OPPORTUNITY TO PROVE YOUR VALUE TO ME, STOCKMAN.

HOW IS THAT, GENERAL?

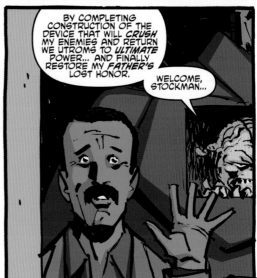

BY COMPLETING CONSTRUCTION OF THE DEVICE THAT WILL *CRUSH* MY ENEMIES AND RETURN WE UTROMS TO *ULTIMATE* POWER... AND FINALLY RESTORE MY *FATHER'S* LOST HONOR.

WELCOME, STOCKMAN...

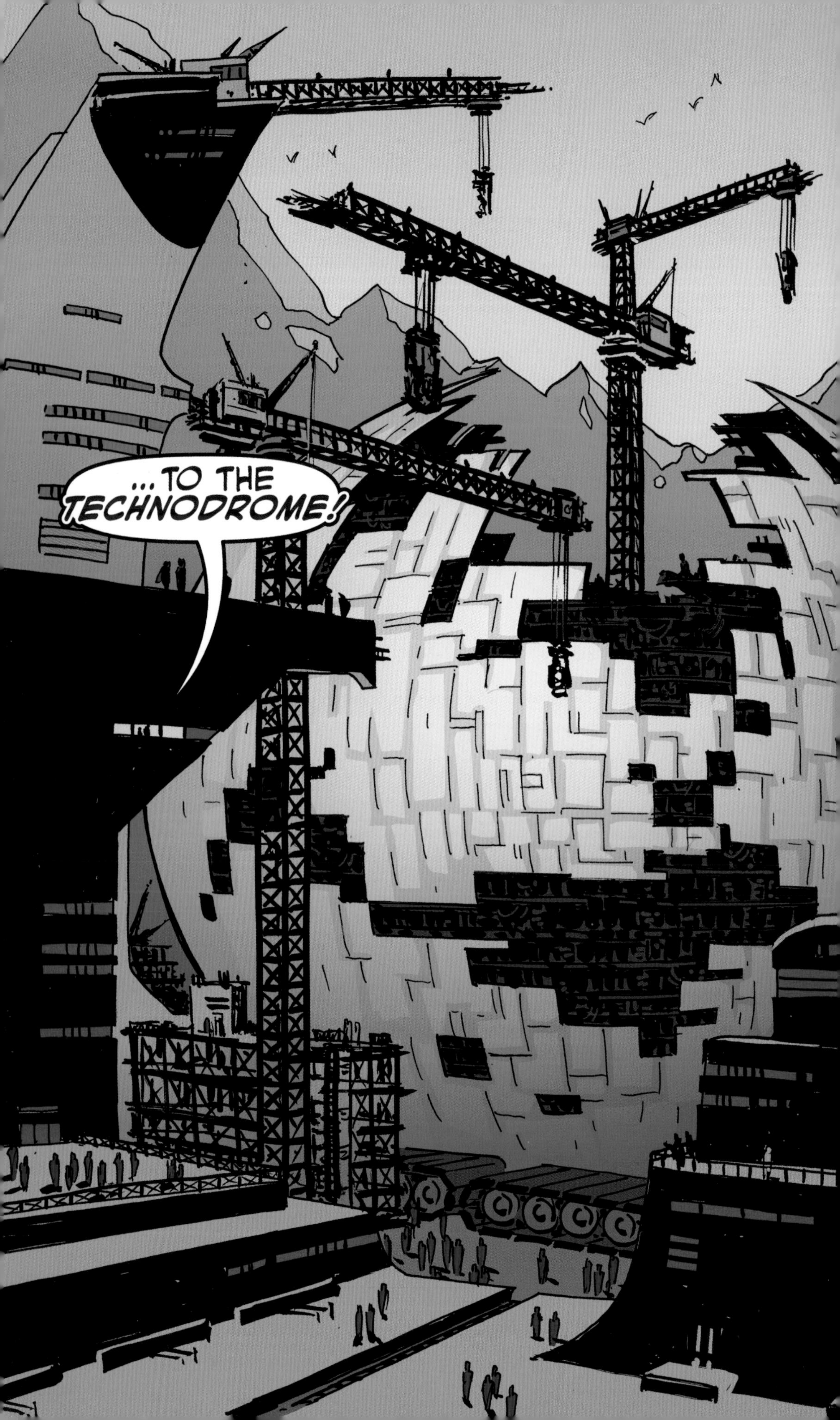
...TO THE TECHNODROME!

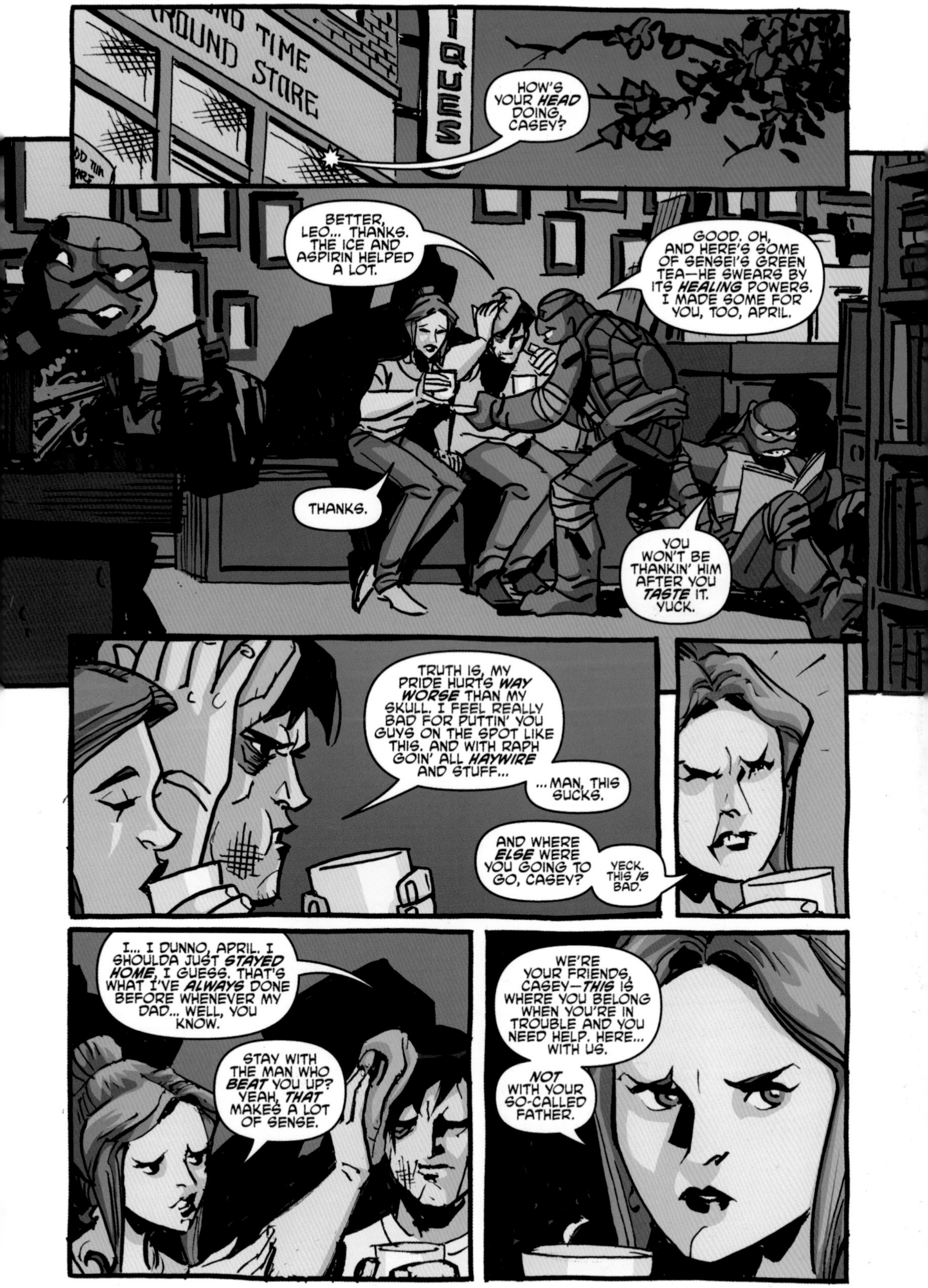

ROUND TIME
ROUND STORE
IQUES
HOW'S YOUR *HEAD* DOING, CASEY?
BETTER, LEO... THANKS. THE ICE AND ASPIRIN HELPED A LOT.
GOOD. OH, AND HERE'S SOME OF SENSEI'S GREEN TEA—HE SWEARS BY ITS *HEALING* POWERS. I MADE SOME FOR YOU, TOO, APRIL.
THANKS.
YOU WON'T BE THANKIN' HIM AFTER YOU *TASTE* IT. YUCK.
TRUTH IS, MY PRIDE HURTS *WAY WORSE* THAN MY SKULL. I FEEL REALLY BAD FOR PUTTIN' YOU GUYS ON THE SPOT LIKE THIS. AND WITH RAPH GOIN' ALL *HAYWIRE* AND STUFF...
...MAN, THIS SUCKS.
AND WHERE *ELSE* WERE YOU GOING TO GO, CASEY?
YECK. THIS *IS* BAD.
I... I DUNNO, APRIL. I SHOULDA JUST *STAYED HOME*, I GUESS. THAT'S WHAT I'VE *ALWAYS* DONE BEFORE WHENEVER MY DAD... WELL, YOU KNOW.
STAY WITH THE MAN WHO *BEAT* YOU UP? YEAH, *THAT* MAKES A LOT OF SENSE.
WE'RE YOUR FRIENDS, CASEY—*THIS* IS WHERE YOU BELONG WHEN YOU'RE IN TROUBLE AND YOU NEED HELP. HERE... WITH US.
NOT WITH YOUR SO-CALLED FATHER.

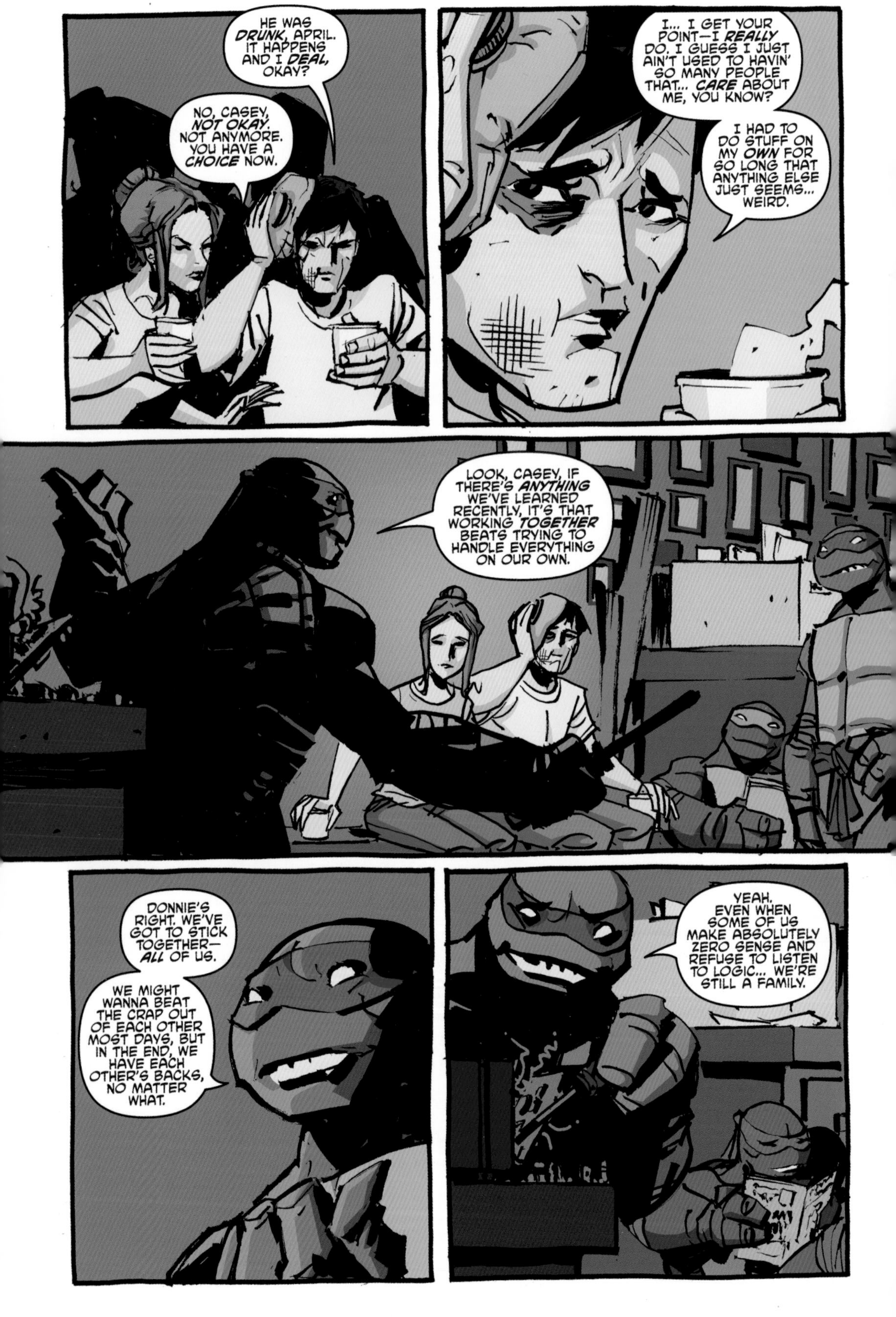

HE WAS DRUNK, APRIL. IT HAPPENS AND I DEAL, OKAY?
NO, CASEY, NOT OKAY. NOT ANYMORE. YOU HAVE A CHOICE NOW.
I... I GET YOUR POINT—I REALLY DO. I GUESS I JUST AIN'T USED TO HAVIN' SO MANY PEOPLE THAT... CARE ABOUT ME, YOU KNOW?
I HAD TO DO STUFF ON MY OWN FOR SO LONG THAT ANYTHING ELSE JUST SEEMS... WEIRD.
LOOK, CASEY, IF THERE'S ANYTHING WE'VE LEARNED RECENTLY, IT'S THAT WORKING TOGETHER BEATS TRYING TO HANDLE EVERYTHING ON OUR OWN.
DONNIE'S RIGHT. WE'VE GOT TO STICK TOGETHER— ALL OF US.
WE MIGHT WANNA BEAT THE CRAP OUT OF EACH OTHER MOST DAYS, BUT IN THE END, WE HAVE EACH OTHER'S BACKS, NO MATTER WHAT.
YEAH. EVEN WHEN SOME OF US MAKE ABSOLUTELY ZERO SENSE AND REFUSE TO LISTEN TO LOGIC... WE'RE STILL A FAMILY.

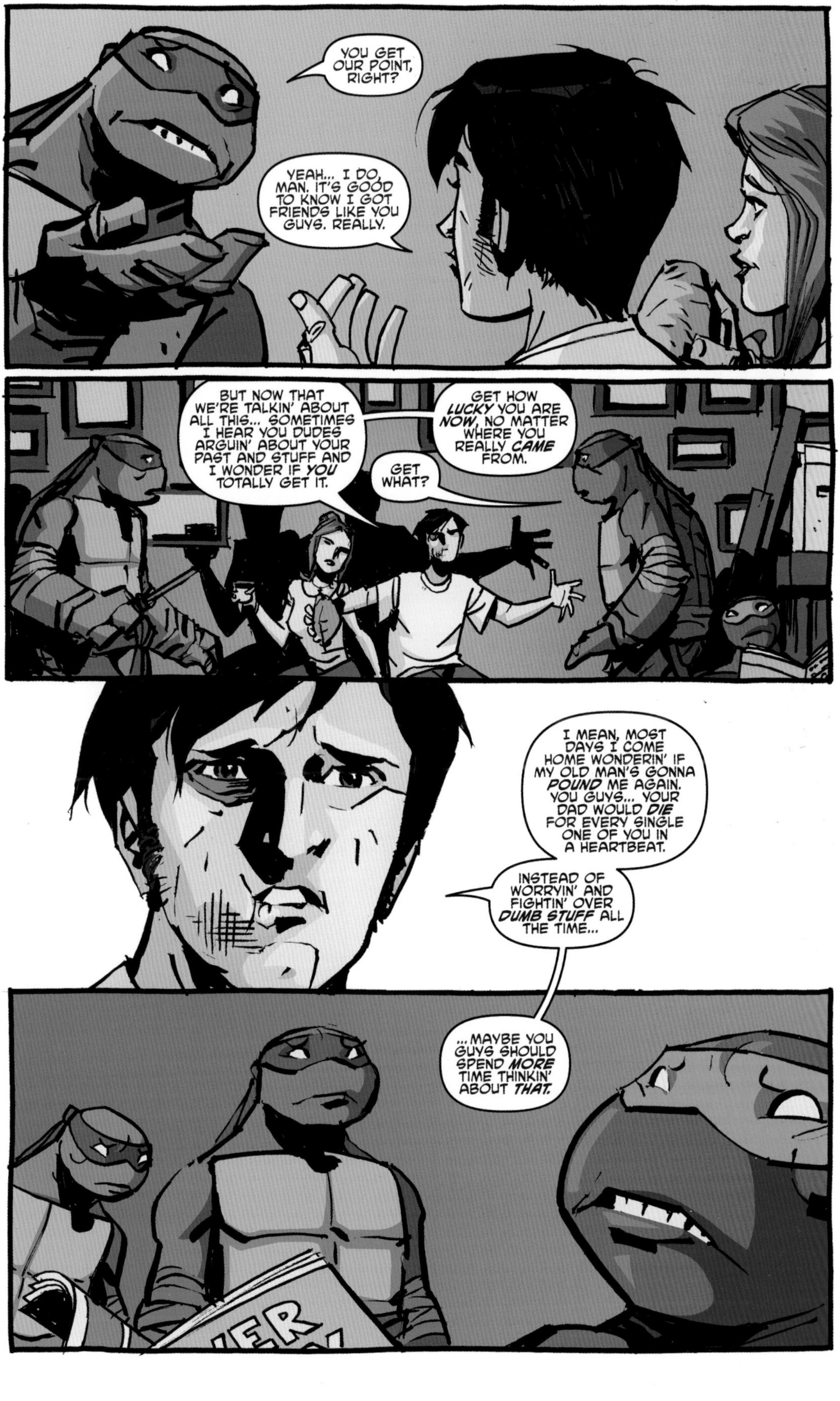
YOU GET OUR POINT, RIGHT?
YEAH... I DO, MAN. IT'S GOOD TO KNOW I GOT FRIENDS LIKE YOU GUYS. REALLY.
BUT NOW THAT WE'RE TALKIN' ABOUT ALL THIS... SOMETIMES I HEAR YOU DUDES ARGUIN' ABOUT YOUR PAST AND STUFF AND I WONDER IF YOU TOTALLY GET IT.
GET WHAT?
GET HOW LUCKY YOU ARE NOW, NO MATTER WHERE YOU REALLY CAME FROM.
I MEAN, MOST DAYS I COME HOME WONDERIN' IF MY OLD MAN'S GONNA POUND ME AGAIN. YOU GUYS... YOUR DAD WOULD DIE FOR EVERY SINGLE ONE OF YOU IN A HEARTBEAT.
INSTEAD OF WORRYIN' AND FIGHTIN' OVER DUMB STUFF ALL THE TIME...
...MAYBE YOU GUYS SHOULD SPEND MORE TIME THINKIN' ABOUT THAT.

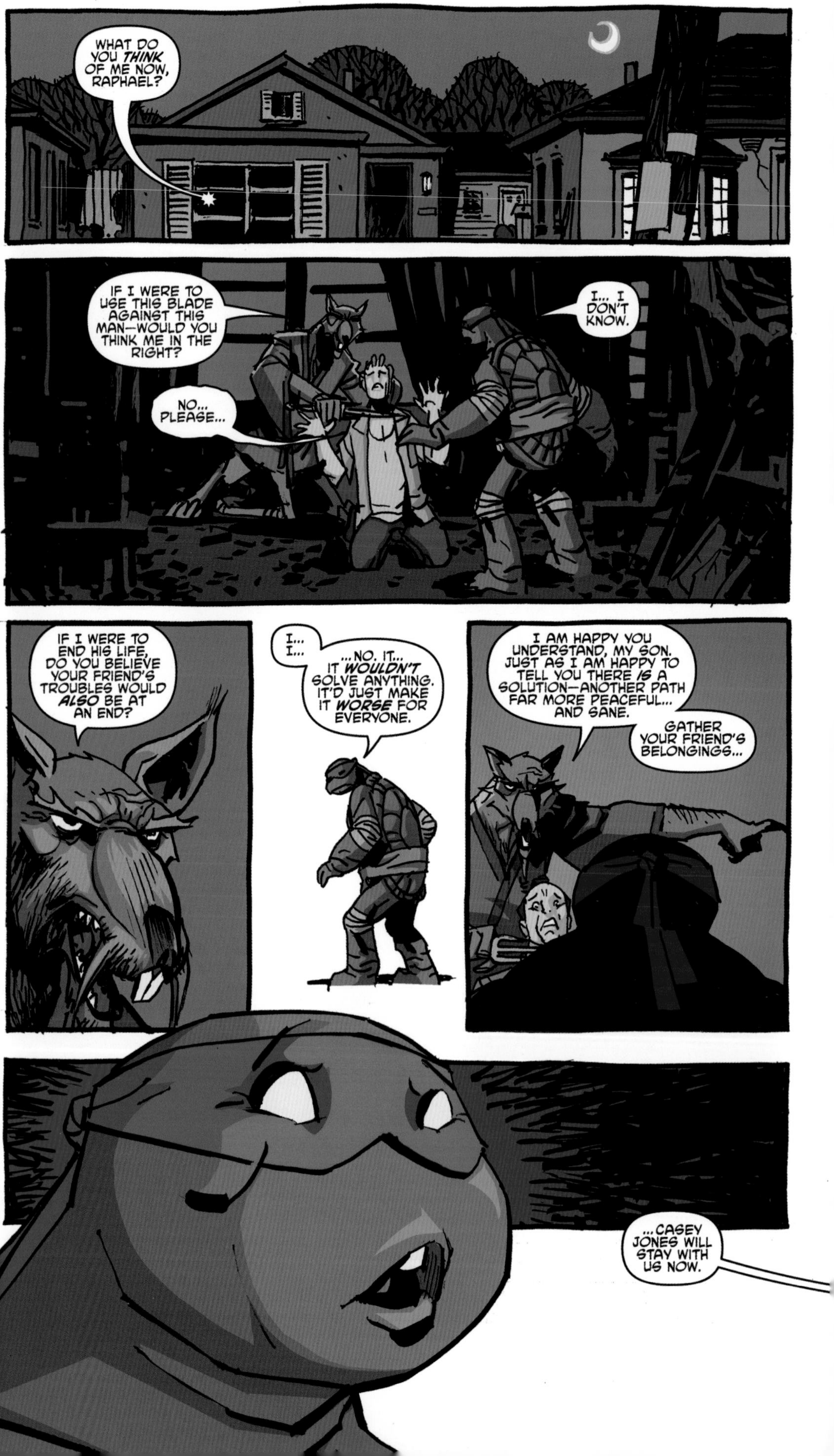
WHAT DO YOU THINK OF ME NOW, RAPHAEL?
IF I WERE TO USE THIS BLADE AGAINST THIS MAN—WOULD YOU THINK ME IN THE RIGHT?
I... I DON'T KNOW.
NO... PLEASE...
IF I WERE TO END HIS LIFE, DO YOU BELIEVE YOUR FRIEND'S TROUBLES WOULD ALSO BE AT AN END?
I... I...
...NO. IT... IT WOULDN'T SOLVE ANYTHING. IT'D JUST MAKE IT WORSE FOR EVERYONE.
I AM HAPPY YOU UNDERSTAND, MY SON. JUST AS I AM HAPPY TO TELL YOU THERE IS A SOLUTION—ANOTHER PATH FAR MORE PEACEFUL... AND SANE.
GATHER YOUR FRIEND'S BELONGINGS...
...CASEY JONES WILL STAY WITH US NOW.

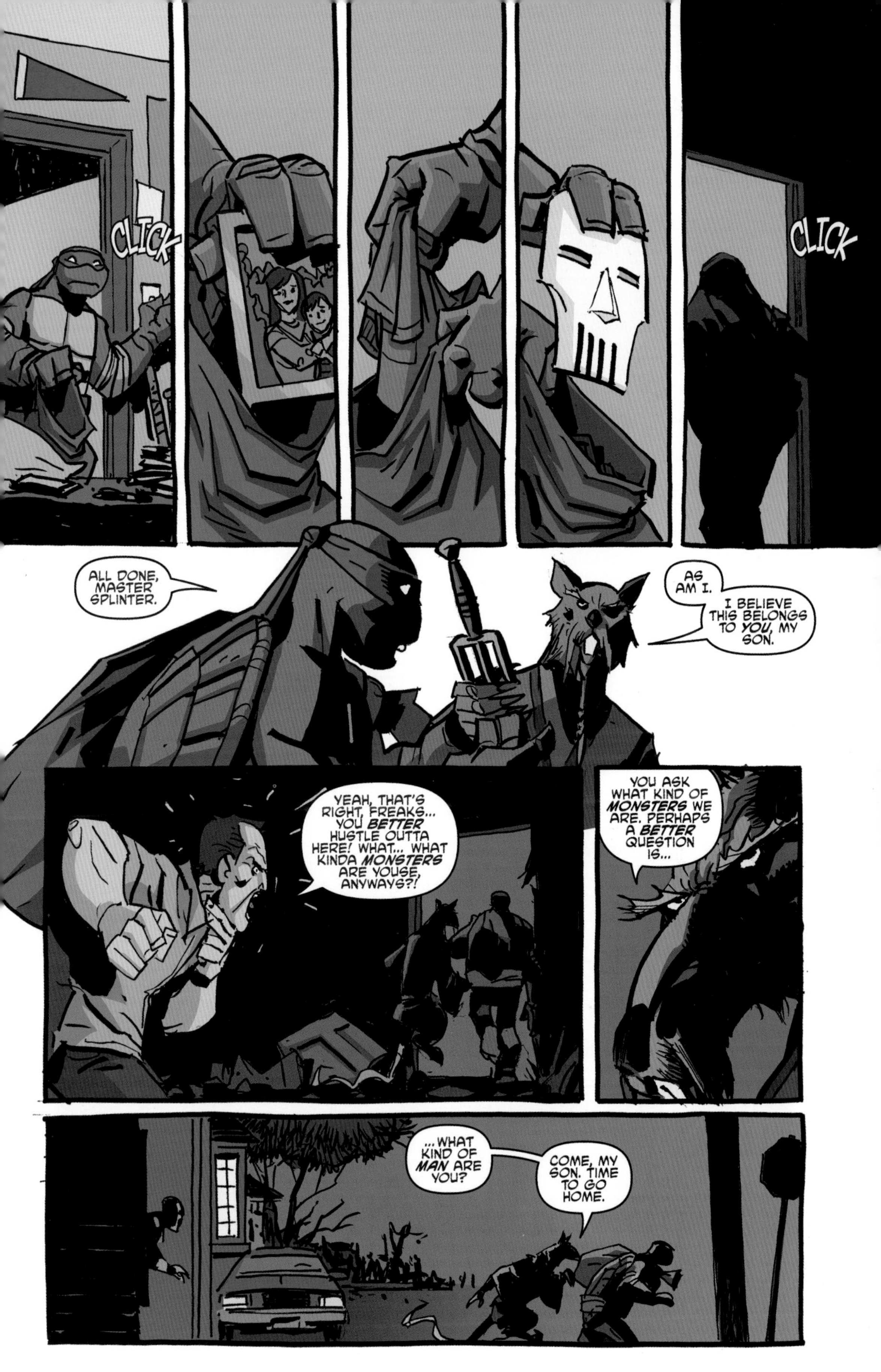
CLICK
CLICK
ALL DONE, MASTER SPLINTER.
AS AM I.
I BELIEVE THIS BELONGS TO YOU, MY SON.
YEAH, THAT'S RIGHT, FREAKS... YOU BETTER HUSTLE OUTTA HERE! WHAT... WHAT KINDA MONSTERS ARE YOUSE, ANYWAYS?!
YOU ASK WHAT KIND OF MONSTERS WE ARE. PERHAPS A BETTER QUESTION IS...
...WHAT KIND OF MAN ARE YOU?
COME, MY SON. TIME TO GO HOME.

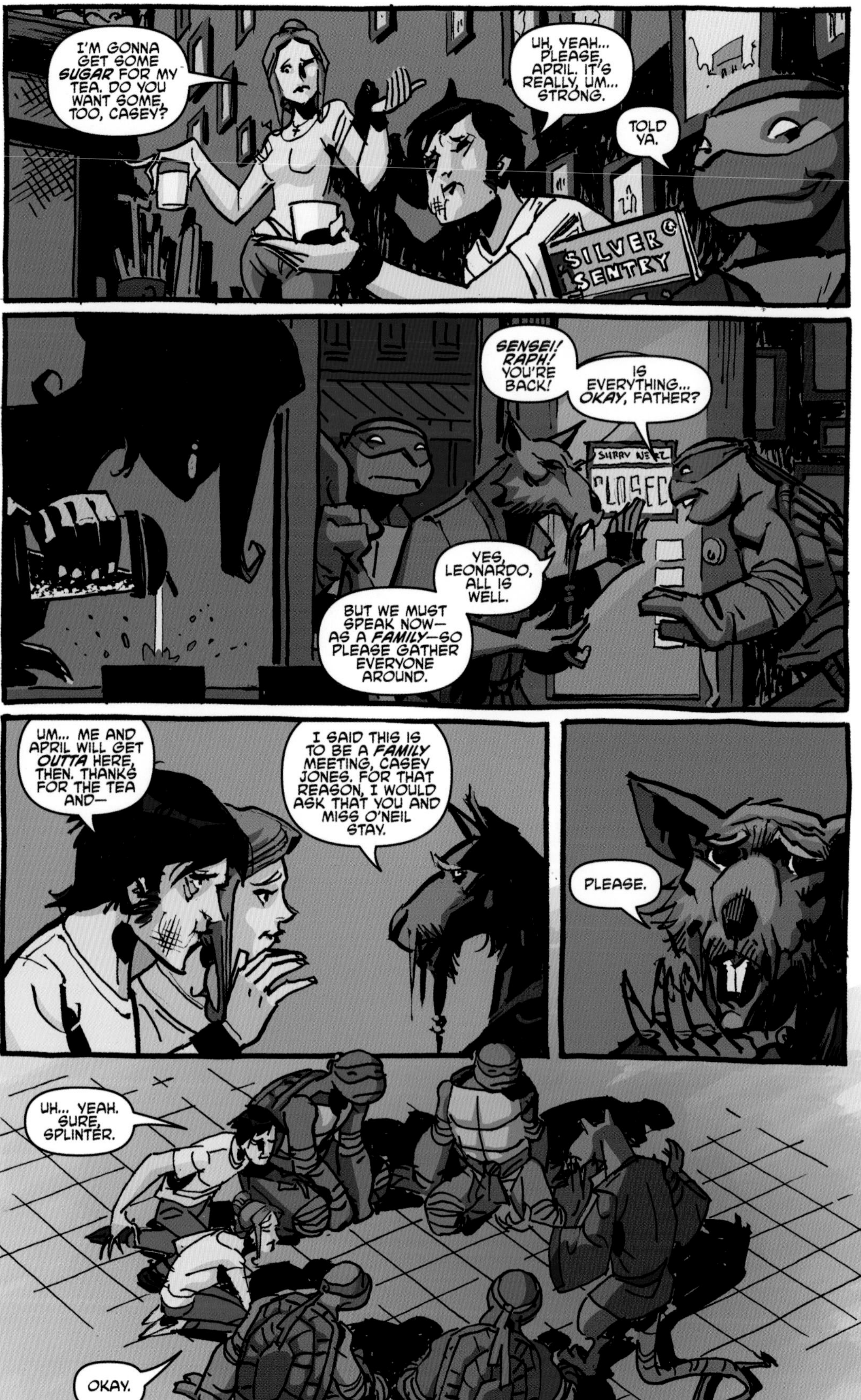
I'M GONNA GET SOME SUGAR FOR MY TEA. DO YOU WANT SOME, TOO, CASEY?
UH, YEAH... PLEASE, APRIL. IT'S REALLY, UM... STRONG.
TOLD YA.
SILVER SENTRY
SENSEI! RAPH! YOU'RE BACK!
IS EVERYTHING... OKAY, FATHER?
CLOSED
YES, LEONARDO, ALL IS WELL.
BUT WE MUST SPEAK NOW— AS A FAMILY—SO PLEASE GATHER EVERYONE AROUND.
UM... ME AND APRIL WILL GET OUTTA HERE, THEN. THANKS FOR THE TEA AND—
I SAID THIS IS TO BE A FAMILY MEETING, CASEY JONES. FOR THAT REASON, I WOULD ASK THAT YOU AND MISS O'NEIL STAY.
PLEASE.
UH... YEAH. SURE, SPLINTER.
OKAY.

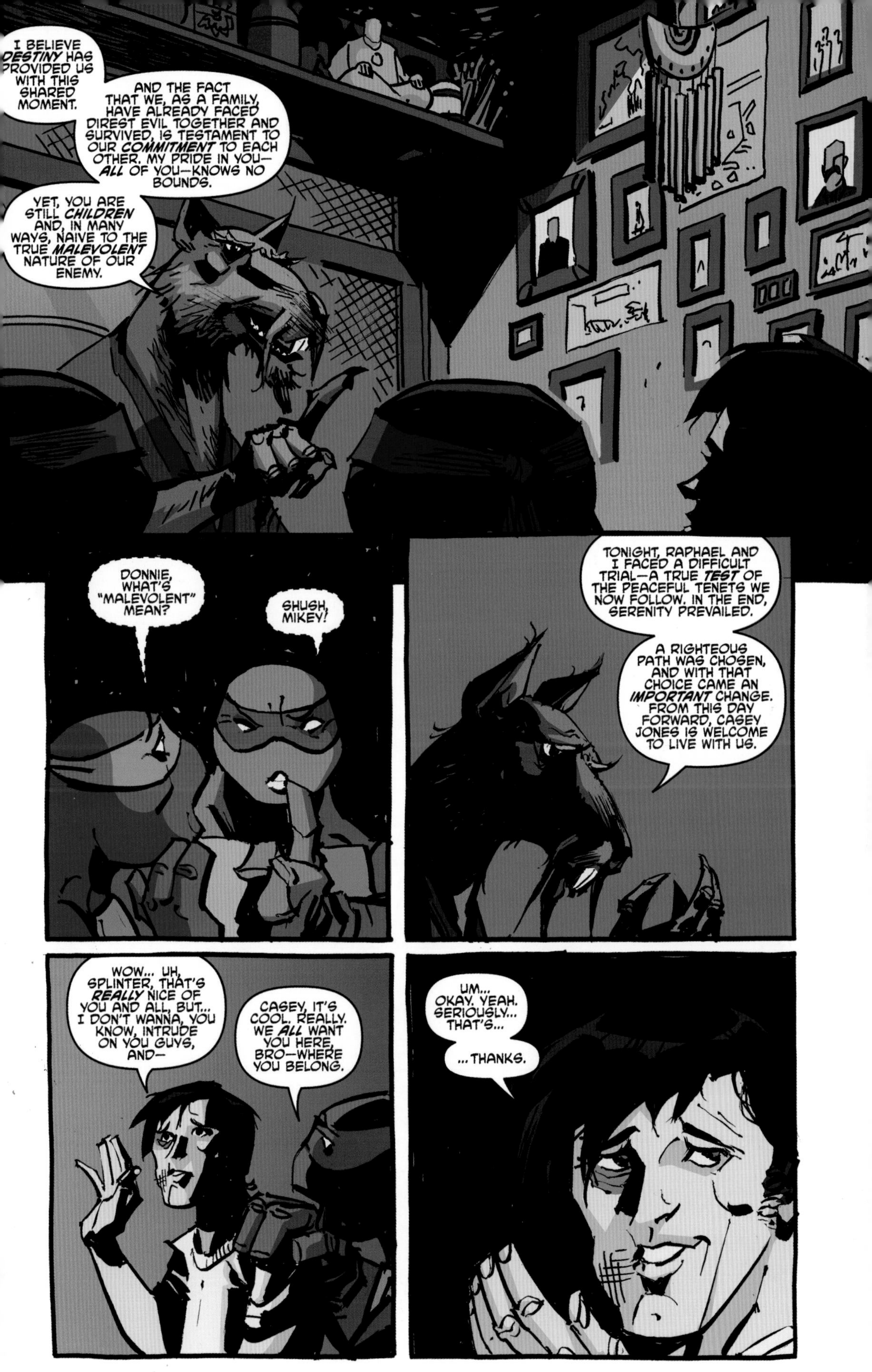
I BELIEVE DESTINY HAS PROVIDED US WITH THIS SHARED MOMENT.
AND THE FACT THAT WE, AS A FAMILY, HAVE ALREADY FACED DIREST EVIL TOGETHER AND SURVIVED, IS TESTAMENT TO OUR COMMITMENT TO EACH OTHER. MY PRIDE IN YOU— ALL OF YOU—KNOWS NO BOUNDS.
YET, YOU ARE STILL CHILDREN AND, IN MANY WAYS, NAIVE TO THE TRUE MALEVOLENT NATURE OF OUR ENEMY.
DONNIE, WHAT'S "MALEVOLENT" MEAN?
SHUSH, MIKEY!
TONIGHT, RAPHAEL AND I FACED A DIFFICULT TRIAL—A TRUE TEST OF THE PEACEFUL TENETS WE NOW FOLLOW. IN THE END, SERENITY PREVAILED.
A RIGHTEOUS PATH WAS CHOSEN, AND WITH THAT CHOICE CAME AN IMPORTANT CHANGE. FROM THIS DAY FORWARD, CASEY JONES IS WELCOME TO LIVE WITH US.
WOW... UH, SPLINTER, THAT'S REALLY NICE OF YOU AND ALL, BUT... I DON'T WANNA, YOU KNOW, INTRUDE ON YOU GUYS, AND—
CASEY, IT'S COOL. REALLY. WE ALL WANT YOU HERE, BRO—WHERE YOU BELONG.
UM... OKAY. YEAH. SERIOUSLY... THAT'S...
...THANKS.

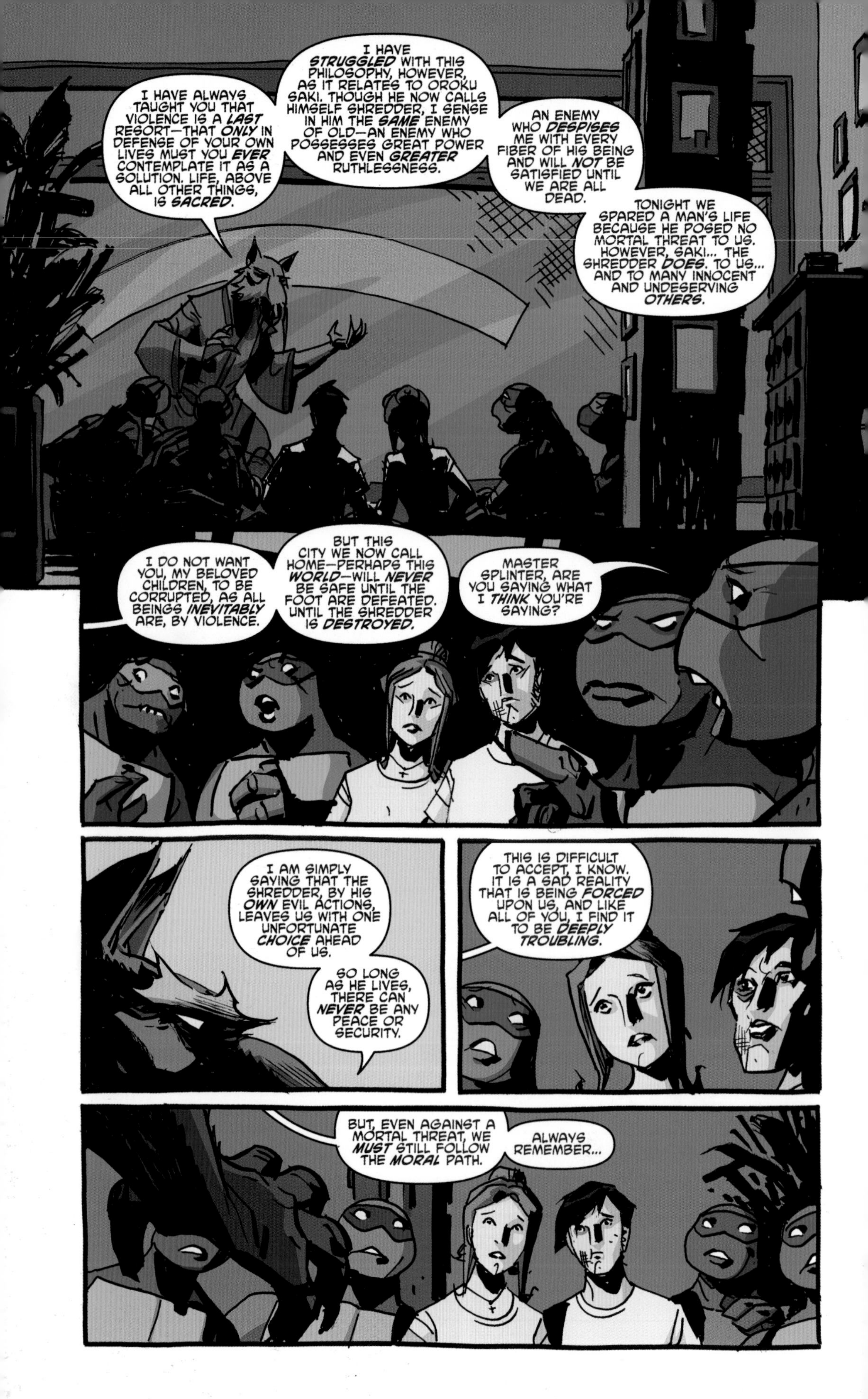
I HAVE ALWAYS TAUGHT YOU THAT VIOLENCE IS A LAST RESORT—THAT ONLY IN DEFENSE OF YOUR OWN LIVES MUST YOU EVER CONTEMPLATE IT AS A SOLUTION. LIFE, ABOVE ALL OTHER THINGS, IS SACRED.
I HAVE STRUGGLED WITH THIS PHILOSOPHY, HOWEVER, AS IT RELATES TO OROKU SAKI. THOUGH HE NOW CALLS HIMSELF SHREDDER, I SENSE IN HIM THE SAME ENEMY OF OLD—AN ENEMY WHO POSSESSES GREAT POWER AND EVEN GREATER RUTHLESSNESS.
AN ENEMY WHO DESPISES ME WITH EVERY FIBER OF HIS BEING AND WILL NOT BE SATISFIED UNTIL WE ARE ALL DEAD.
TONIGHT WE SPARED A MAN'S LIFE BECAUSE HE POSED NO MORTAL THREAT TO US. HOWEVER, SAKI... THE SHREDDER DOES. TO US... AND TO MANY INNOCENT AND UNDESERVING OTHERS.
I DO NOT WANT YOU, MY BELOVED CHILDREN, TO BE CORRUPTED, AS ALL BEINGS INEVITABLY ARE, BY VIOLENCE.
BUT THIS CITY WE NOW CALL HOME—PERHAPS THIS WORLD—WILL NEVER BE SAFE UNTIL THE FOOT ARE DEFEATED. UNTIL THE SHREDDER IS DESTROYED.
MASTER SPLINTER, ARE YOU SAYING WHAT I THINK YOU'RE SAYING?
I AM SIMPLY SAYING THAT THE SHREDDER, BY HIS OWN EVIL ACTIONS, LEAVES US WITH ONE UNFORTUNATE CHOICE AHEAD OF US.
SO LONG AS HE LIVES, THERE CAN NEVER BE ANY PEACE OR SECURITY.
THIS IS DIFFICULT TO ACCEPT, I KNOW. IT IS A SAD REALITY THAT IS BEING FORCED UPON US, AND LIKE ALL OF YOU, I FIND IT TO BE DEEPLY TROUBLING.
BUT, EVEN AGAINST A MORTAL THREAT, WE MUST STILL FOLLOW THE MORAL PATH.
ALWAYS REMEMBER...

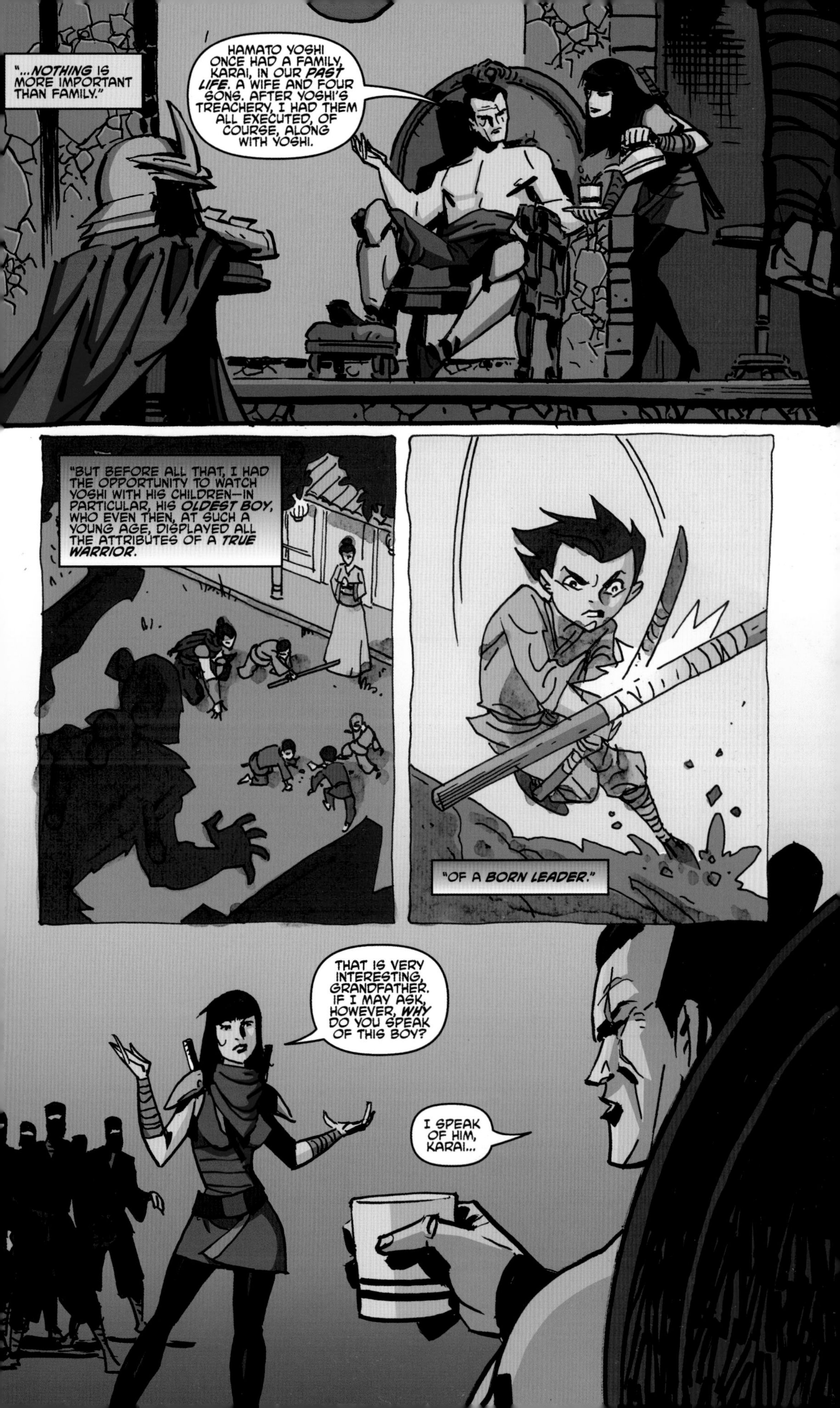
"...NOTHING IS MORE IMPORTANT THAN FAMILY."
HAMATO YOSHI ONCE HAD A FAMILY, KARAI, IN OUR PAST LIFE. A WIFE AND FOUR SONS. AFTER YOSHI'S TREACHERY, I HAD THEM ALL EXECUTED, OF COURSE, ALONG WITH YOSHI.
"BUT BEFORE ALL THAT, I HAD THE OPPORTUNITY TO WATCH YOSHI WITH HIS CHILDREN—IN PARTICULAR, HIS OLDEST BOY, WHO EVEN THEN, AT SUCH A YOUNG AGE, DISPLAYED ALL THE ATTRIBUTES OF A TRUE WARRIOR.
"OF A BORN LEADER."
THAT IS VERY INTERESTING, GRANDFATHER. IF I MAY ASK, HOWEVER, WHY DO YOU SPEAK OF THIS BOY?
I SPEAK OF HIM, KARAI...

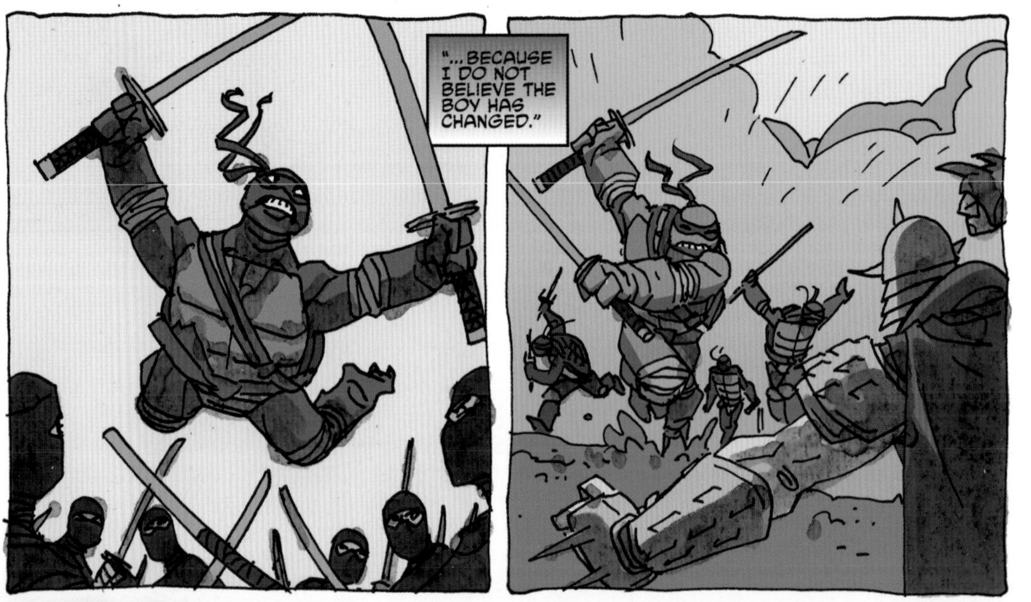
"...BECAUSE I DO NOT BELIEVE THE BOY HAS CHANGED."
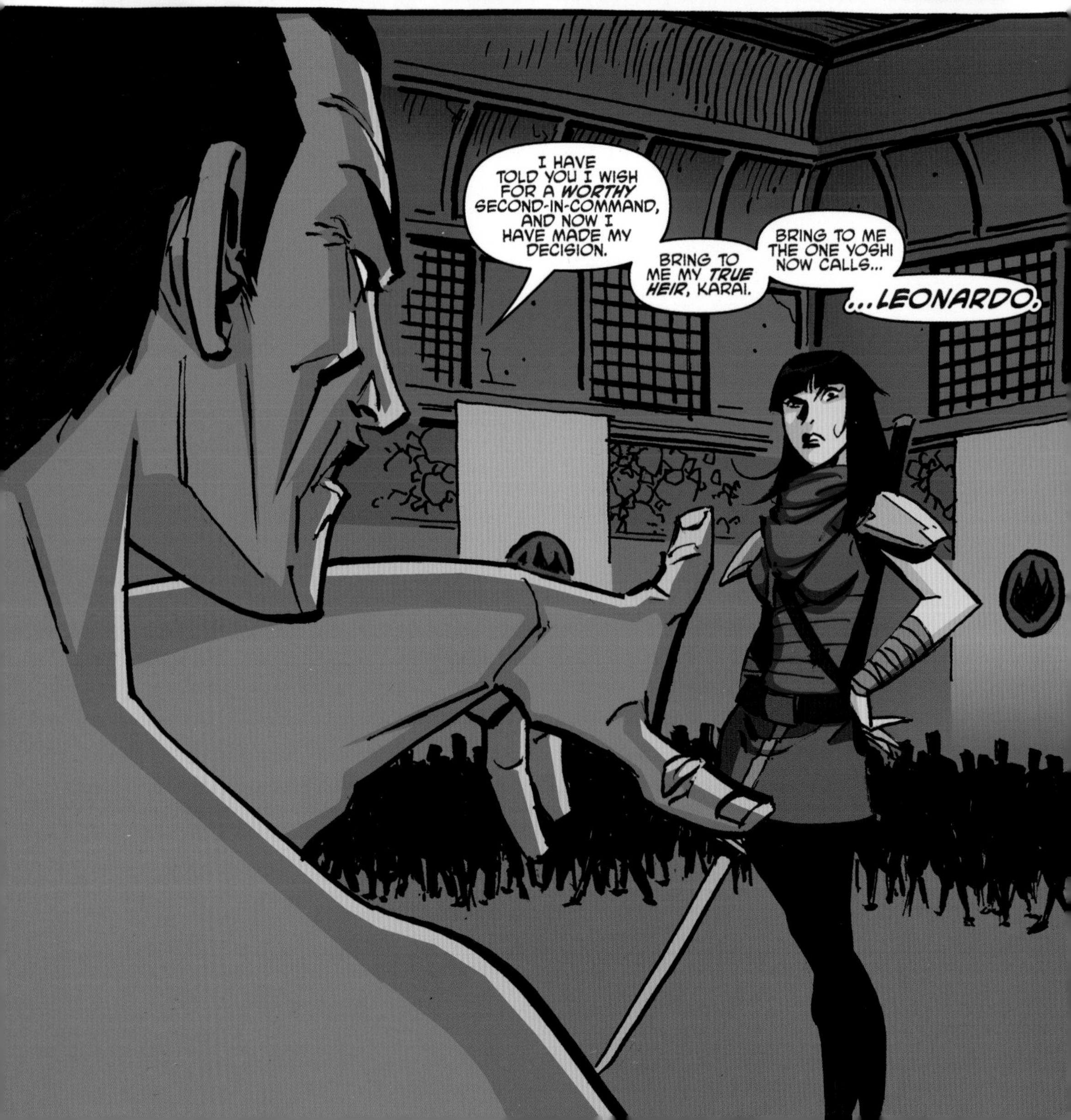
I HAVE TOLD YOU I WISH FOR A *WORTHY* SECOND-IN-COMMAND, AND NOW I HAVE MADE MY DECISION.
BRING TO ME MY *TRUE HEIR*, KARAI.
BRING TO ME THE ONE YOSHI NOW CALLS...
...LEONARDO.

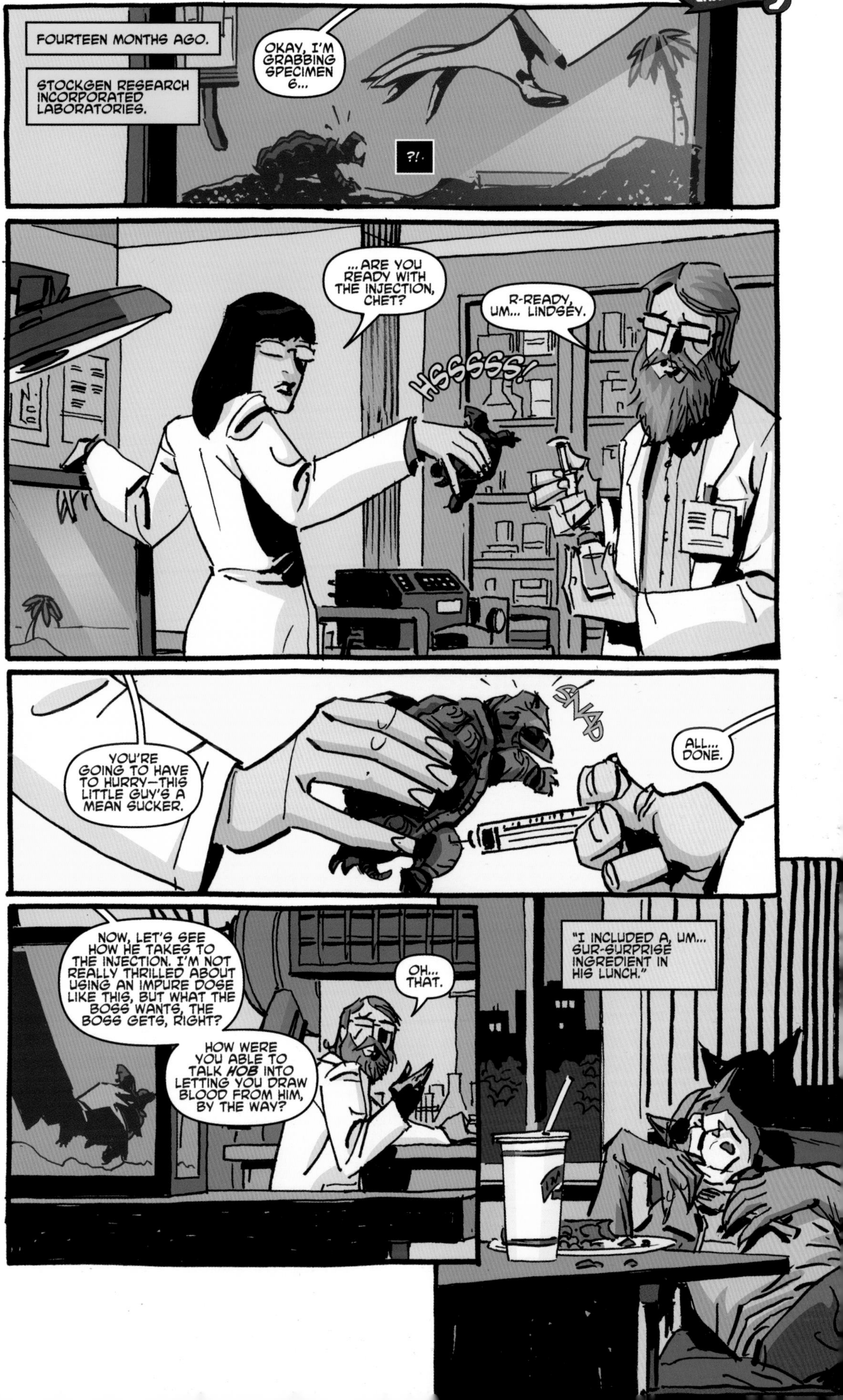
FOURTEEN MONTHS AGO.
STOCKGEN RESEARCH INCORPORATED LABORATORIES.
OKAY, I'M GRABBING SPECIMEN 6...
?!.
...ARE YOU READY WITH THE INJECTION, CHET?
R-READY, UM... LINDSEY.
HSSSSS!
YOU'RE GOING TO HAVE TO HURRY—THIS LITTLE GUY'S A MEAN SUCKER.
SNAP
ALL... DONE.
NOW, LET'S SEE HOW HE TAKES TO THE INJECTION. I'M NOT REALLY THRILLED ABOUT USING AN IMPURE DOSE LIKE THIS, BUT WHAT THE BOSS WANTS, THE BOSS GETS, RIGHT?
HOW WERE YOU ABLE TO TALK HOB INTO LETTING YOU DRAW BLOOD FROM HIM, BY THE WAY?
OH... THAT.
"I INCLUDED A, UM... SUR-SURPRISE INGREDIENT IN HIS LUNCH."

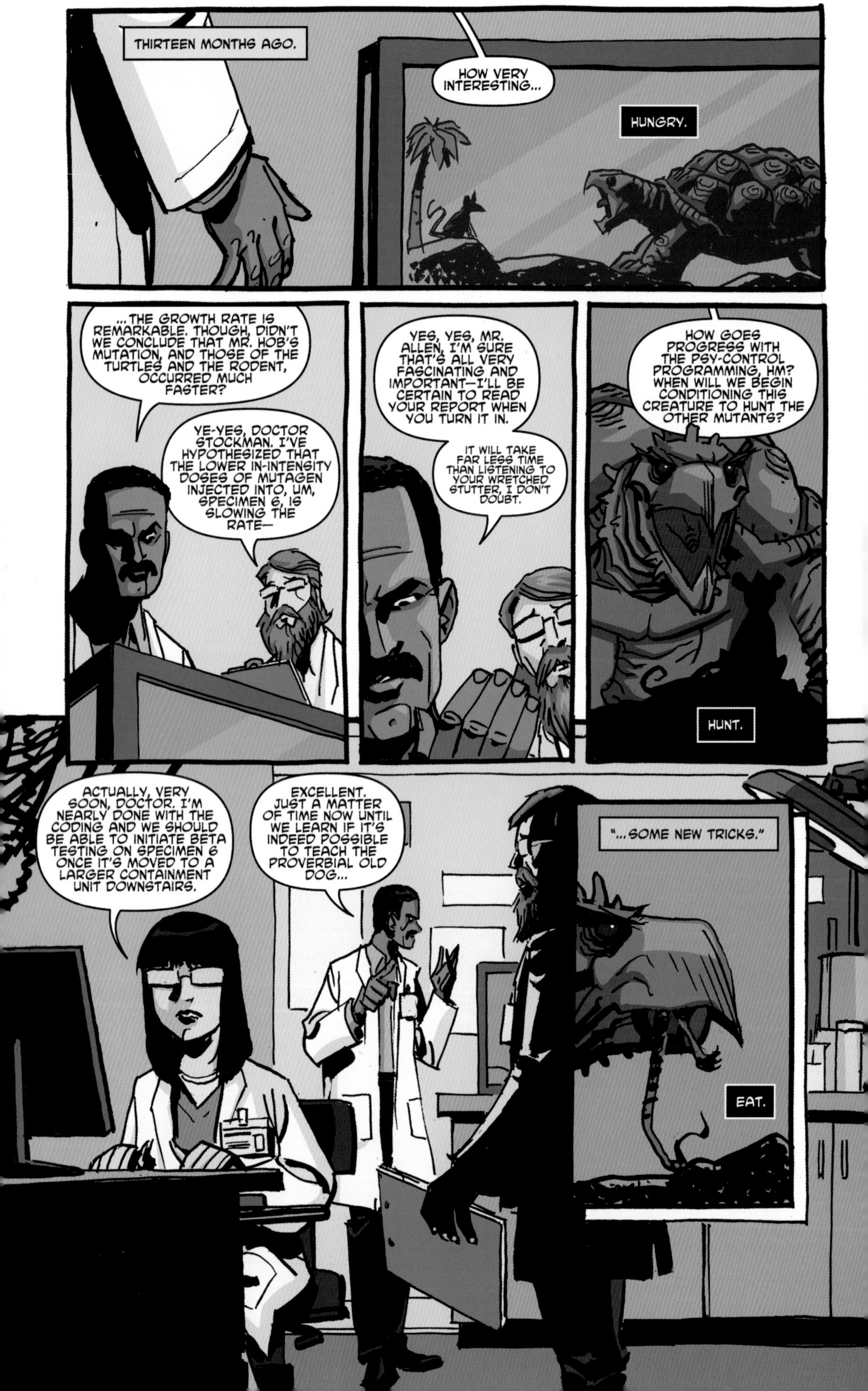
THIRTEEN MONTHS AGO.
HOW VERY INTERESTING...
HUNGRY.
...THE GROWTH RATE IS REMARKABLE. THOUGH, DIDN'T WE CONCLUDE THAT MR. HOB'S MUTATION, AND THOSE OF THE TURTLES AND THE RODENT, OCCURRED MUCH FASTER?
YE-YES, DOCTOR STOCKMAN. I'VE HYPOTHESIZED THAT THE LOWER IN-INTENSITY DOSES OF MUTAGEN INJECTED INTO, UM, SPECIMEN 6, IS SLOWING THE RATE—
YES, YES, MR. ALLEN, I'M SURE THAT'S ALL VERY FASCINATING AND IMPORTANT—I'LL BE CERTAIN TO READ YOUR REPORT WHEN YOU TURN IT IN.
IT WILL TAKE FAR LESS TIME THAN LISTENING TO YOUR WRETCHED STUTTER, I DON'T DOUBT.
HOW GOES PROGRESS WITH THE PSY-CONTROL PROGRAMMING, HM? WHEN WILL WE BEGIN CONDITIONING THIS CREATURE TO HUNT THE OTHER MUTANTS?
HUNT.
ACTUALLY, VERY SOON, DOCTOR. I'M NEARLY DONE WITH THE CODING AND WE SHOULD BE ABLE TO INITIATE BETA TESTING ON SPECIMEN 6 ONCE IT'S MOVED TO A LARGER CONTAINMENT UNIT DOWNSTAIRS.
EXCELLENT. JUST A MATTER OF TIME NOW UNTIL WE LEARN IF IT'S INDEED POSSIBLE TO TEACH THE PROVERBIAL OLD DOG...
"...SOME NEW TRICKS."
EAT.

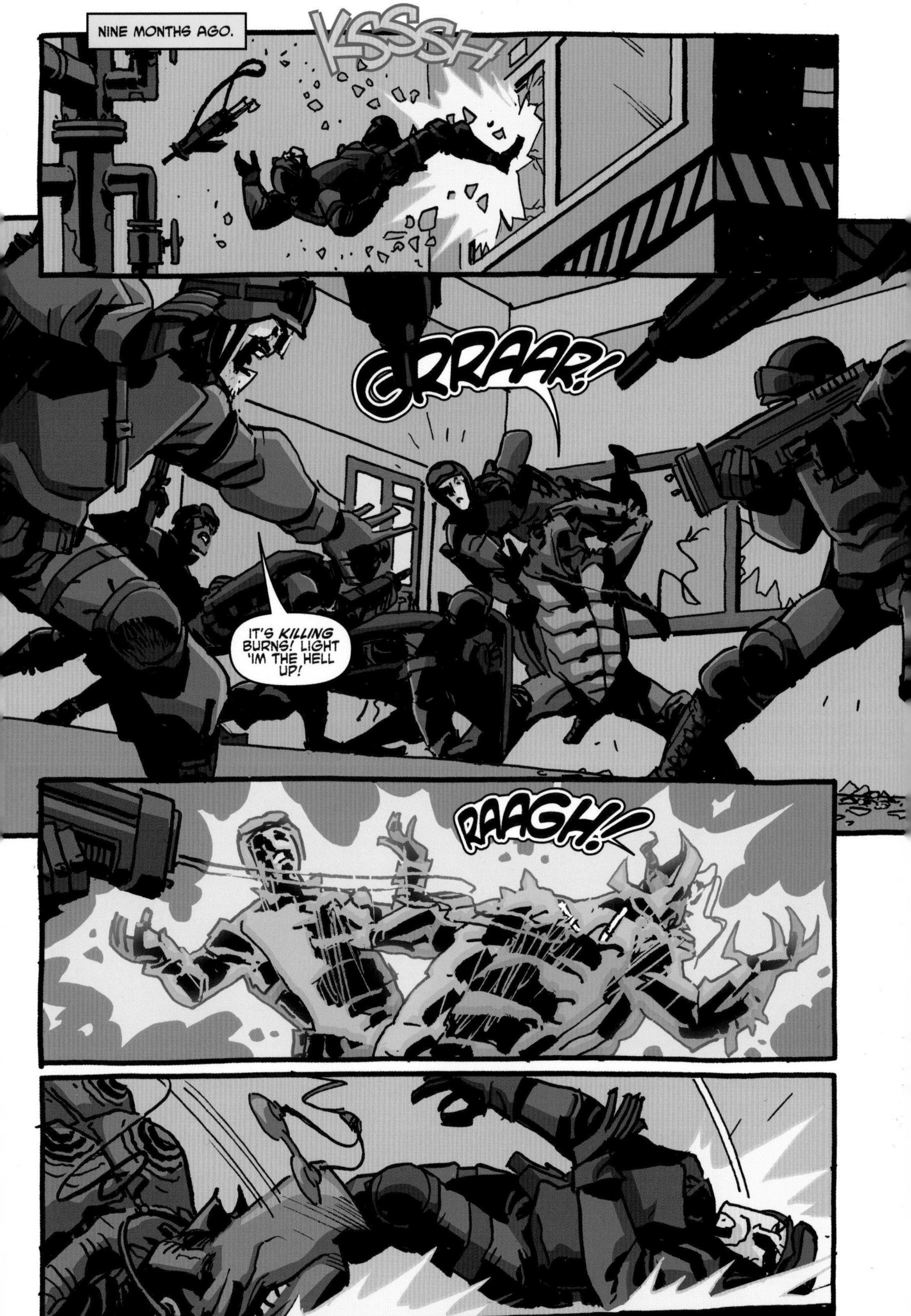
NINE MONTHS AGO.
KSSSH
GRRAAR!
IT'S KILLING BURNS! LIGHT 'IM THE HELL UP!
RAAGH!!

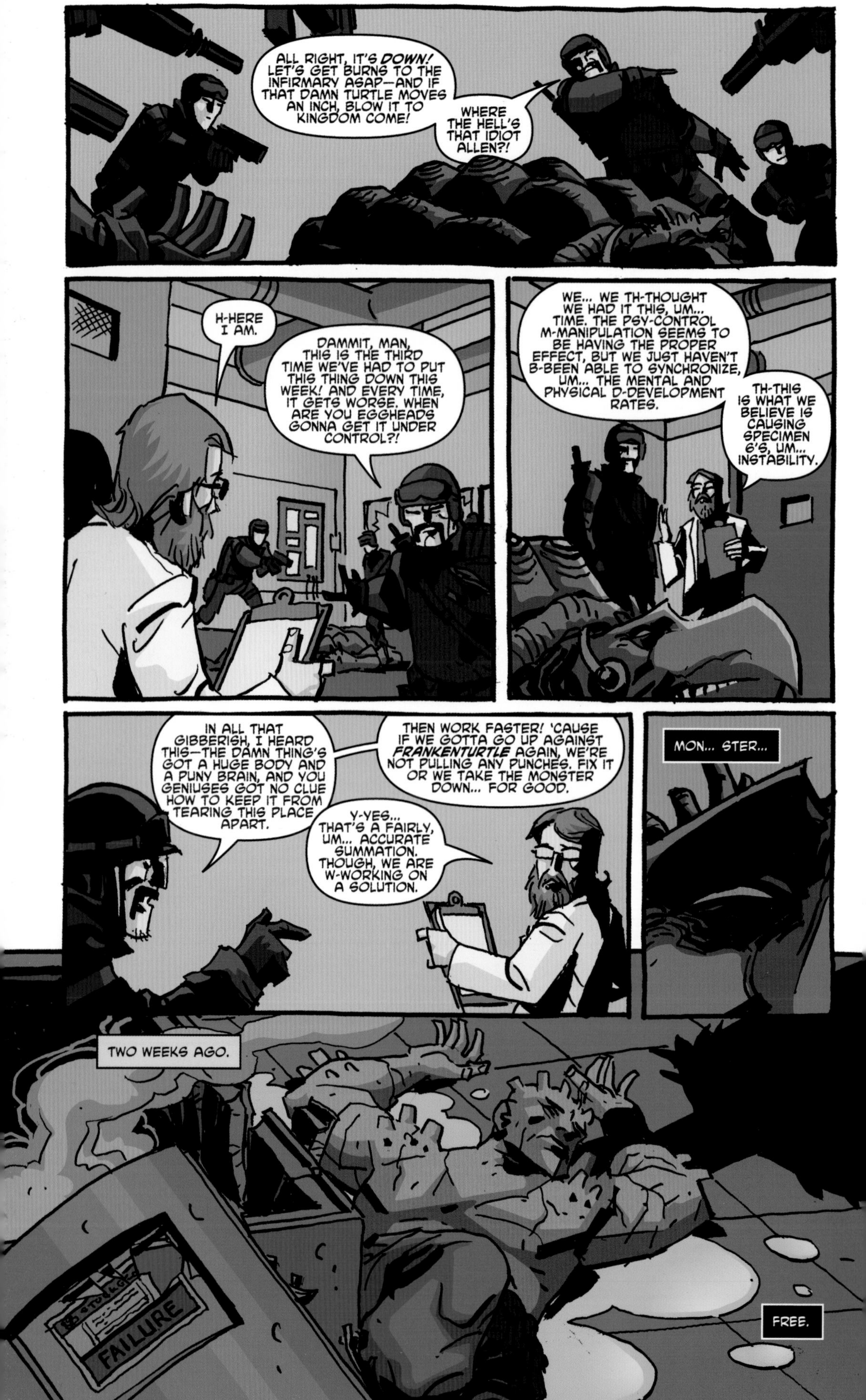

ALL RIGHT, IT'S DOWN! LET'S GET BURNS TO THE INFIRMARY ASAP—AND IF THAT DAMN TURTLE MOVES AN INCH, BLOW IT TO KINGDOM COME!
WHERE THE HELL'S THAT IDIOT ALLEN?!
H-HERE I AM.
DAMMIT, MAN, THIS IS THE THIRD TIME WE'VE HAD TO PUT THIS THING DOWN THIS WEEK! AND EVERY TIME, IT GETS WORSE. WHEN ARE YOU EGGHEADS GONNA GET IT UNDER CONTROL?!
WE... WE TH-THOUGHT WE HAD IT THIS, UM... TIME. THE PSY-CONTROL M-MANIPULATION SEEMS TO BE HAVING THE PROPER EFFECT, BUT WE JUST HAVEN'T B-BEEN ABLE TO SYNCHRONIZE, UM... THE MENTAL AND PHYSICAL D-DEVELOPMENT RATES.
TH-THIS IS WHAT WE BELIEVE IS CAUSING SPECIMEN 6'S, UM... INSTABILITY.
IN ALL THAT GIBBERISH, I HEARD THIS—THE DAMN THING'S GOT A HUGE BODY AND A PUNY BRAIN, AND YOU GENIUSES GOT NO CLUE HOW TO KEEP IT FROM TEARING THIS PLACE APART.
Y-YES... THAT'S A FAIRLY, UM... ACCURATE SUMMATION. THOUGH, WE ARE W-WORKING ON A SOLUTION.
THEN WORK FASTER! 'CAUSE IF WE GOTTA GO UP AGAINST FRANKENTURTLE AGAIN, WE'RE NOT PULLING ANY PUNCHES. FIX IT OR WE TAKE THE MONSTER DOWN... FOR GOOD.
MON... STER...
TWO WEEKS AGO.
FAILURE
FREE.

LAST NIGHT.

KNOCK KNOCK

PIZZERIA

THE MIKESTER! BUMP IT, BABY!

HEY, WOODY.

WHOA. WHY SO GLUM, CHUM?

IT'S... IT'S NOTHIN'. JUST SOME THINGS WITH MASTER SPLINTER.

YOUR DAD? WHAT'S UP WITH THAT OLD RAT-MAN?

HAVE YOU SEEN MY DOG

HELP MISSING DO

MISSING CAT

IF YOU SEE MR. WHISKA PLEASE CALL.

IT'S JUST SOME... SOME NINJA STUFF.

NINJA STUFF? LIKE KUNG-FU FIGHTIN'?

YEAH... THAT, AND SOME OTHER WORSE STUFF WE MIGHT HAVE TO DO. IT SUCKS.

LOOK, MAN, I DON'T PRETEND TO UNDERSTAND WHAT YOU AND YOUR BROS ARE UP TO—I'M JUST A PIZZA GUY... BUT, I DO KNOW A GOOD HEART WHEN I SEE ONE, AND YOURS IS AS GOOD AS THEY COME, MIKE.

KEEP THE POSITIVE ENERGY FLOWING, LISTEN TO THAT GOOD HEART OF YOURS, AND THINGS'LL WORK OUT JUST FINE, YOU'LL SEE.

I... I HOPE SO.

'SIDES, YOU'VE ALWAYS GOT OL' WOODY'S KICKA BUTTA PIZZA PIES TO CHEERA YOU UPPA.

RIGHTEOUS! THANKS, MAN.

DON'T MENTION IT.

53

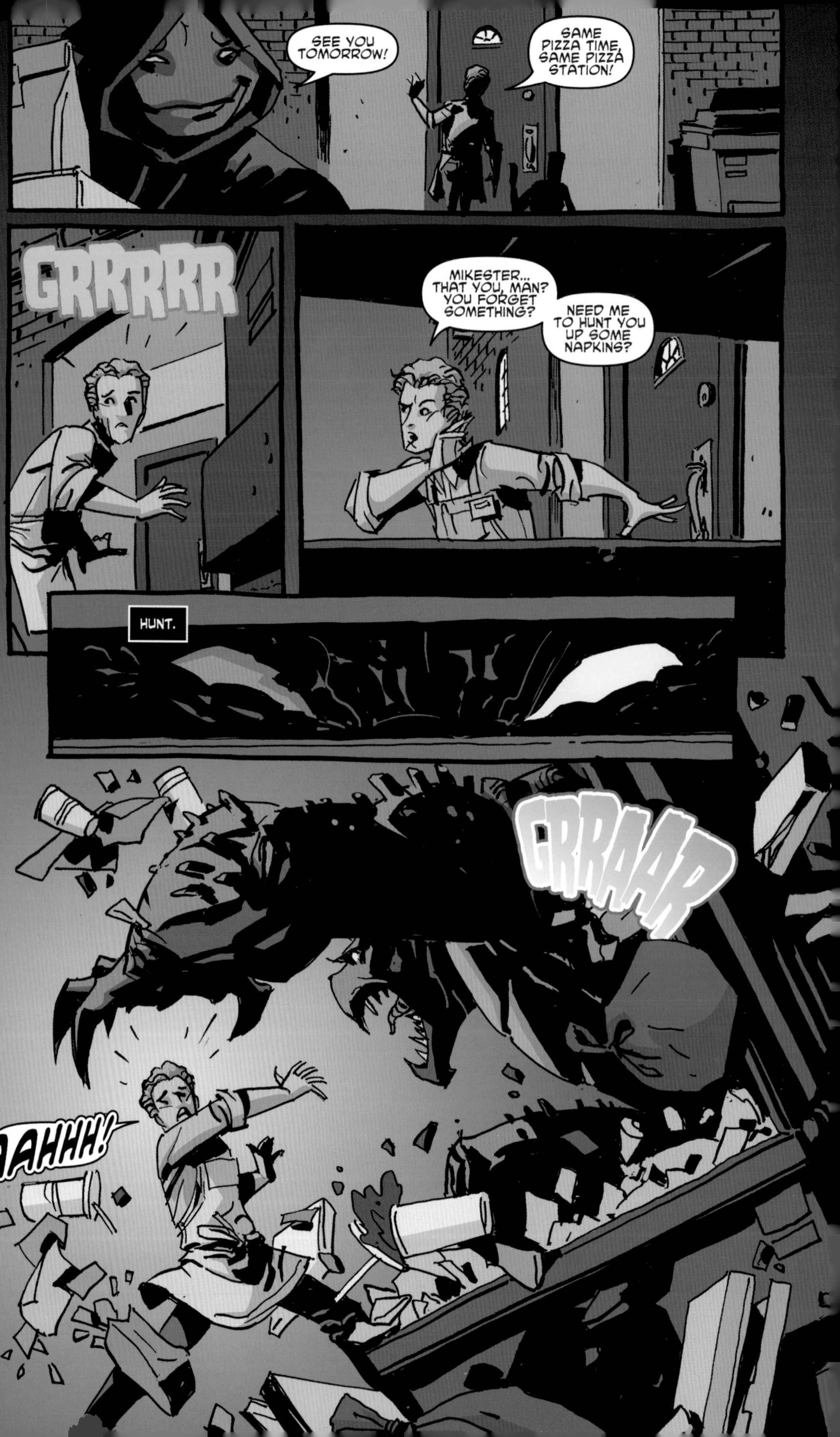

SEE YOU TOMORROW!
SAME PIZZA TIME, SAME PIZZA STATION!
GRRRRR
MIKESTER... THAT YOU, MAN? YOU FORGET SOMETHING?
NEED ME TO HUNT YOU UP SOME NAPKINS?
HUNT.
GRRAAR
AAHHH!

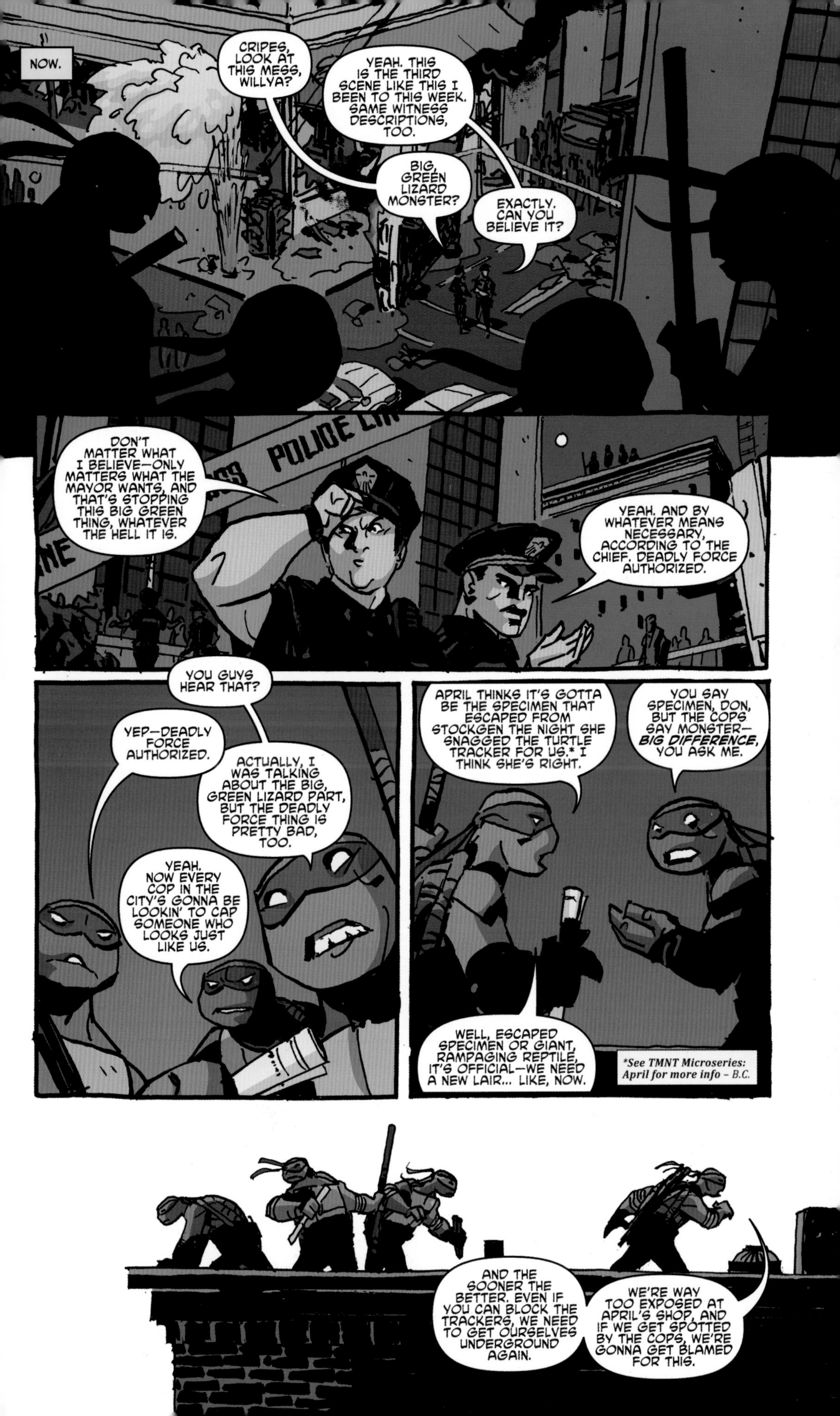
NOW.
CRIPES, LOOK AT THIS MESS, WILLYA?
YEAH. THIS IS THE THIRD SCENE LIKE THIS I BEEN TO THIS WEEK. SAME WITNESS DESCRIPTIONS, TOO.
BIG, GREEN LIZARD MONSTER?
EXACTLY. CAN YOU BELIEVE IT?
POLICE LIN
DON'T MATTER WHAT I BELIEVE—ONLY MATTERS WHAT THE MAYOR WANTS, AND THAT'S STOPPING THIS BIG GREEN THING, WHATEVER THE HELL IT IS.
YEAH. AND BY WHATEVER MEANS NECESSARY, ACCORDING TO THE CHIEF. DEADLY FORCE AUTHORIZED.
YOU GUYS HEAR THAT?
YEP—DEADLY FORCE AUTHORIZED.
ACTUALLY, I WAS TALKING ABOUT THE BIG, GREEN LIZARD PART, BUT THE DEADLY FORCE THING IS PRETTY BAD, TOO.
YEAH. NOW EVERY COP IN THE CITY'S GONNA BE LOOKIN' TO CAP SOMEONE WHO LOOKS JUST LIKE US.
APRIL THINKS IT'S GOTTA BE THE SPECIMEN THAT ESCAPED FROM STOCKGEN THE NIGHT SHE SNAGGED THE TURTLE TRACKER FOR US.* I THINK SHE'S RIGHT.
YOU SAY SPECIMEN, DON, BUT THE COPS SAY MONSTER—*BIG DIFFERENCE*, YOU ASK ME.
WELL, ESCAPED SPECIMEN OR GIANT, RAMPAGING REPTILE, IT'S OFFICIAL—WE NEED A NEW LAIR... LIKE, NOW.
*See TMNT Microseries: April for more info – B.C.
AND THE SOONER THE BETTER. EVEN IF YOU CAN BLOCK THE TRACKERS, WE NEED TO GET OURSELVES UNDERGROUND AGAIN.
WE'RE WAY TOO EXPOSED AT APRIL'S SHOP, AND IF WE GET SPOTTED BY THE COPS, WE'RE GONNA GET BLAMED FOR THIS.

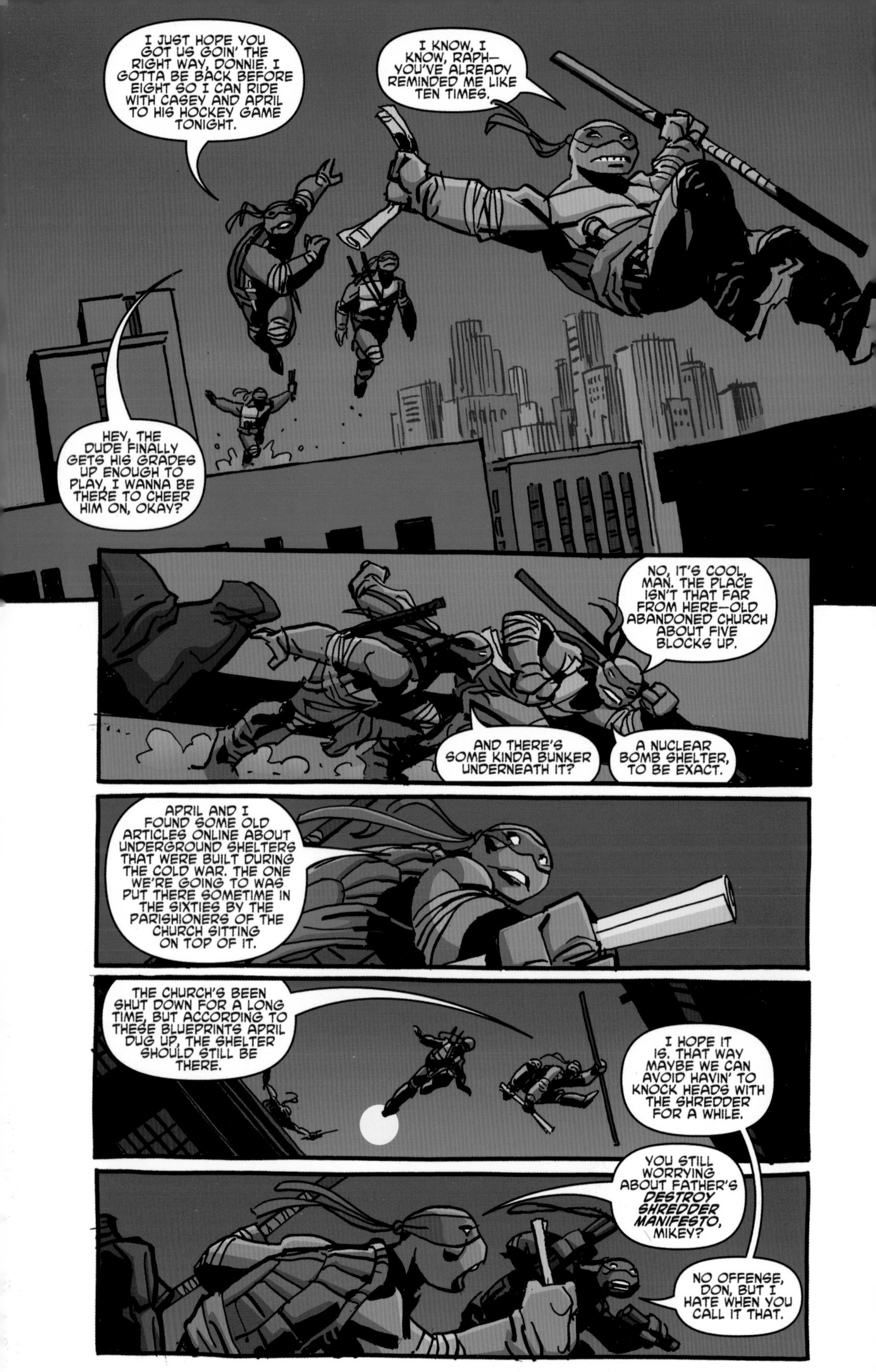
I JUST HOPE YOU GOT US GOIN' THE RIGHT WAY, DONNIE. I GOTTA BE BACK BEFORE EIGHT SO I CAN RIDE WITH CASEY AND APRIL TO HIS HOCKEY GAME TONIGHT.
I KNOW, I KNOW, RAPH— YOU'VE ALREADY REMINDED ME LIKE TEN TIMES.
HEY, THE DUDE FINALLY GETS HIS GRADES UP ENOUGH TO PLAY, I WANNA BE THERE TO CHEER HIM ON, OKAY?
NO, IT'S COOL, MAN. THE PLACE ISN'T THAT FAR FROM HERE—OLD ABANDONED CHURCH ABOUT FIVE BLOCKS UP.
AND THERE'S SOME KINDA BUNKER UNDERNEATH IT?
A NUCLEAR BOMB SHELTER, TO BE EXACT.
APRIL AND I FOUND SOME OLD ARTICLES ONLINE ABOUT UNDERGROUND SHELTERS THAT WERE BUILT DURING THE COLD WAR. THE ONE WE'RE GOING TO WAS PUT THERE SOMETIME IN THE SIXTIES BY THE PARISHIONERS OF THE CHURCH SITTING ON TOP OF IT.
THE CHURCH'S BEEN SHUT DOWN FOR A LONG TIME, BUT ACCORDING TO THESE BLUEPRINTS APRIL DUG UP, THE SHELTER SHOULD STILL BE THERE.
I HOPE IT IS. THAT WAY MAYBE WE CAN AVOID HAVIN' TO KNOCK HEADS WITH THE SHREDDER FOR A WHILE.
YOU STILL WORRYING ABOUT FATHER'S *DESTROY SHREDDER MANIFESTO*, MIKEY?
NO OFFENSE, DON, BUT I HATE WHEN YOU CALL IT THAT.

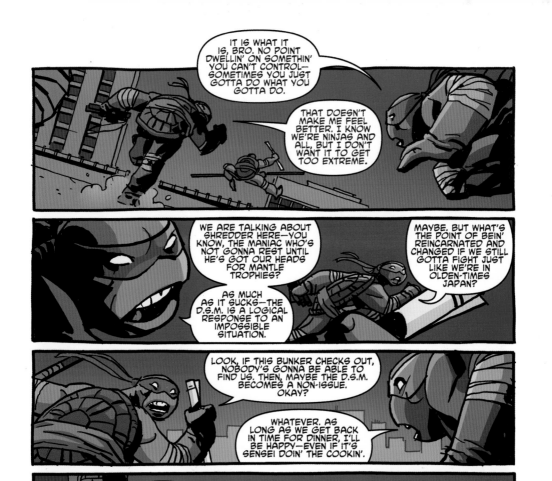

IT IS WHAT IT IS, BRO. NO POINT DWELLIN' ON SOMETHIN' YOU CAN'T CONTROL— SOMETIMES YOU JUST GOTTA DO WHAT YOU GOTTA DO.

THAT DOESN'T MAKE ME FEEL BETTER. I KNOW WE'RE NINJAS AND ALL, BUT I DON'T WANT IT TO GET TOO EXTREME.

WE ARE TALKING ABOUT SHREDDER HERE—YOU KNOW, THE MANIAC WHO'S NOT GONNA REST UNTIL HE'S GOT OUR HEADS FOR MANTLE TROPHIES?

AS MUCH AS IT SUCKS—THE D.S.M. IS A LOGICAL RESPONSE TO AN IMPOSSIBLE SITUATION.

MAYBE. BUT WHAT'S THE POINT OF BEIN' REINCARNATED AND CHANGED IF WE STILL GOTTA FIGHT JUST LIKE WE'RE IN OLDEN-TIMES JAPAN?

LOOK, IF THIS BUNKER CHECKS OUT, NOBODY'S GONNA BE ABLE TO FIND US. THEN, MAYBE THE D.S.M. BECOMES A NON-ISSUE. OKAY?

WHATEVER. AS LONG AS WE GET BACK IN TIME FOR DINNER, I'LL BE HAPPY—EVEN IF IT'S SENSEI DOIN' THE COOKIN'.

WHAT? NO PIZZAS?

NOPE. I STOPPED AT WOODY'S SHOP EARLIER TO SAY HI, BUT HE WASN'T THERE. GUESS HE GOT THE NIGHT OFF OR SOMETHIN'.

WELL, ALL I CAN SAY IS, I REALLY HOPE DINNER'S SOMETHING NEW TONIGHT.

I MEAN, I'D NEVER SAY IT TO HIS FACE, BUT IF THERE'S ONE THING I'M MORE SICK OF THAN MIKEY'S PIZZAS...

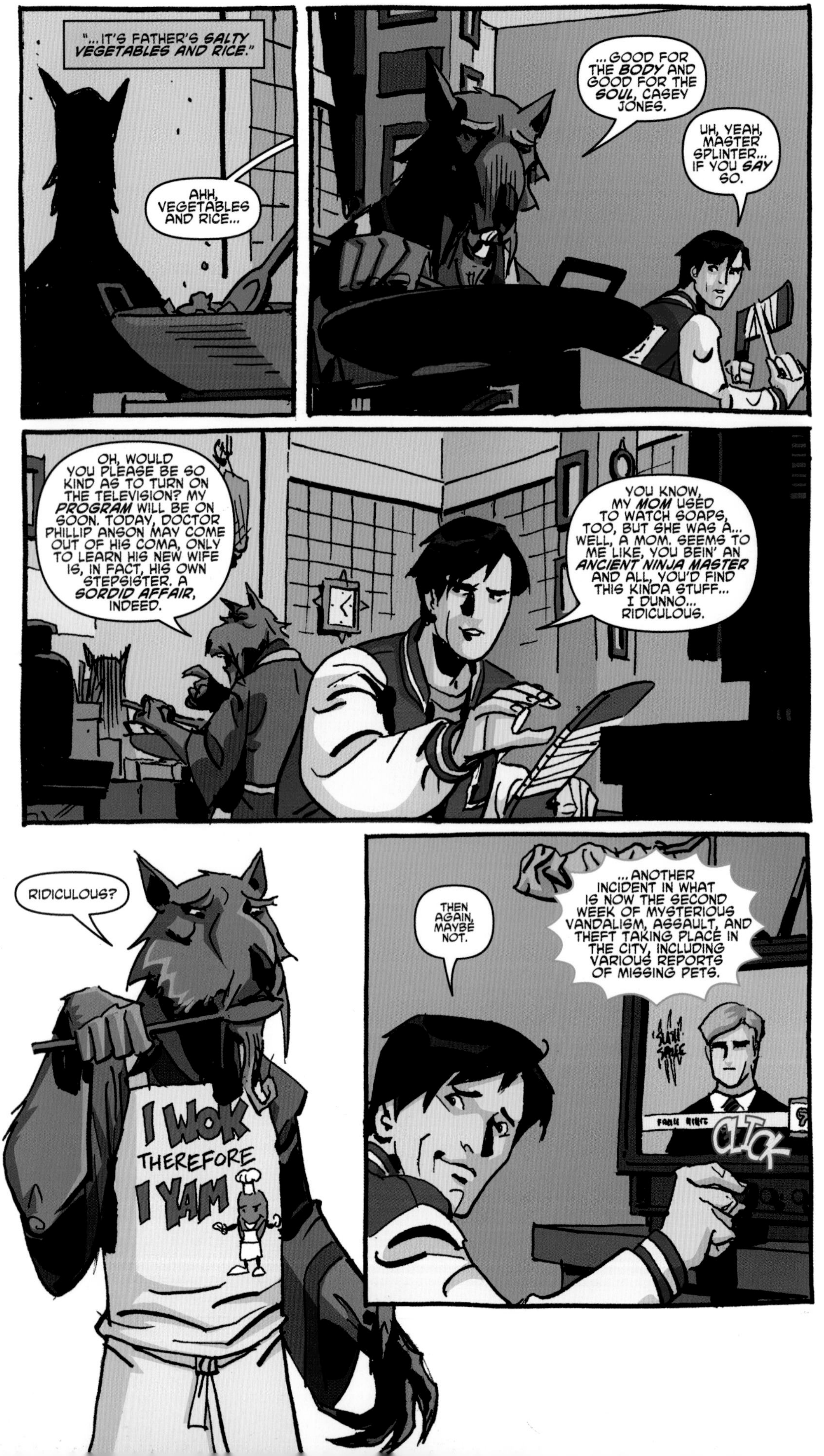
"...IT'S FATHER'S SALTY VEGETABLES AND RICE."
AHH, VEGETABLES AND RICE...
...GOOD FOR THE BODY AND GOOD FOR THE SOUL, CASEY JONES.
UH, YEAH, MASTER SPLINTER... IF YOU SAY SO.
OH, WOULD YOU PLEASE BE SO KIND AS TO TURN ON THE TELEVISION? MY PROGRAM WILL BE ON SOON. TODAY, DOCTOR PHILLIP ANSON MAY COME OUT OF HIS COMA, ONLY TO LEARN HIS NEW WIFE IS, IN FACT, HIS OWN STEPSISTER. A SORDID AFFAIR, INDEED.
YOU KNOW, MY MOM USED TO WATCH SOAPS, TOO, BUT SHE WAS A... WELL, A MOM. SEEMS TO ME LIKE, YOU BEIN' AN ANCIENT NINJA MASTER AND ALL, YOU'D FIND THIS KINDA STUFF... I DUNNO... RIDICULOUS.
RIDICULOUS?
I WOK THEREFORE I YAM
THEN AGAIN, MAYBE NOT.
...ANOTHER INCIDENT IN WHAT IS NOW THE SECOND WEEK OF MYSTERIOUS VANDALISM, ASSAULT, AND THEFT TAKING PLACE IN THE CITY, INCLUDING VARIOUS REPORTS OF MISSING PETS.
CLICK

SLASH SPREE

FRANK WHITE

ACCORDING TO THE POLICE, AN UNIDENTIFIED INDIVIDUAL VICIOUSLY ACCOSTED AN EMPLOYEE AT A *SMALL PIZZERIA* LATE LAST NIGHT. THOUGH THE VICTIM SUFFERED ONLY MINOR INJURIES, HE WAS SEVERELY TRAUMATIZED AND IS BEING TREATED FOR SHOCK.

THIS LATEST ATTACK APPEARS TO BE PART OF A RECENT DESTRUCTIVE SPREE. SEVERAL WITNESSES HAVE DESCRIBED A *"LIZARD-LIKE CREATURE OF IMMENSE SIZE."* SOME CITIZENS HAVE BEGUN CALLING THE MYSTERY VANDAL *"SLASH"* IN REFERENCE TO THE SEVERE SLASHING DAMAGE CAUSED TO PROPERTY DURING MANY OF THE INCIDENTS.

YOU GUYS ARE *NOT* GONNA BELIEVE WHAT HAPPENED TO MY VAN.

WHAT IS IT, MISS O'NEIL?

I'VE GOT A FLAT TIRE AND... AND *SOMETHING ELSE.*

A FLAT AIN'T *THAT* BIG A DEAL, APRIL. C'MON... LET'S GO CHECK IT OUT.

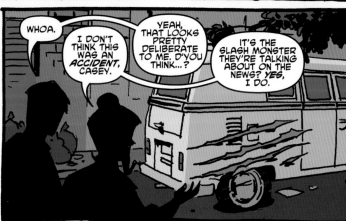

WHOA.

I DON'T THINK THIS WAS AN *ACCIDENT,* CASEY.

YEAH, THAT LOOKS PRETTY DELIBERATE TO ME. D'YOU THINK...?

IT'S THE SLASH MONSTER THEY'RE TALKING ABOUT ON THE NEWS? *YES,* I DO.

REMEMBER HOW I SAID *SOMETHING* GOT OUT OF STOCKGEN? WELL BASED ON THE SIZE OF THE CONTAINER IT WAS IN, THAT SOMETHING WAS *REALLY BIG*... AND OBVIOUSLY EXTREMELY VIOLENT AND DANGEROUS.

I'M PRETTY CERTAIN *THAT'S* WHAT'S RUNNING AROUND THE CITY. I THINK IT'S HUNTING. AND, CRAZY AS IT SOUNDS, I THINK IT'S HUNTING *US.*

WELL, HOPEFULLY THE COPS GET IT BEFORE IT GETS ANY OF US. IF IT CAN DO *THIS* TO YOUR VAN, IMAGINE WHAT IT COULD DO TO A PERSON...

...OR A TURTLE.

YEAH...

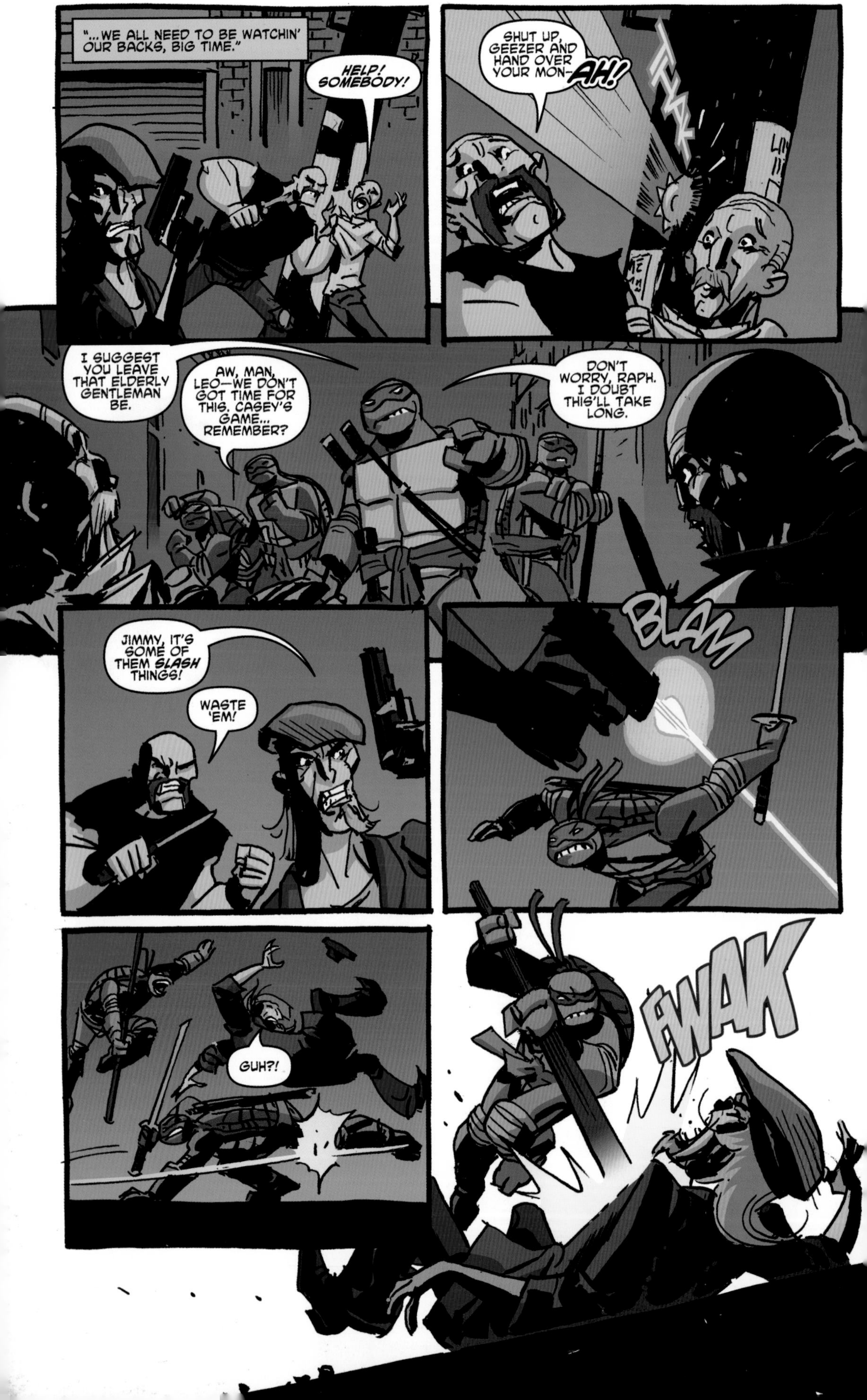
"...WE ALL NEED TO BE WATCHIN' OUR BACKS, BIG TIME."
HELP! SOMEBODY!
SHUT UP, GEEZER AND HAND OVER YOUR MON--AH!
THAK
I SUGGEST YOU LEAVE THAT ELDERLY GENTLEMAN BE.
AW, MAN, LEO--WE DON'T GOT TIME FOR THIS. CASEY'S GAME... REMEMBER?
DON'T WORRY, RAPH. I DOUBT THIS'LL TAKE LONG.
JIMMY, IT'S SOME OF THEM SLASH THINGS!
WASTE 'EM!
BLAM
GUH?!
FWAK

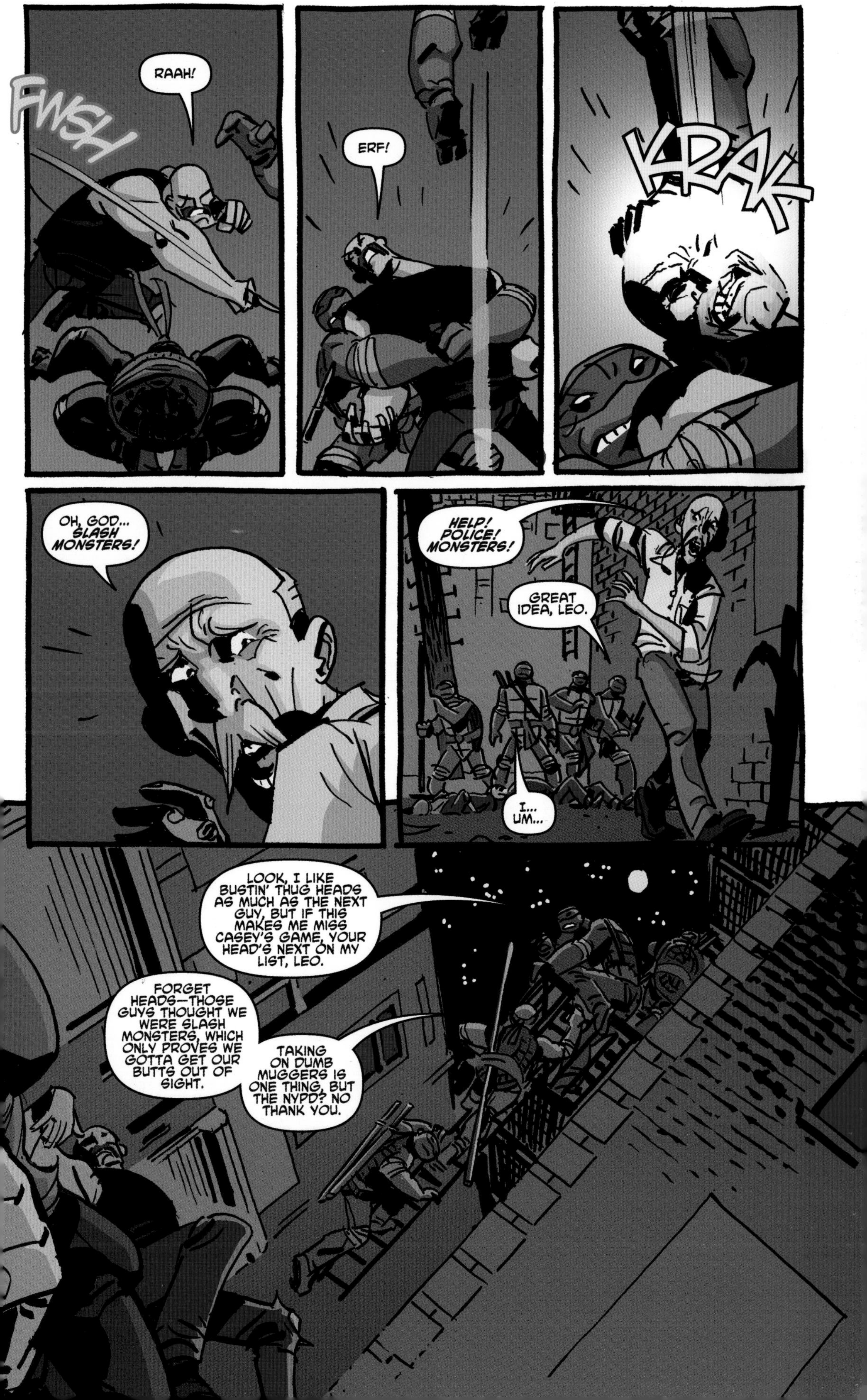
RAAH!
FWSH
ERF!
KRAK
OH, GOD... SLASH MONSTERS!
HELP! POLICE! MONSTERS!
GREAT IDEA, LEO.
I... UM...
LOOK, I LIKE BUSTIN' THUG HEADS AS MUCH AS THE NEXT GUY, BUT IF THIS MAKES ME MISS CASEY'S GAME, YOUR HEAD'S NEXT ON MY LIST, LEO.
FORGET HEADS—THOSE GUYS THOUGHT WE WERE SLASH MONSTERS, WHICH ONLY PROVES WE GOTTA GET OUR BUTTS OUT OF SIGHT.
TAKING ON DUMB MUGGERS IS ONE THING, BUT THE NYPD? NO THANK YOU.

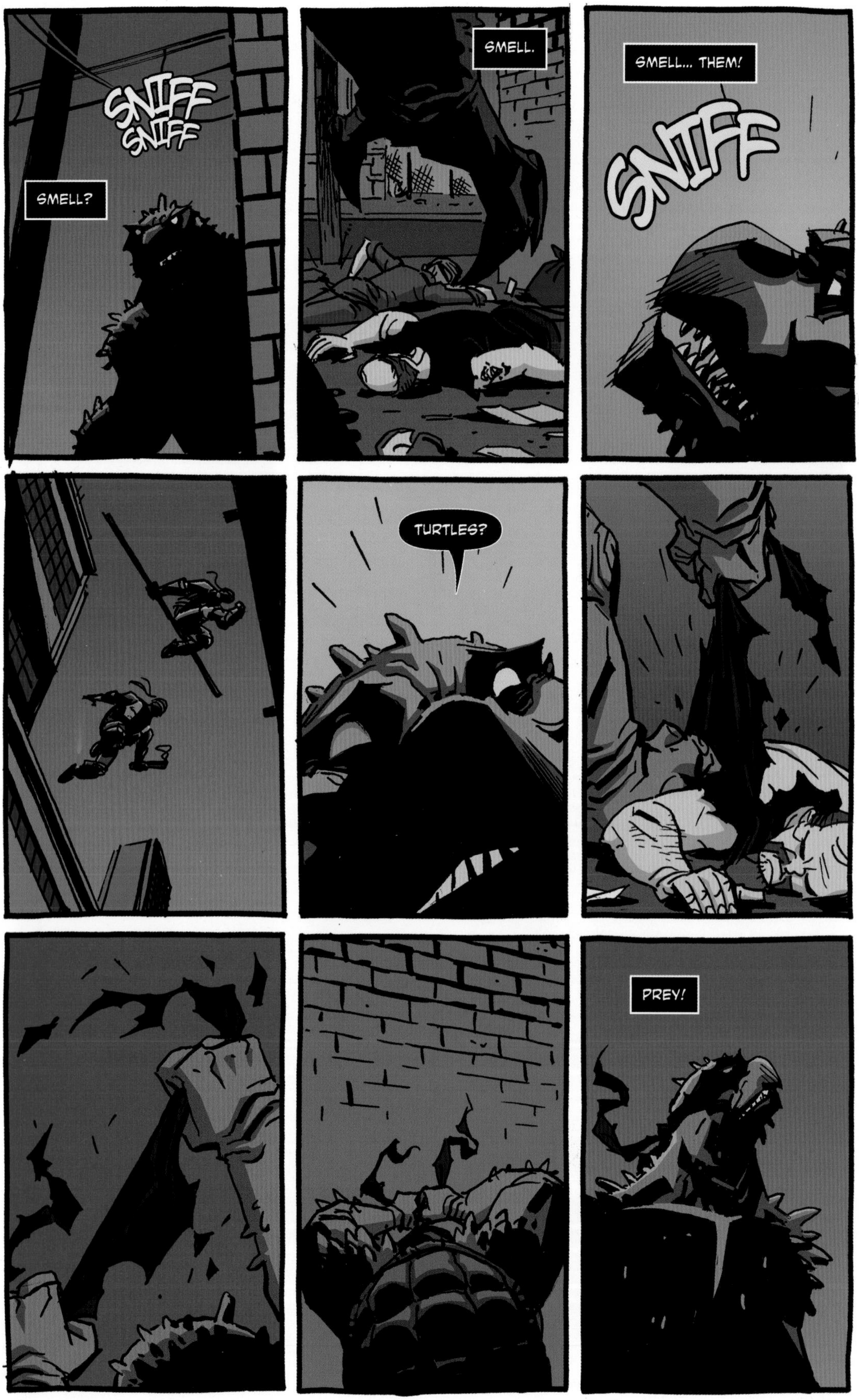
SNIFF SNIFF
SMELL?
SMELL.
SMELL... THEM!
SNIFF
TURTLES?
PREY!

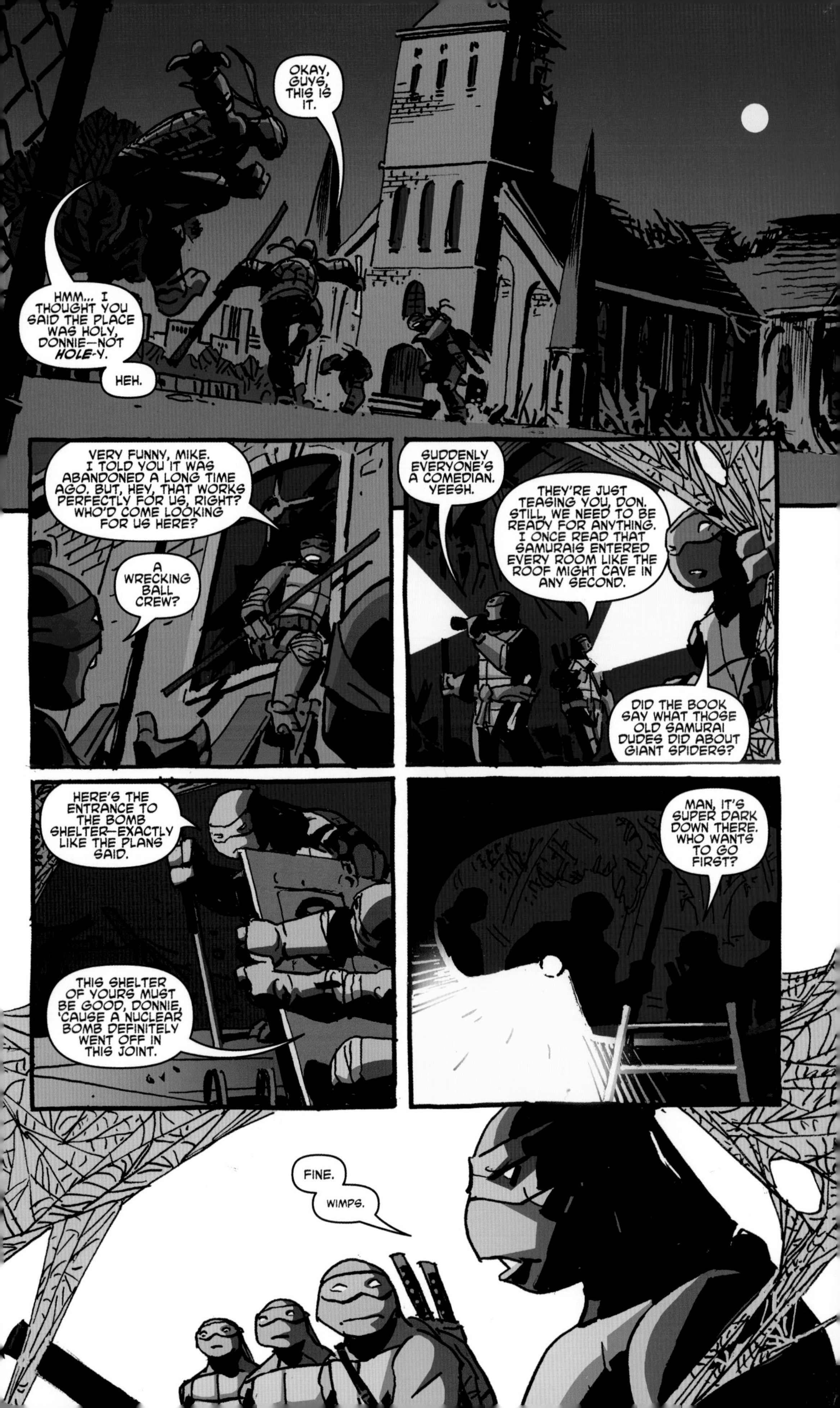
OKAY, GUYS, THIS IS IT.
HMM... I THOUGHT YOU SAID THE PLACE WAS HOLY, DONNIE—NOT *HOLE*-Y.
HEH.
VERY FUNNY, MIKE. I TOLD YOU IT WAS ABANDONED A LONG TIME AGO. BUT, HEY, THAT WORKS PERFECTLY FOR US, RIGHT? WHO'D COME LOOKING FOR US HERE?
A WRECKING BALL CREW?
SUDDENLY EVERYONE'S A COMEDIAN. YEESH.
THEY'RE JUST TEASING YOU, DON. STILL, WE NEED TO BE READY FOR ANYTHING. I ONCE READ THAT SAMURAIS ENTERED EVERY ROOM LIKE THE ROOF MIGHT CAVE IN ANY SECOND.
DID THE BOOK SAY WHAT THOSE OLD SAMURAI DUDES DID ABOUT GIANT SPIDERS?
HERE'S THE ENTRANCE TO THE BOMB SHELTER—EXACTLY LIKE THE PLANS SAID.
THIS SHELTER OF YOURS MUST BE GOOD, DONNIE, 'CAUSE A NUCLEAR BOMB DEFINITELY WENT OFF IN THIS JOINT.
MAN, IT'S SUPER DARK DOWN THERE. WHO WANTS TO GO FIRST?
FINE.
WIMPS.

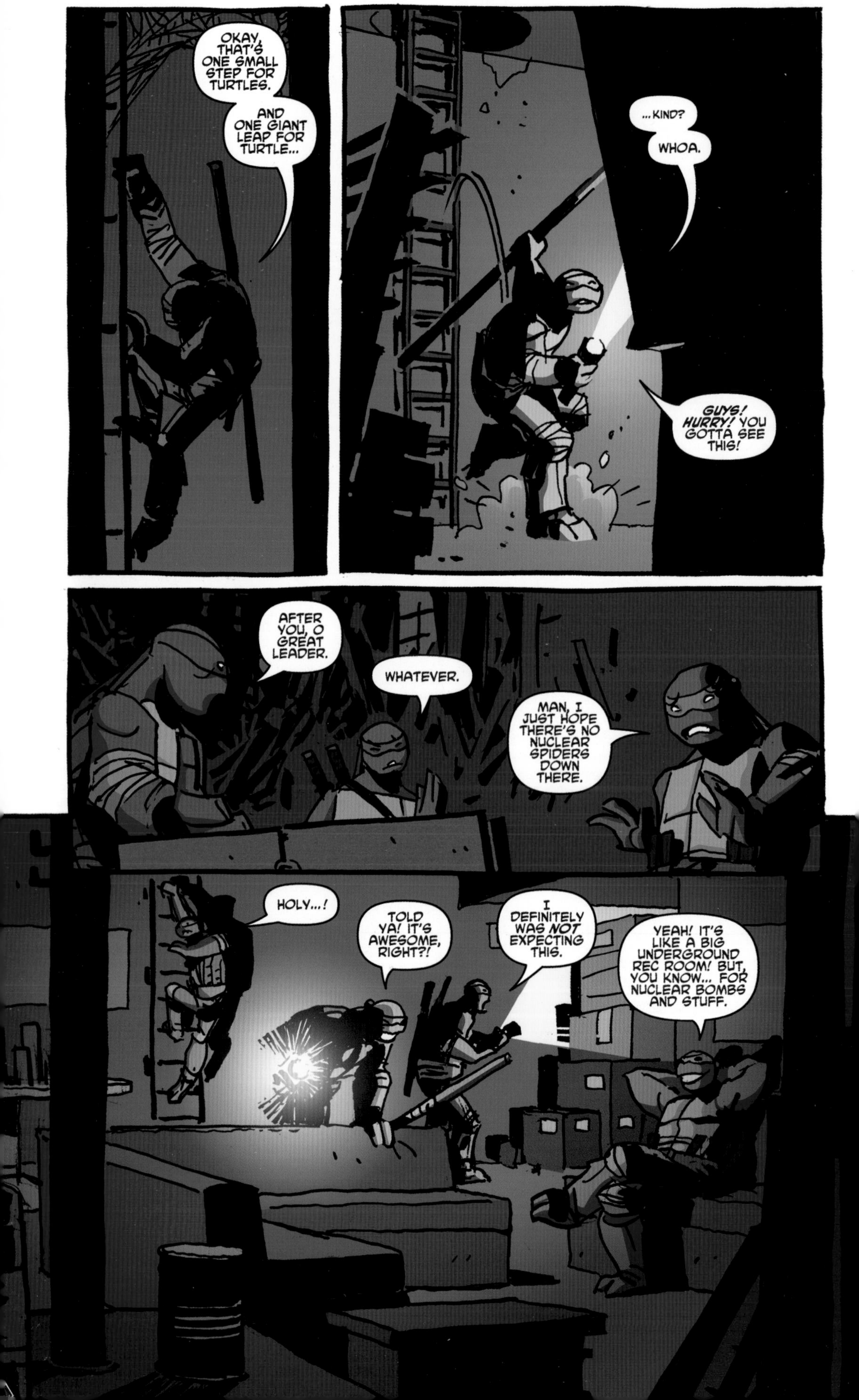
OKAY, THAT'S ONE SMALL STEP FOR TURTLES.
AND ONE GIANT LEAP FOR TURTLE...
...KIND?
WHOA.
GUYS! HURRY! YOU GOTTA SEE THIS!
AFTER YOU, O GREAT LEADER.
WHATEVER.
MAN, I JUST HOPE THERE'S NO NUCLEAR SPIDERS DOWN THERE.
HOLY...!
TOLD YA! IT'S AWESOME, RIGHT?!
I DEFINITELY WAS NOT EXPECTING THIS.
YEAH! IT'S LIKE A BIG UNDERGROUND REC ROOM! BUT, YOU KNOW... FOR NUCLEAR BOMBS AND STUFF.

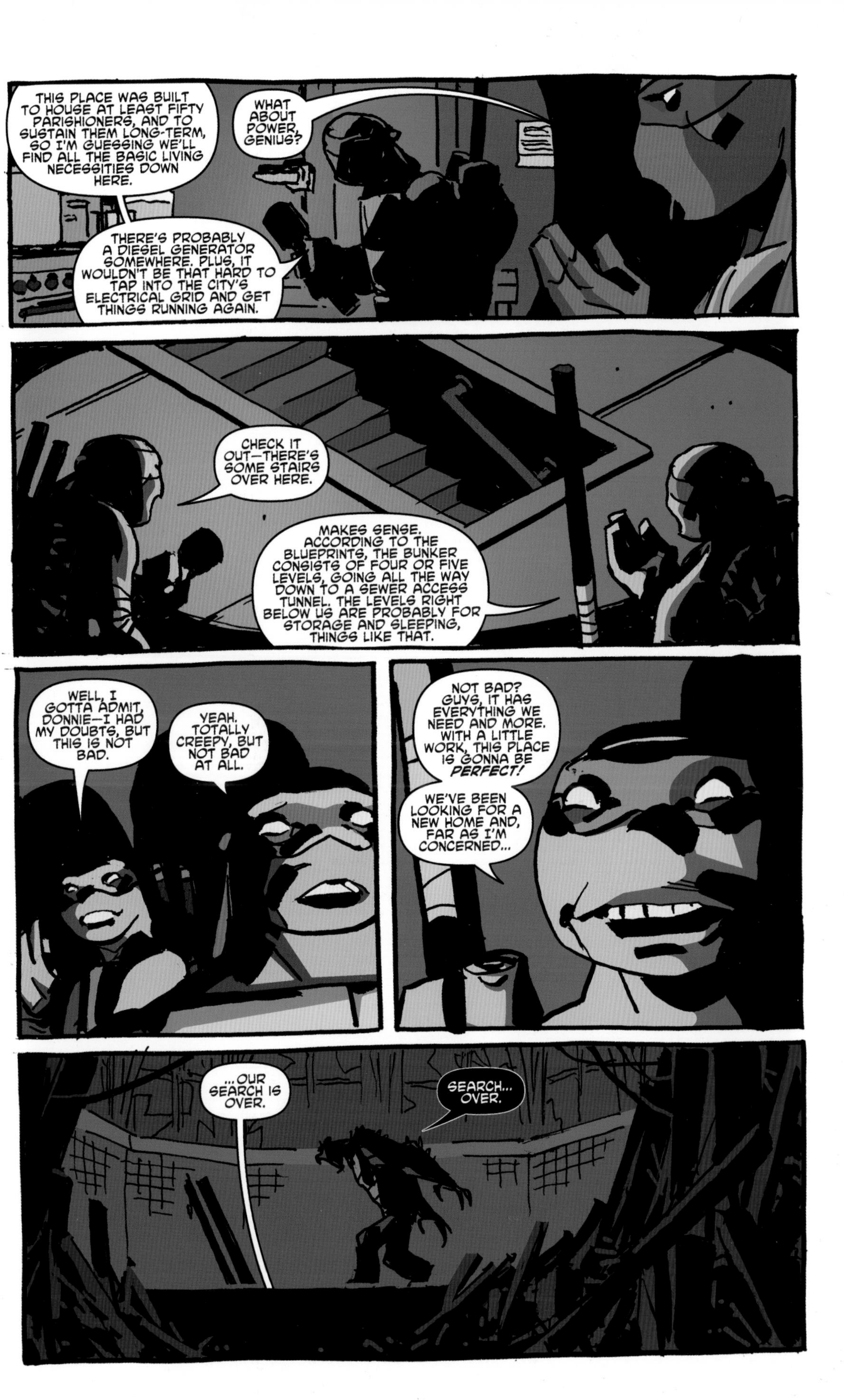
THIS PLACE WAS BUILT TO HOUSE AT LEAST FIFTY PARISHIONERS, AND TO SUSTAIN THEM LONG-TERM, SO I'M GUESSING WE'LL FIND ALL THE BASIC LIVING NECESSITIES DOWN HERE.
WHAT ABOUT POWER, GENIUS?
THERE'S PROBABLY A DIESEL GENERATOR SOMEWHERE. PLUS, IT WOULDN'T BE THAT HARD TO TAP INTO THE CITY'S ELECTRICAL GRID AND GET THINGS RUNNING AGAIN.
CHECK IT OUT—THERE'S SOME STAIRS OVER HERE.
MAKES SENSE. ACCORDING TO THE BLUEPRINTS, THE BUNKER CONSISTS OF FOUR OR FIVE LEVELS, GOING ALL THE WAY DOWN TO A SEWER ACCESS TUNNEL. THE LEVELS RIGHT BELOW US ARE PROBABLY FOR STORAGE AND SLEEPING, THINGS LIKE THAT.
WELL, I GOTTA ADMIT, DONNIE—I HAD MY DOUBTS, BUT THIS IS NOT BAD.
YEAH. TOTALLY CREEPY, BUT NOT BAD AT ALL.
NOT BAD? GUYS, IT HAS EVERYTHING WE NEED AND MORE. WITH A LITTLE WORK, THIS PLACE IS GONNA BE *PERFECT!*
WE'VE BEEN LOOKING FOR A NEW HOME AND, FAR AS I'M CONCERNED...
...OUR SEARCH IS OVER.
SEARCH... OVER.

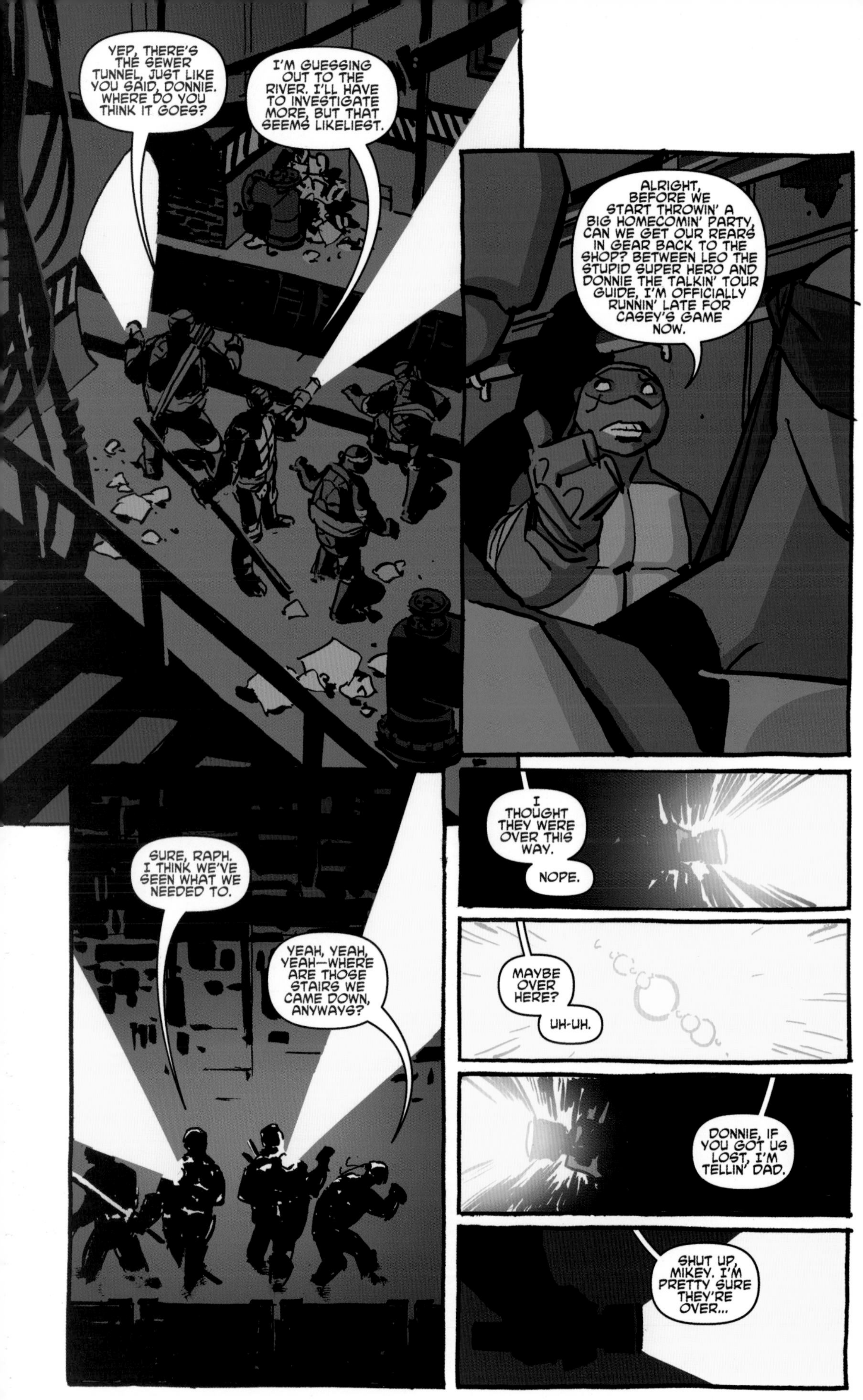
YEP, THERE'S THE SEWER TUNNEL, JUST LIKE YOU SAID, DONNIE. WHERE DO YOU THINK IT GOES?
I'M GUESSING OUT TO THE RIVER. I'LL HAVE TO INVESTIGATE MORE, BUT THAT SEEMS LIKELIEST.
ALRIGHT, BEFORE WE START THROWIN' A BIG HOMECOMIN' PARTY, CAN WE GET OUR REARS IN GEAR BACK TO THE SHOP? BETWEEN LEO THE STUPID SUPER HERO AND DONNIE THE TALKIN' TOUR GUIDE, I'M OFFICIALLY RUNNIN' LATE FOR CASEY'S GAME NOW.
SURE, RAPH. I THINK WE'VE SEEN WHAT WE NEEDED TO.
YEAH, YEAH, YEAH—WHERE ARE THOSE STAIRS WE CAME DOWN, ANYWAYS?
I THOUGHT THEY WERE OVER THIS WAY.
NOPE.
MAYBE OVER HERE?
UH-UH.
DONNIE, IF YOU GOT US LOST, I'M TELLIN' DAD.
SHUT UP, MIKEY. I'M PRETTY SURE THEY'RE OVER...

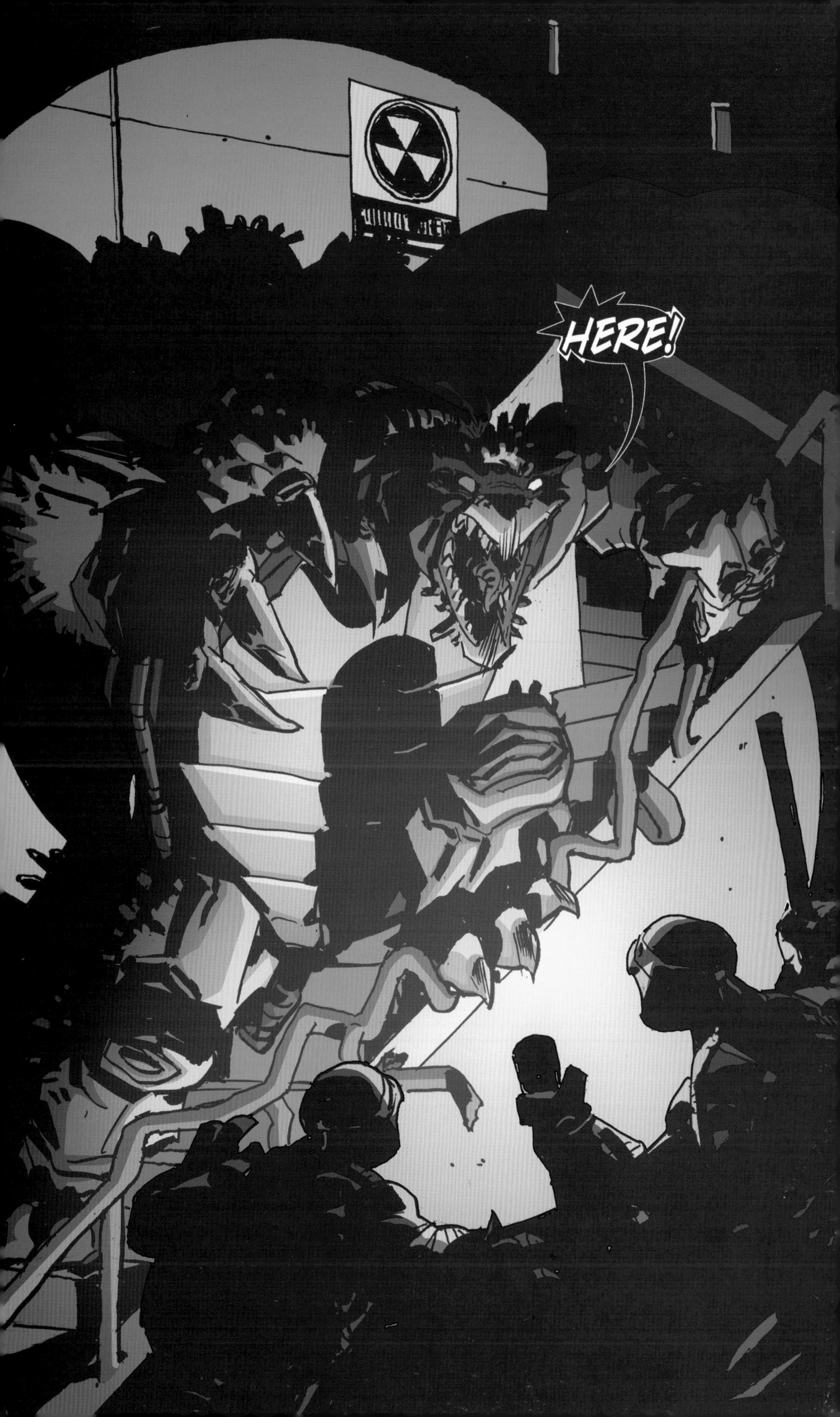
HERE!

WHOP

WHAT THE HELL?!

WHAT IS THAT?!

GRRAR

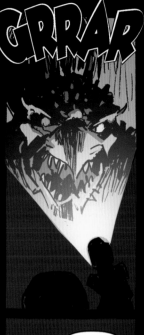

FWWAK

IT'S SOME KIND OF MONSTER! GRAB THE FLASHLIGHTS!

MONSTER?! IS IT A NUCLEAR SPIDER?!

JUST GET THE DAMN FLASHLIGHT, MIKEY!

OH... CRUD.

KRAK

GUYS?!

IT'S FAST!

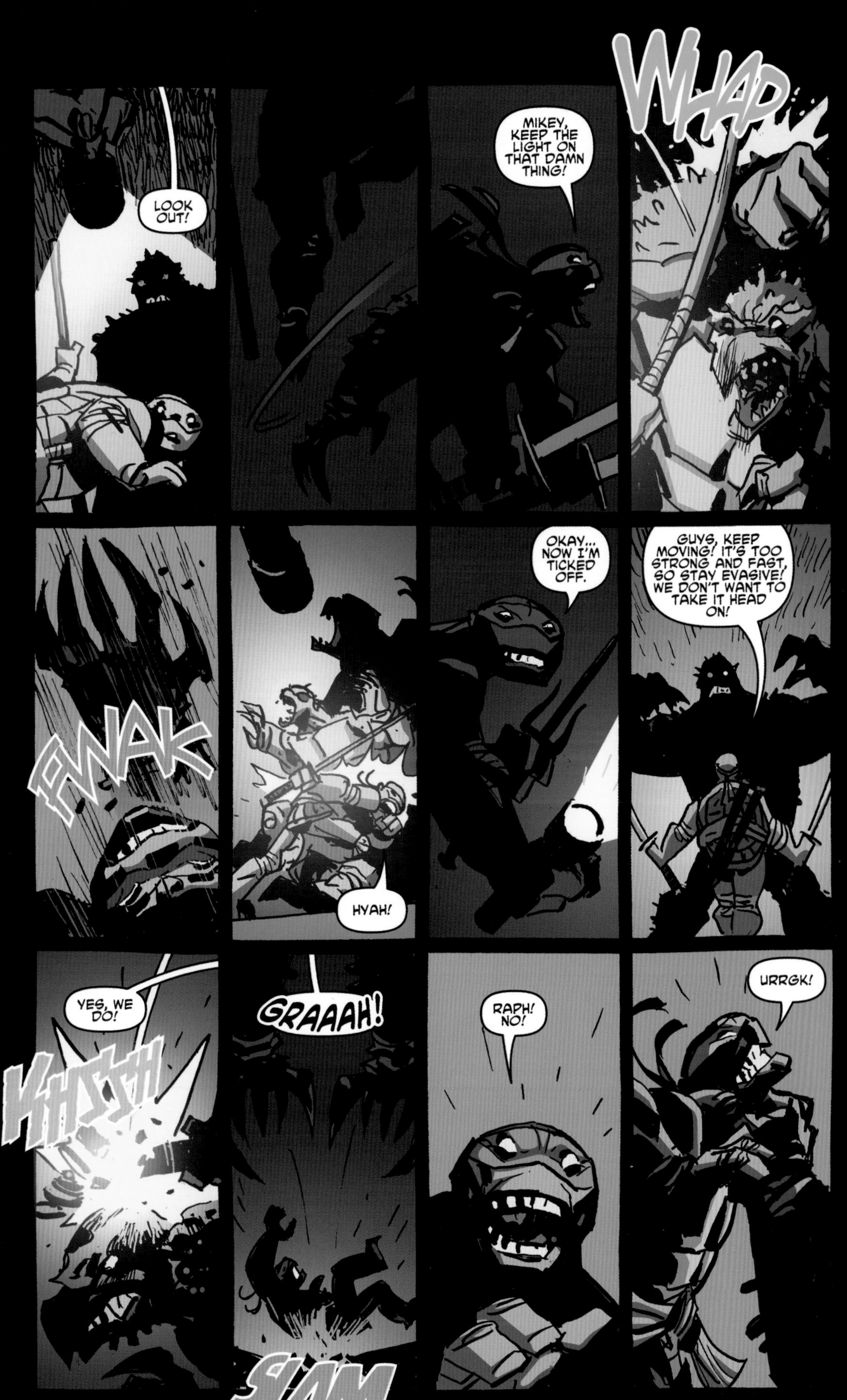

LOOK OUT!
MIKEY, KEEP THE LIGHT ON THAT DAMN THING!
WHAP
FWAK
HYAH!
OKAY... NOW I'M TICKED OFF.
GUYS, KEEP MOVING! IT'S TOO STRONG AND FAST, SO STAY EVASIVE! WE DON'T WANT TO TAKE IT HEAD ON!
YES, WE DO!
KHSSH
GRAAAH!
SLAM
RAPH! NO!
URRGK!

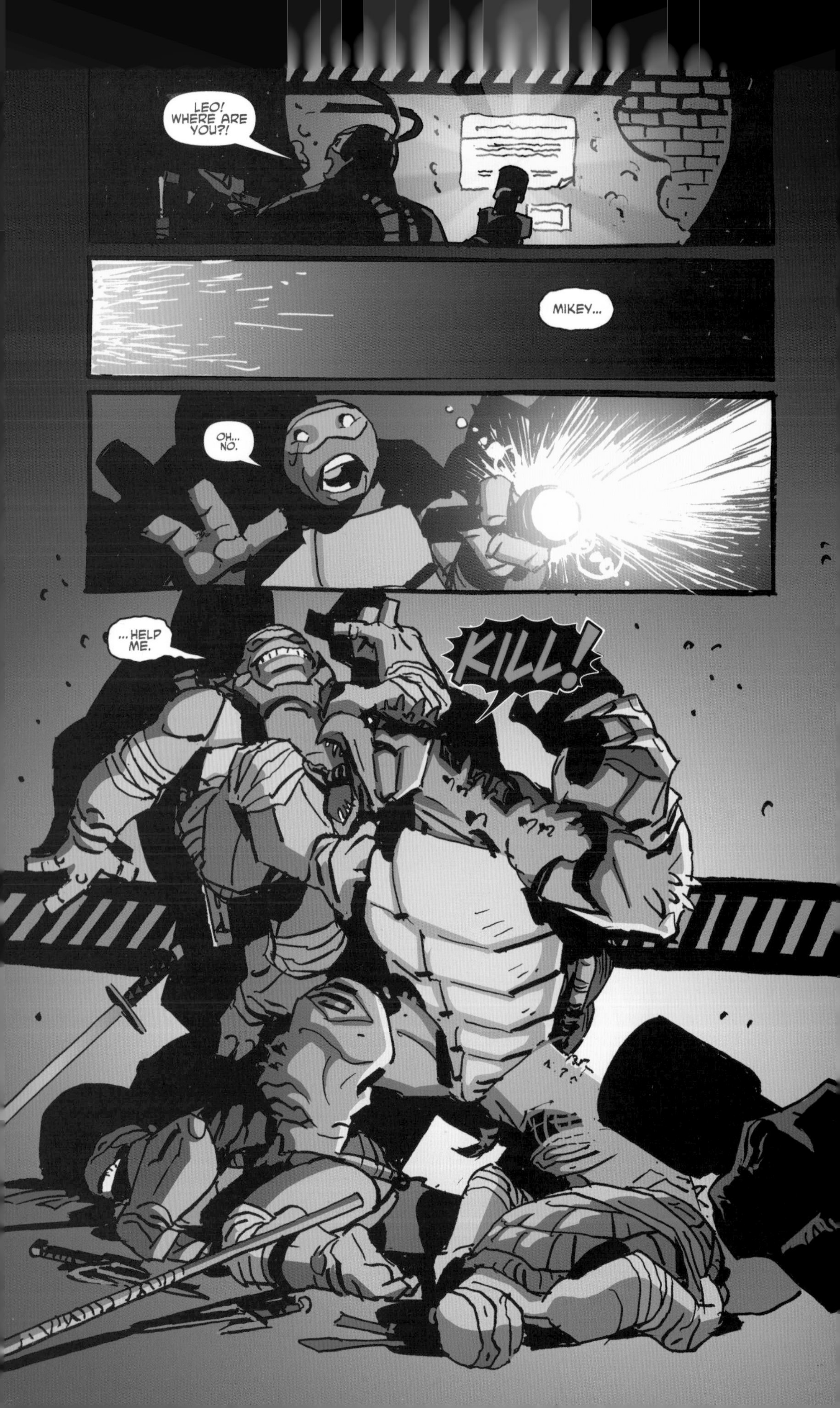
LEO! WHERE ARE YOU?!
MIKEY...
OH... NO.
...HELP ME.
KILL!

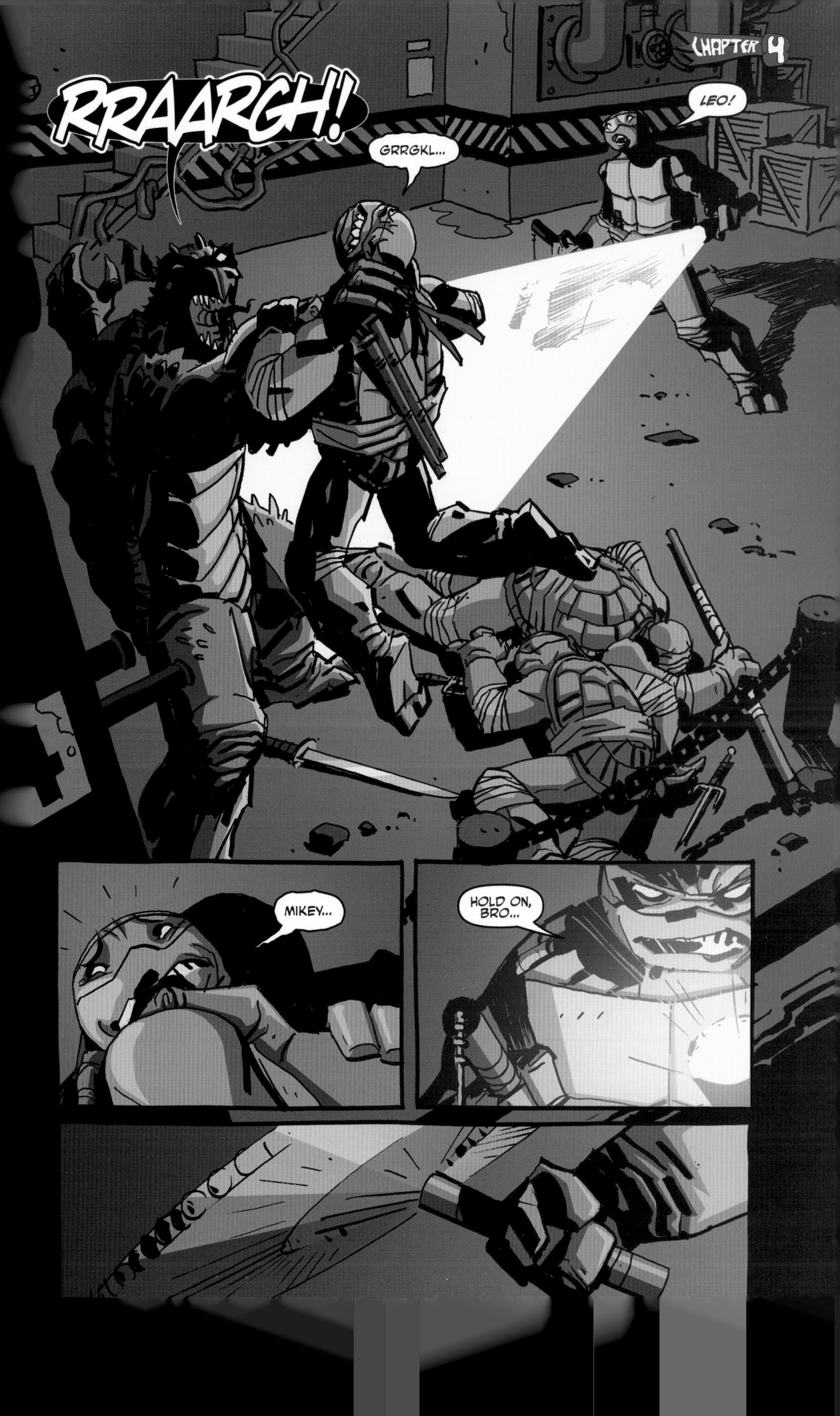
RRAARGH!
GRRGKL...
LEO!
MIKEY...
HOLD ON, BRO...

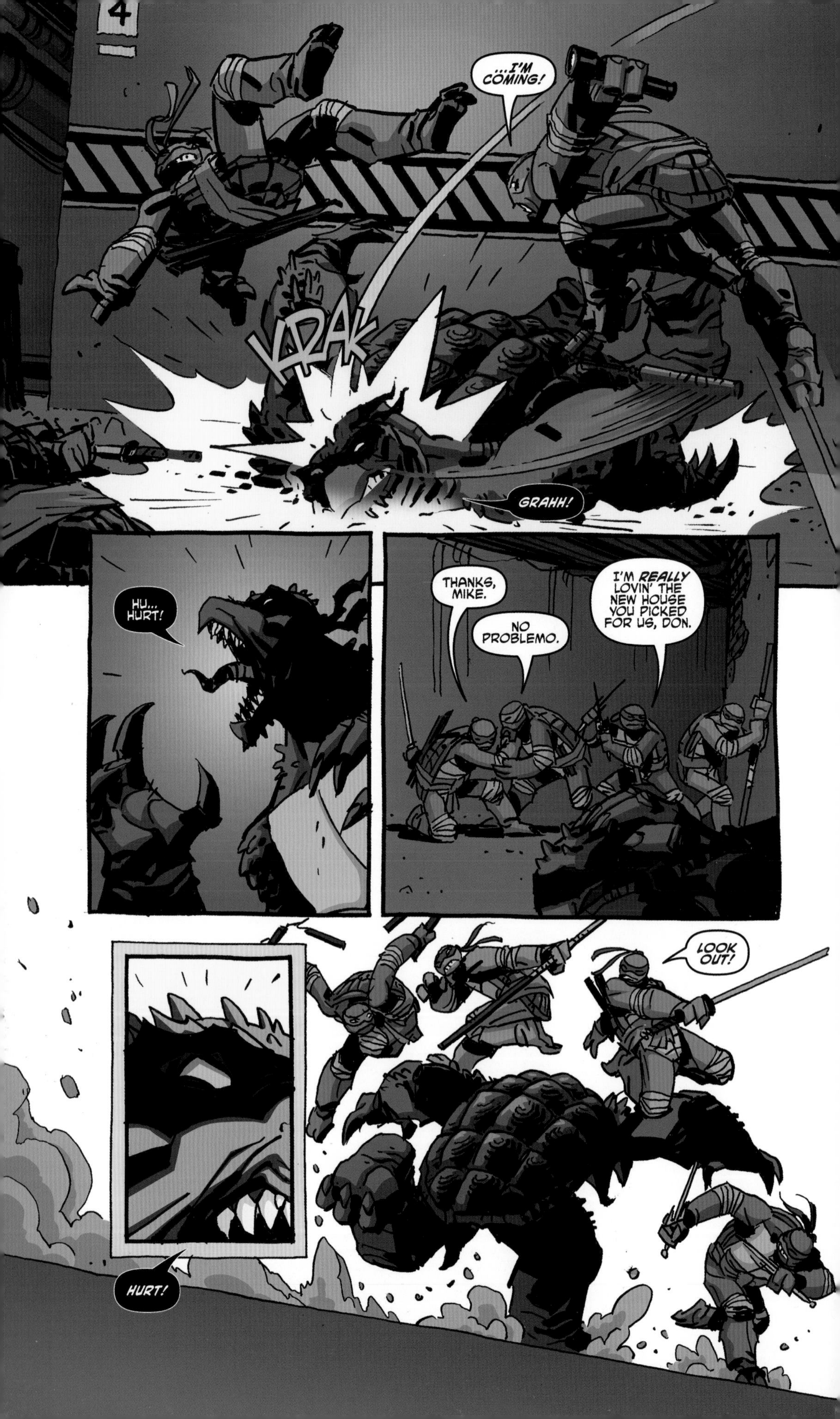

4
...I'M COMING!
KRAK
GRAHH!
HU... HURT!
THANKS, MIKE.
NO PROBLEMO.
I'M REALLY LOVIN' THE NEW HOUSE YOU PICKED FOR US, DON.
LOOK OUT!
HURT!

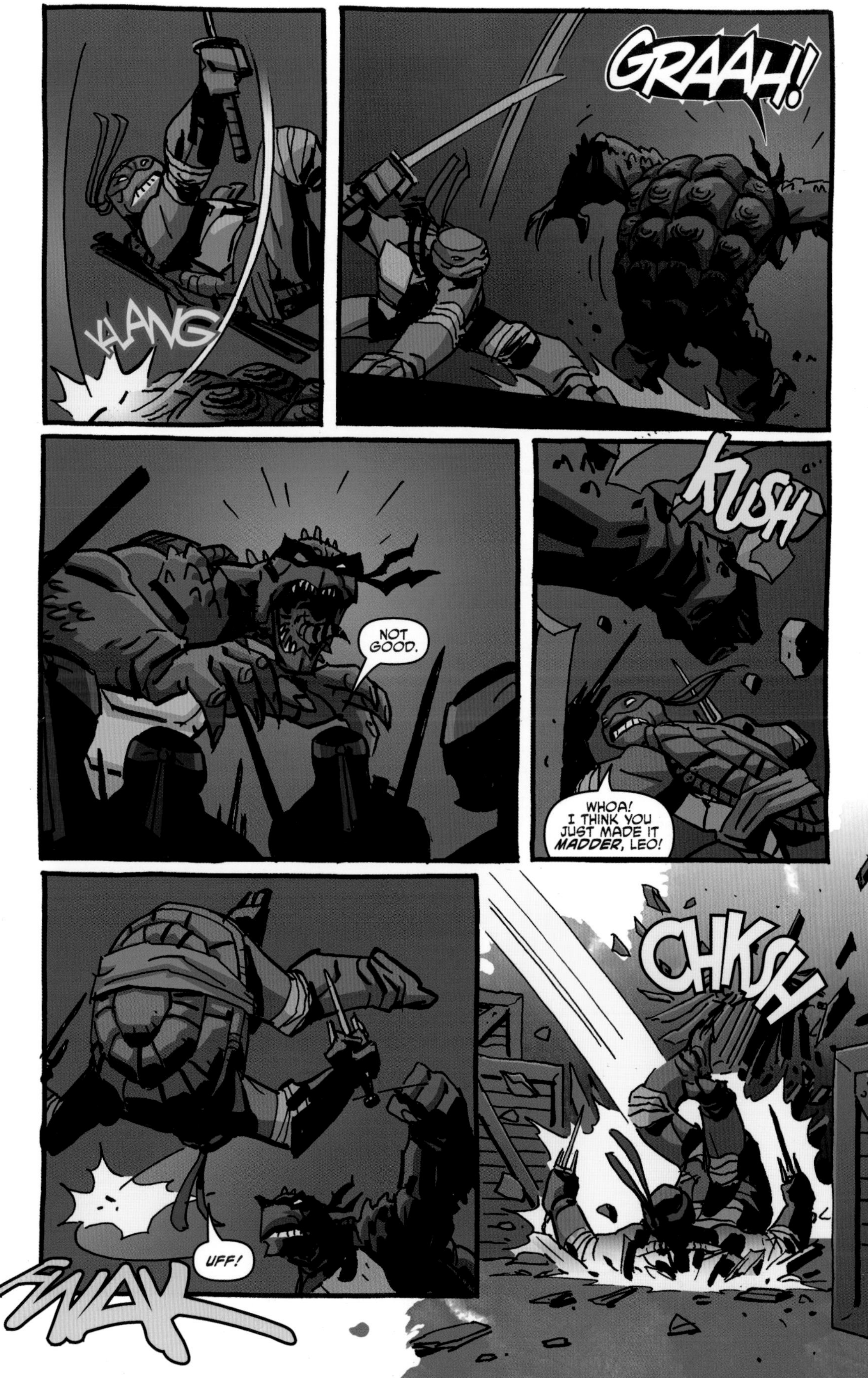
KLANG
GRAAH!
NOT GOOD.
KRUSH
WHOA! I THINK YOU JUST MADE IT *MADDER*, LEO!
SWAK
UFF!
CHKSH

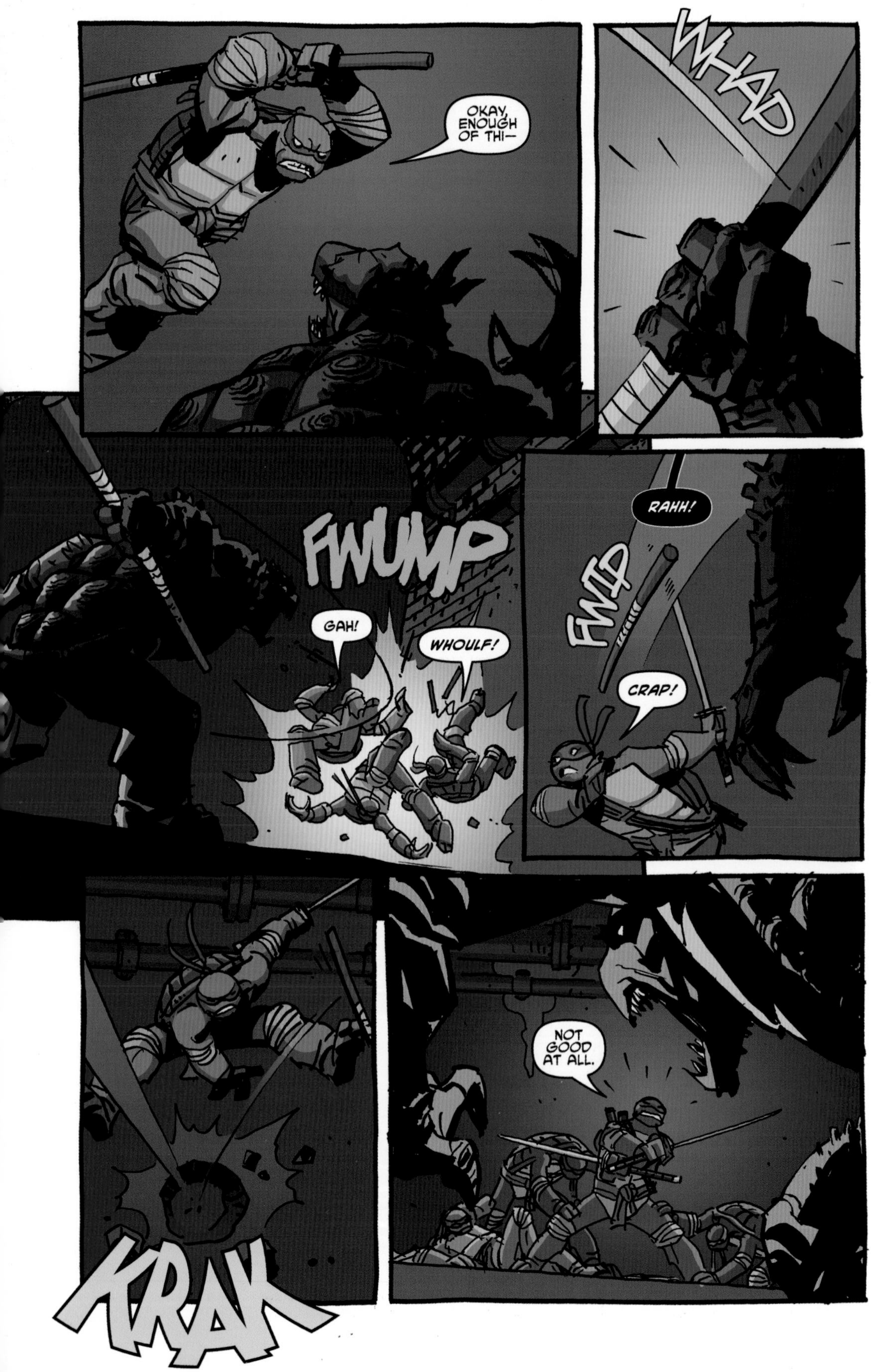
OKAY, ENOUGH OF THI—
WHAP
FWUMP
GAH!
WHOULF!
RAHH!
FWIP
CRAP!
KRAK
NOT GOOD AT ALL.

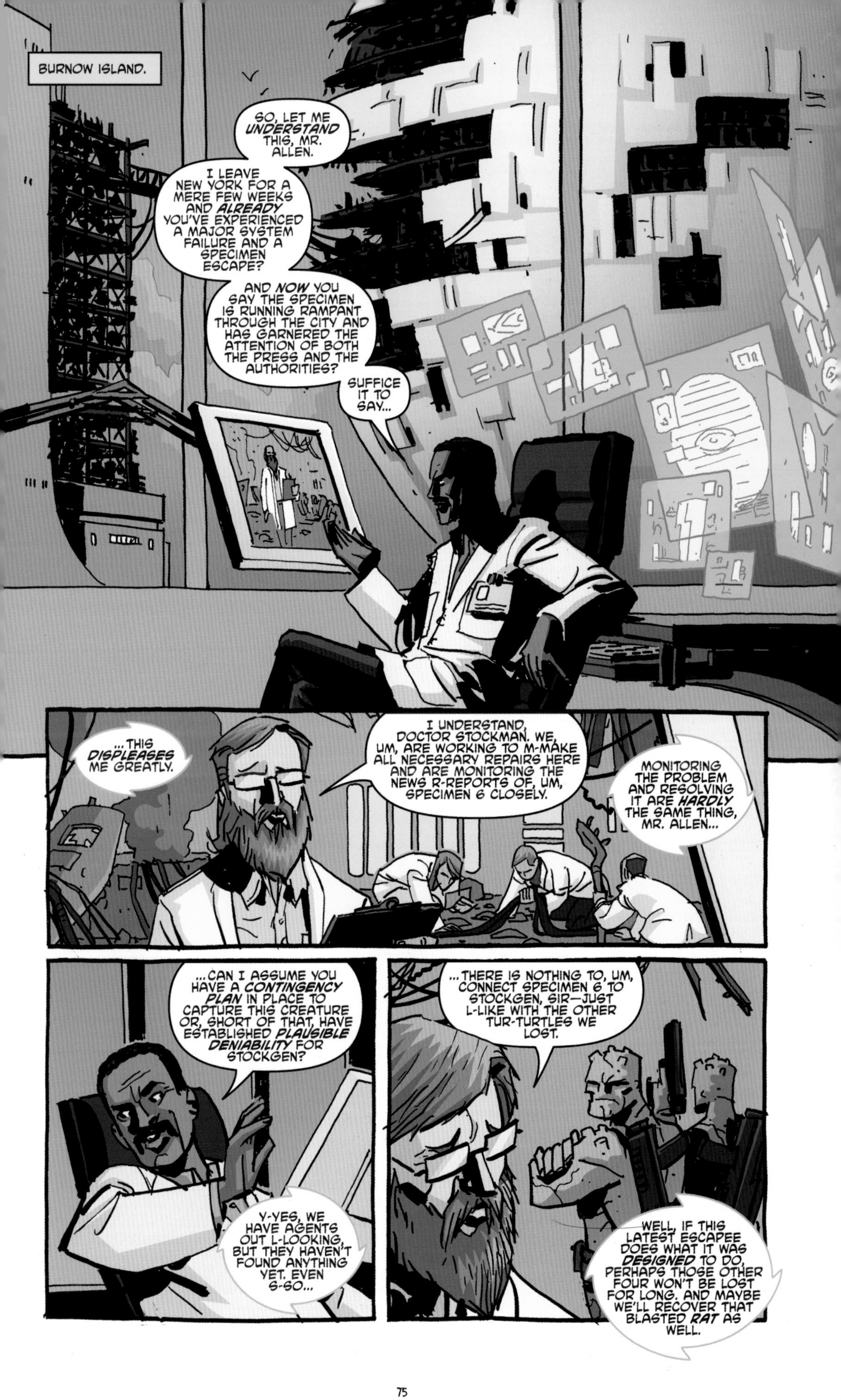
BURNOW ISLAND.
SO, LET ME UNDERSTAND THIS, MR. ALLEN.
I LEAVE NEW YORK FOR A MERE FEW WEEKS AND ALREADY YOU'VE EXPERIENCED A MAJOR SYSTEM FAILURE AND A SPECIMEN ESCAPE?
AND NOW YOU SAY THE SPECIMEN IS RUNNING RAMPANT THROUGH THE CITY AND HAS GARNERED THE ATTENTION OF BOTH THE PRESS AND THE AUTHORITIES?
SUFFICE IT TO SAY...
...THIS DISPLEASES ME GREATLY.
I UNDERSTAND, DOCTOR STOCKMAN. WE, UM, ARE WORKING TO M-MAKE ALL NECESSARY REPAIRS HERE AND ARE MONITORING THE NEWS R-REPORTS OF, UM, SPECIMEN 6 CLOSELY.
MONITORING THE PROBLEM AND RESOLVING IT ARE HARDLY THE SAME THING, MR. ALLEN...
...CAN I ASSUME YOU HAVE A CONTINGENCY PLAN IN PLACE TO CAPTURE THIS CREATURE OR, SHORT OF THAT, HAVE ESTABLISHED PLAUSIBLE DENIABILITY FOR STOCKGEN?
Y-YES, WE HAVE AGENTS OUT L-LOOKING, BUT THEY HAVEN'T FOUND ANYTHING YET. EVEN S-SO...
...THERE IS NOTHING TO, UM, CONNECT SPECIMEN 6 TO STOCKGEN, SIR—JUST L-LIKE WITH THE OTHER TUR-TURTLES WE LOST.
WELL, IF THIS LATEST ESCAPEE DOES WHAT IT WAS DESIGNED TO DO, PERHAPS THOSE OTHER FOUR WON'T BE LOST FOR LONG. AND MAYBE WE'LL RECOVER THAT BLASTED RAT AS WELL.

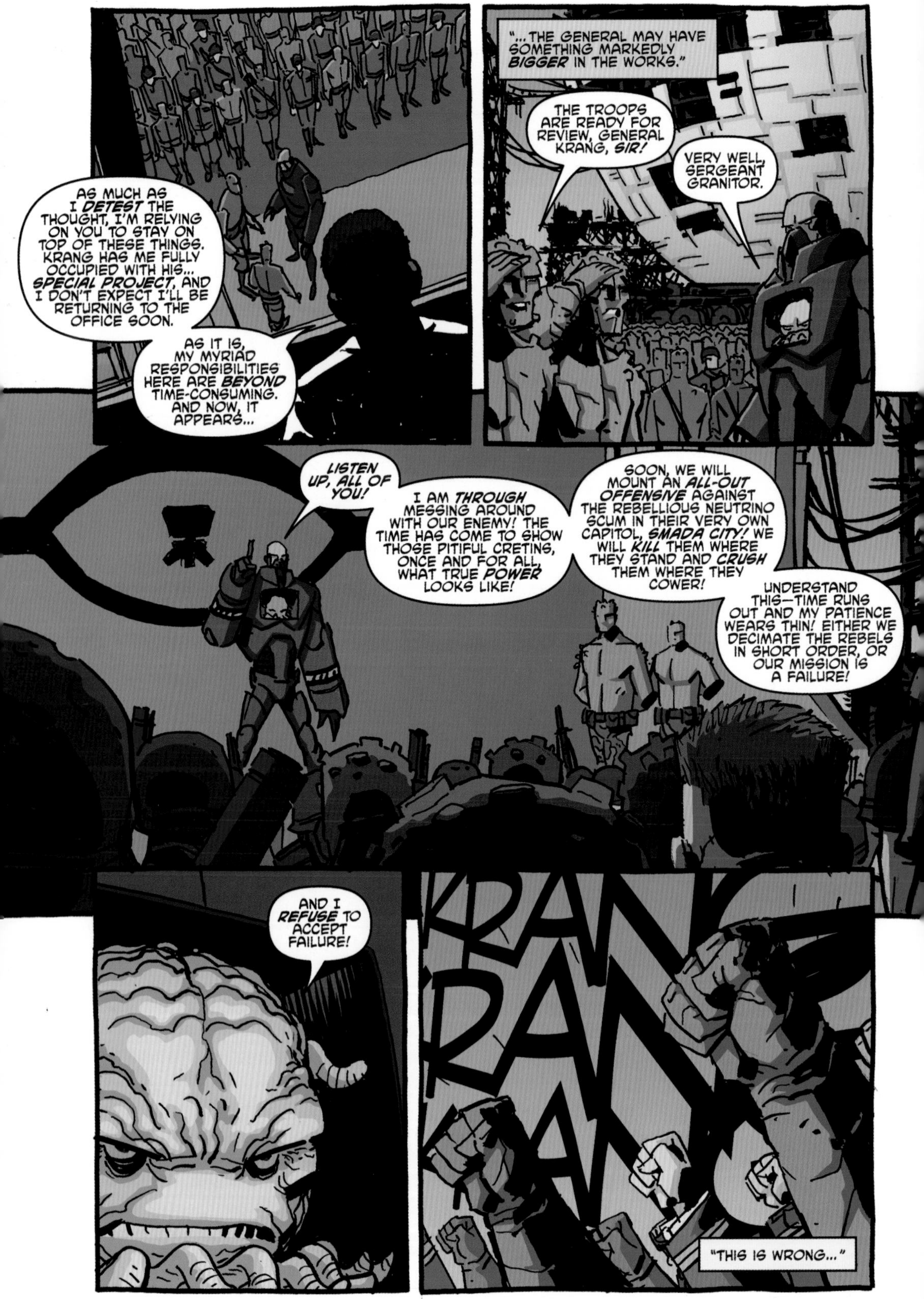
AS MUCH AS I DETEST THE THOUGHT, I'M RELYING ON YOU TO STAY ON TOP OF THESE THINGS. KRANG HAS ME FULLY OCCUPIED WITH HIS... SPECIAL PROJECT, AND I DON'T EXPECT I'LL BE RETURNING TO THE OFFICE SOON.
AS IT IS, MY MYRIAD RESPONSIBILITIES HERE ARE BEYOND TIME-CONSUMING. AND NOW, IT APPEARS...
"...THE GENERAL MAY HAVE SOMETHING MARKEDLY BIGGER IN THE WORKS."
THE TROOPS ARE READY FOR REVIEW, GENERAL KRANG, SIR!
VERY WELL, SERGEANT GRANITOR.
LISTEN UP, ALL OF YOU!
I AM THROUGH MESSING AROUND WITH OUR ENEMY! THE TIME HAS COME TO SHOW THOSE PITIFUL CRETINS, ONCE AND FOR ALL, WHAT TRUE POWER LOOKS LIKE!
SOON, WE WILL MOUNT AN ALL-OUT OFFENSIVE AGAINST THE REBELLIOUS NEUTRINO SCUM IN THEIR VERY OWN CAPITOL, SMADA CITY! WE WILL KILL THEM WHERE THEY STAND AND CRUSH THEM WHERE THEY COWER!
UNDERSTAND THIS—TIME RUNS OUT AND MY PATIENCE WEARS THIN! EITHER WE DECIMATE THE REBELS IN SHORT ORDER, OR OUR MISSION IS A FAILURE!
AND I REFUSE TO ACCEPT FAILURE!
KRANG
KRANG
KRANG
"THIS IS WRONG..."

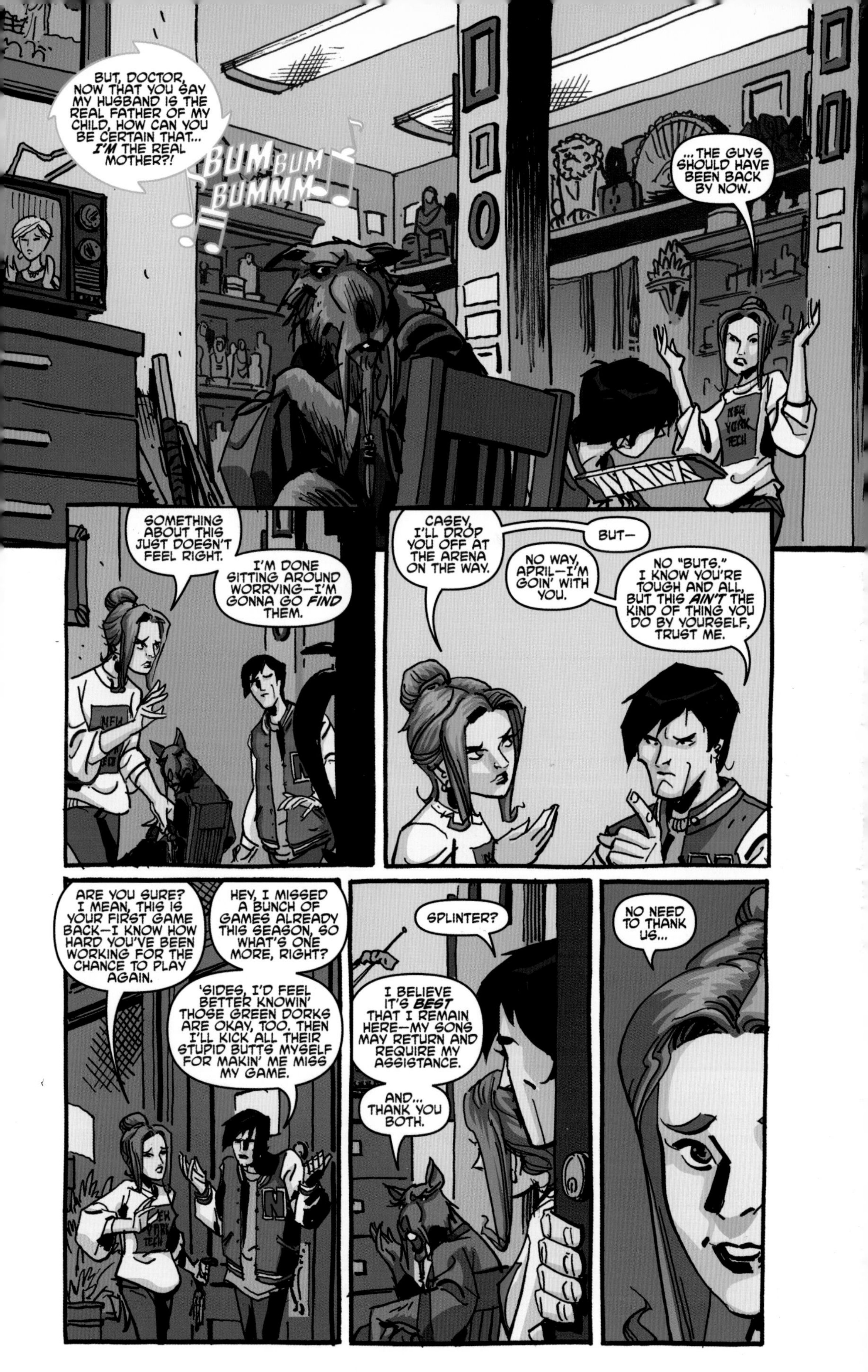
BUT, DOCTOR, NOW THAT YOU SAY MY HUSBAND IS THE REAL FATHER OF MY CHILD, HOW CAN YOU BE CERTAIN THAT... I'M THE REAL MOTHER?!
BUM BUM BUMMM
...THE GUYS SHOULD HAVE BEEN BACK BY NOW.
SOMETHING ABOUT THIS JUST DOESN'T FEEL RIGHT.
I'M DONE SITTING AROUND WORRYING—I'M GONNA GO FIND THEM.
CASEY, I'LL DROP YOU OFF AT THE ARENA ON THE WAY.
BUT—
NO WAY, APRIL—I'M GOIN' WITH YOU.
NO "BUTS." I KNOW YOU'RE TOUGH AND ALL, BUT THIS AIN'T THE KIND OF THING YOU DO BY YOURSELF, TRUST ME.
ARE YOU SURE? I MEAN, THIS IS YOUR FIRST GAME BACK—I KNOW HOW HARD YOU'VE BEEN WORKING FOR THE CHANCE TO PLAY AGAIN.
HEY, I MISSED A BUNCH OF GAMES ALREADY THIS SEASON, SO WHAT'S ONE MORE, RIGHT?
'SIDES, I'D FEEL BETTER KNOWIN' THOSE GREEN DORKS ARE OKAY, TOO. THEN I'LL KICK ALL THEIR STUPID BUTTS MYSELF FOR MAKIN' ME MISS MY GAME.
SPLINTER?
I BELIEVE IT'S BEST THAT I REMAIN HERE—MY SONS MAY RETURN AND REQUIRE MY ASSISTANCE.
AND... THANK YOU BOTH.
NO NEED TO THANK US...
NEW YORK TECH

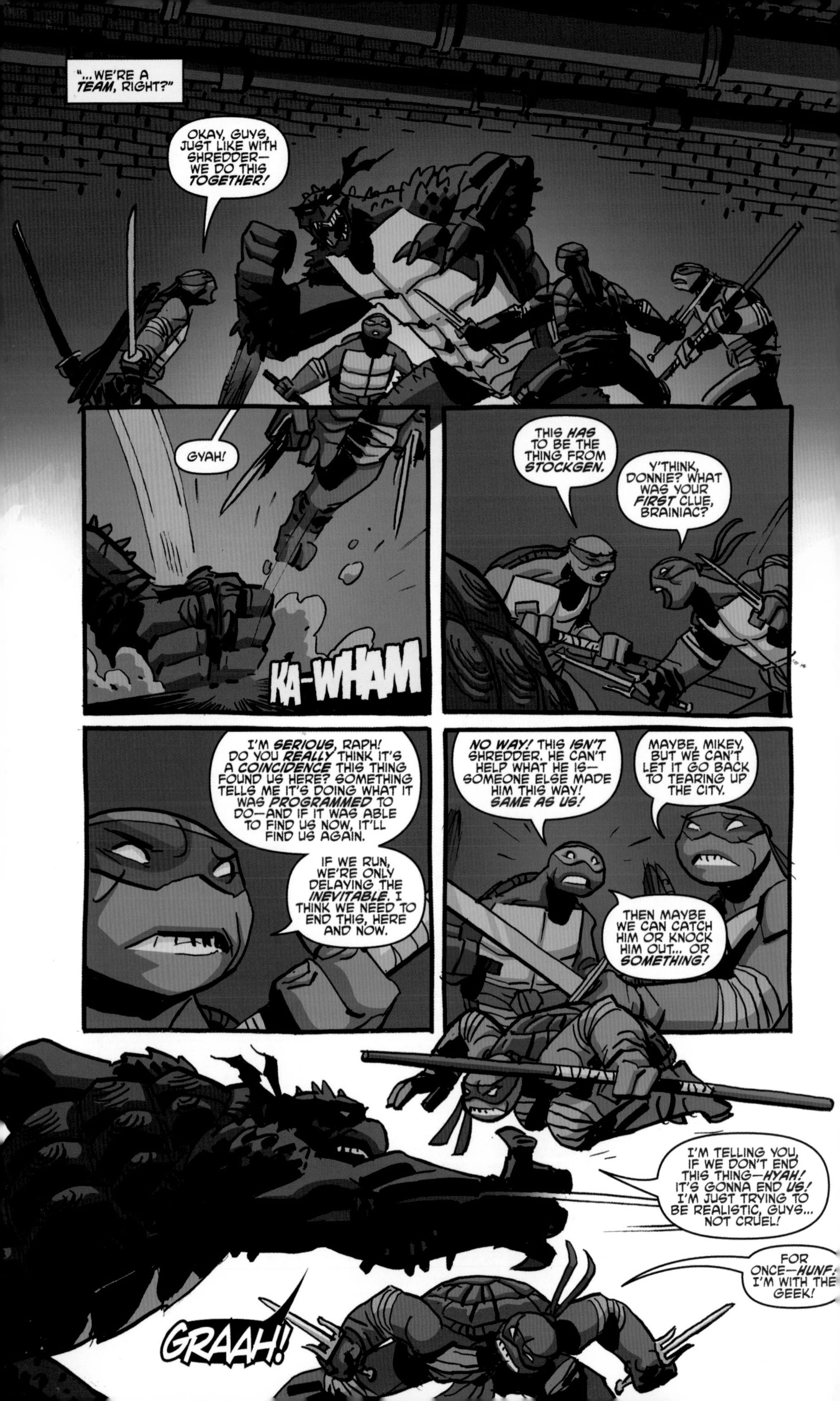
"...WE'RE A TEAM, RIGHT?"
OKAY, GUYS, JUST LIKE WITH SHREDDER— WE DO THIS TOGETHER!
GYAH!
KA-WHAM
THIS HAS TO BE THE THING FROM STOCKGEN.
Y'THINK, DONNIE? WHAT WAS YOUR FIRST CLUE, BRAINIAC?
I'M SERIOUS, RAPH! DO YOU REALLY THINK IT'S A COINCIDENCE THIS THING FOUND US HERE? SOMETHING TELLS ME IT'S DOING WHAT IT WAS PROGRAMMED TO DO—AND IF IT WAS ABLE TO FIND US NOW, IT'LL FIND US AGAIN.
IF WE RUN, WE'RE ONLY DELAYING THE INEVITABLE. I THINK WE NEED TO END THIS, HERE AND NOW.
NO WAY! THIS ISN'T SHREDDER. HE CAN'T HELP WHAT HE IS— SOMEONE ELSE MADE HIM THIS WAY! SAME AS US!
MAYBE, MIKEY, BUT WE CAN'T LET IT GO BACK TO TEARING UP THE CITY.
THEN MAYBE WE CAN CATCH HIM OR KNOCK HIM OUT... OR SOMETHING!
I'M TELLING YOU, IF WE DON'T END THIS THING—HYAH! IT'S GONNA END US! I'M JUST TRYING TO BE REALISTIC, GUYS... NOT CRUEL!
FOR ONCE—HUNF! I'M WITH THE GEEK!
GRAAH!

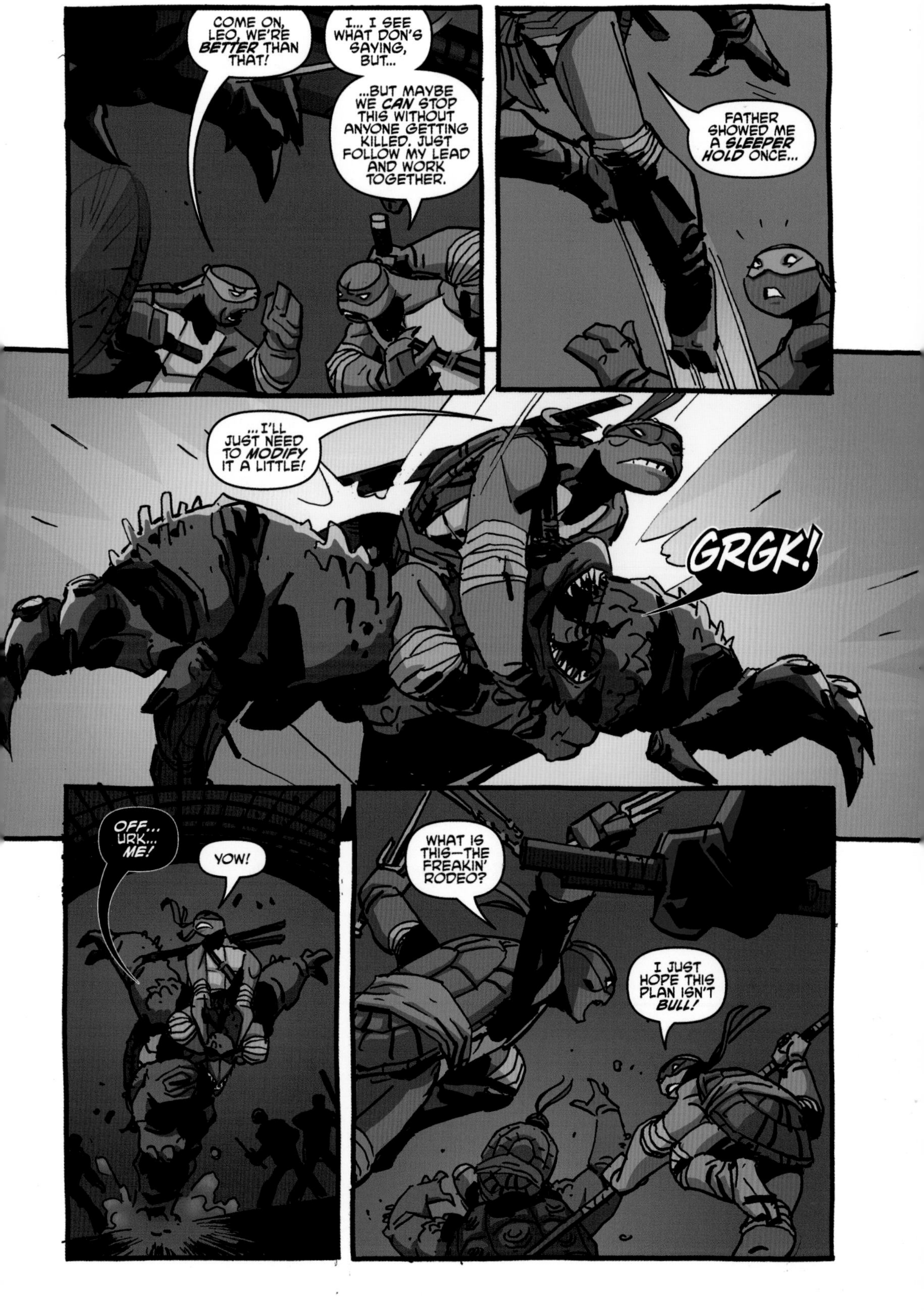
COME ON, LEO, WE'RE BETTER THAN THAT!
I... I SEE WHAT DON'S SAYING, BUT...
...BUT MAYBE WE CAN STOP THIS WITHOUT ANYONE GETTING KILLED. JUST FOLLOW MY LEAD AND WORK TOGETHER.
FATHER SHOWED ME A SLEEPER HOLD ONCE...
...I'LL JUST NEED TO MODIFY IT A LITTLE!
GRGK!
OFF... URK... ME!
YOW!
WHAT IS THIS—THE FREAKIN' RODEO?
I JUST HOPE THIS PLAN ISN'T BULL!

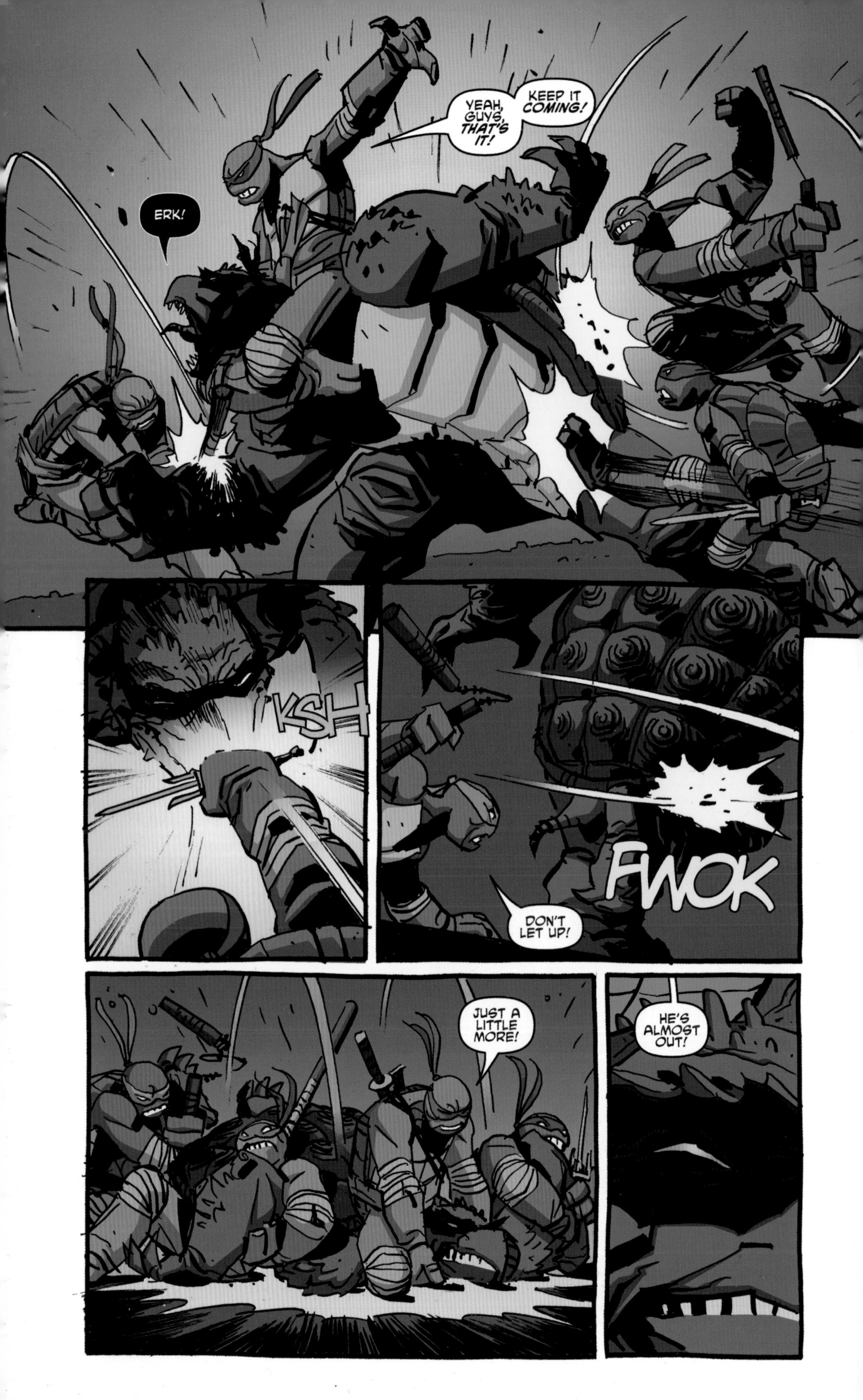

ERK!
YEAH, GUYS, THAT'S IT!
KEEP IT COMING!
KSH
FWOK
DON'T LET UP!
JUST A LITTLE MORE!
HE'S ALMOST OUT!

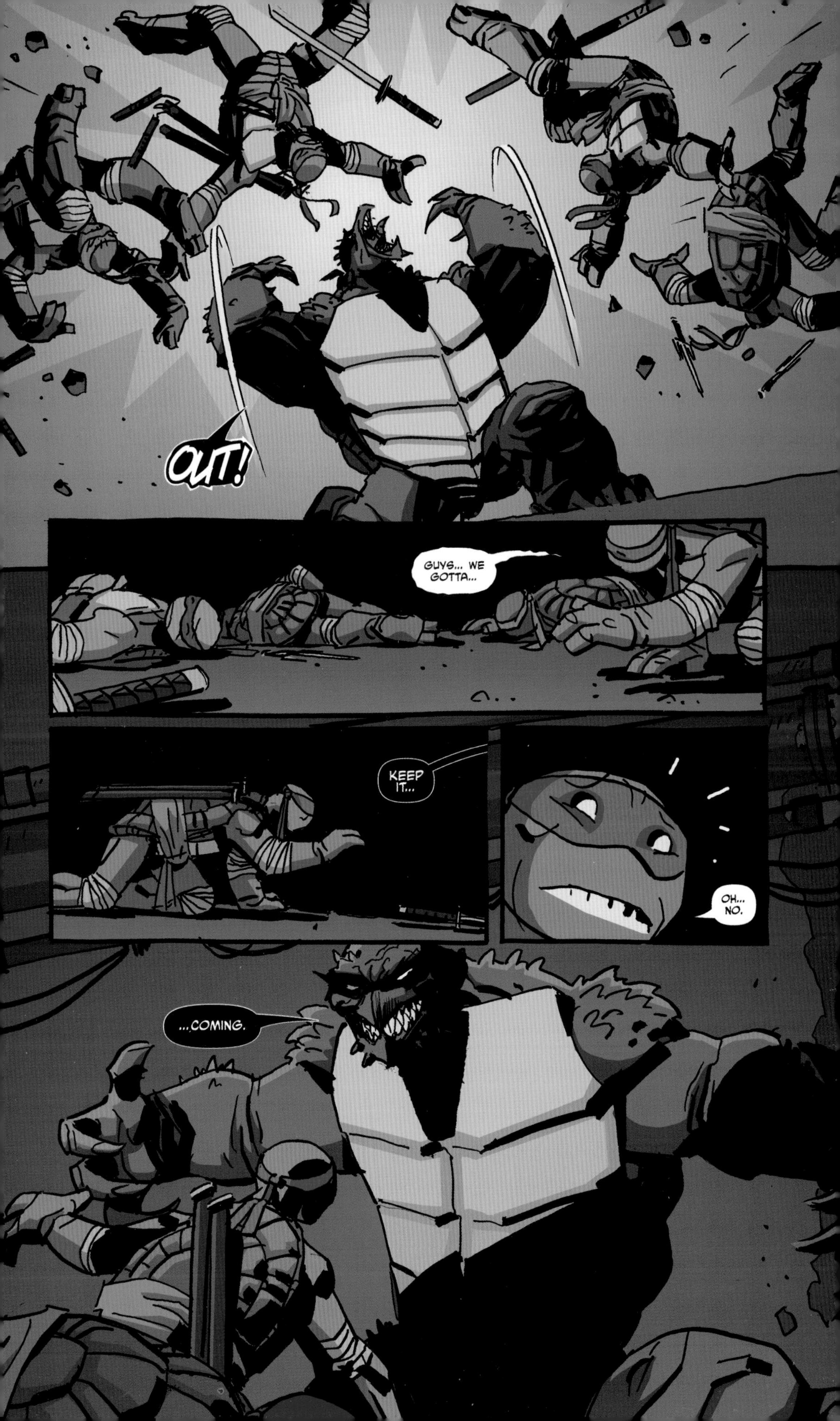
OUT!
GUYS... WE GOTTA...
KEEP IT...
OH... NO.
...COMING.

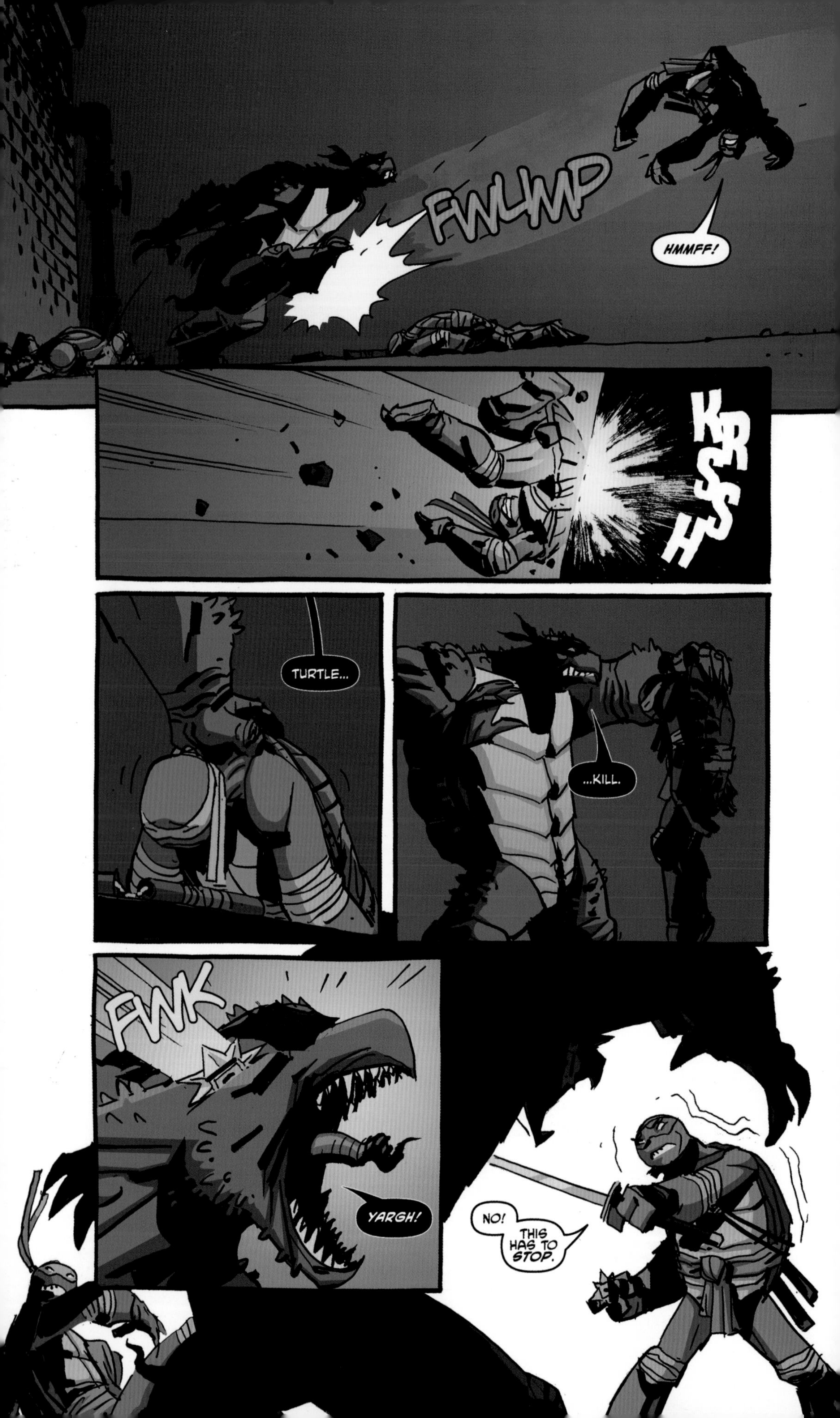
FWUMP
HMMFF!
KRSSH
TURTLE...
...KILL.
FWK
YARGH!
NO! THIS HAS TO STOP.

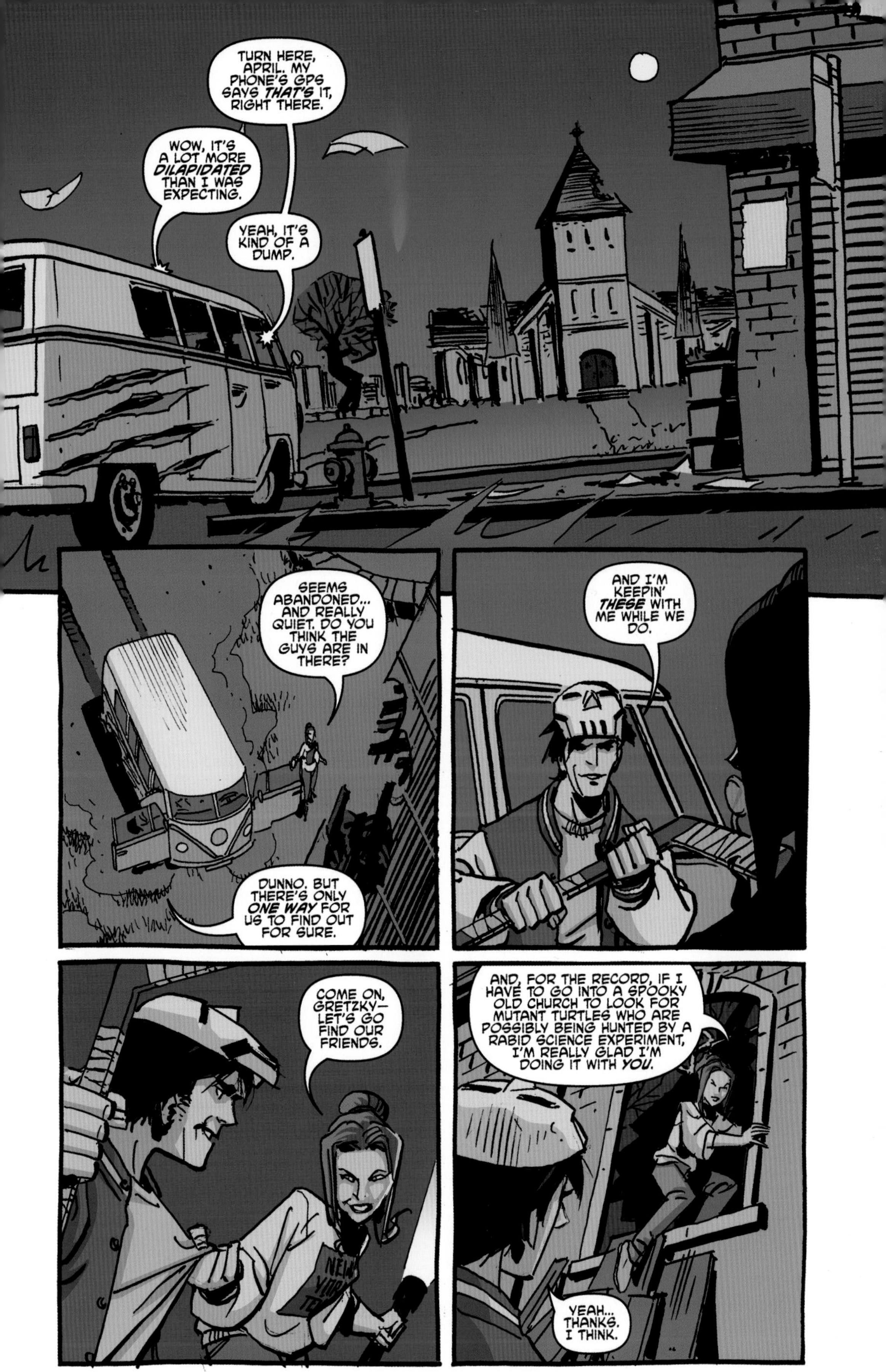
TURN HERE, APRIL. MY PHONE'S GPS SAYS *THAT'S* IT, RIGHT THERE.
WOW, IT'S A LOT MORE *DILAPIDATED* THAN I WAS EXPECTING.
YEAH, IT'S KIND OF A DUMP.
SEEMS ABANDONED... AND REALLY QUIET. DO YOU THINK THE GUYS ARE IN THERE?
DUNNO. BUT THERE'S ONLY *ONE WAY* FOR US TO FIND OUT FOR SURE.
AND I'M KEEPIN' *THESE* WITH ME WHILE WE DO.
COME ON, GRETZKY— LET'S GO FIND OUR FRIENDS.
AND, FOR THE RECORD, IF I HAVE TO GO INTO A SPOOKY OLD CHURCH TO LOOK FOR MUTANT TURTLES WHO ARE POSSIBLY BEING HUNTED BY A RABID SCIENCE EXPERIMENT, I'M REALLY GLAD I'M DOING IT WITH *YOU*.
YEAH... THANKS. I THINK.

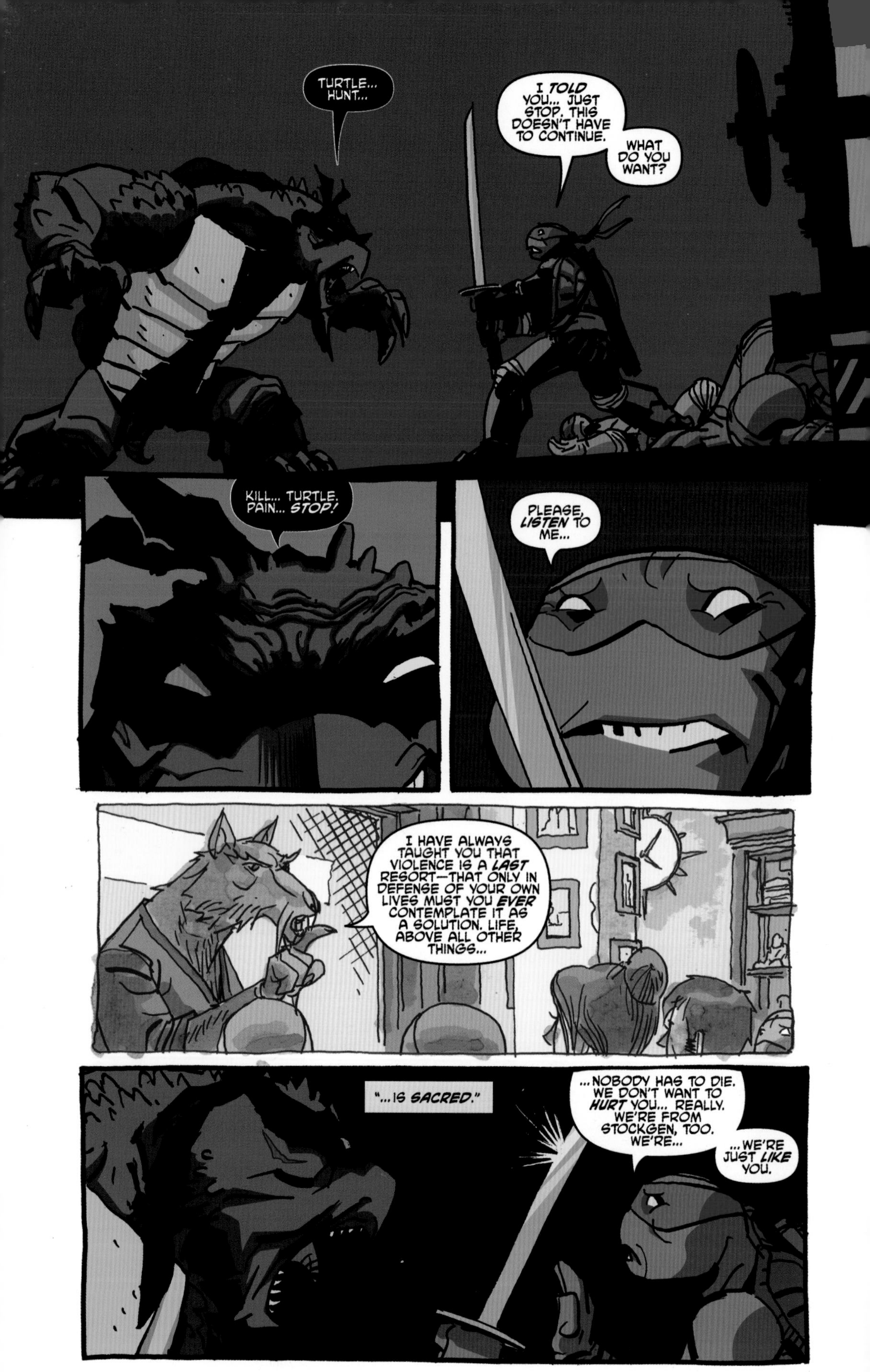
TURTLE... HUNT...
I TOLD YOU... JUST STOP. THIS DOESN'T HAVE TO CONTINUE.
WHAT DO YOU WANT?
KILL... TURTLE. PAIN... STOP!
PLEASE, LISTEN TO ME...
I HAVE ALWAYS TAUGHT YOU THAT VIOLENCE IS A LAST RESORT—THAT ONLY IN DEFENSE OF YOUR OWN LIVES MUST YOU EVER CONTEMPLATE IT AS A SOLUTION. LIFE, ABOVE ALL OTHER THINGS...
"...IS SACRED."
...NOBODY HAS TO DIE. WE DON'T WANT TO HURT YOU... REALLY. WE'RE FROM STOCKGEN, TOO. WE'RE...
...WE'RE JUST LIKE YOU.

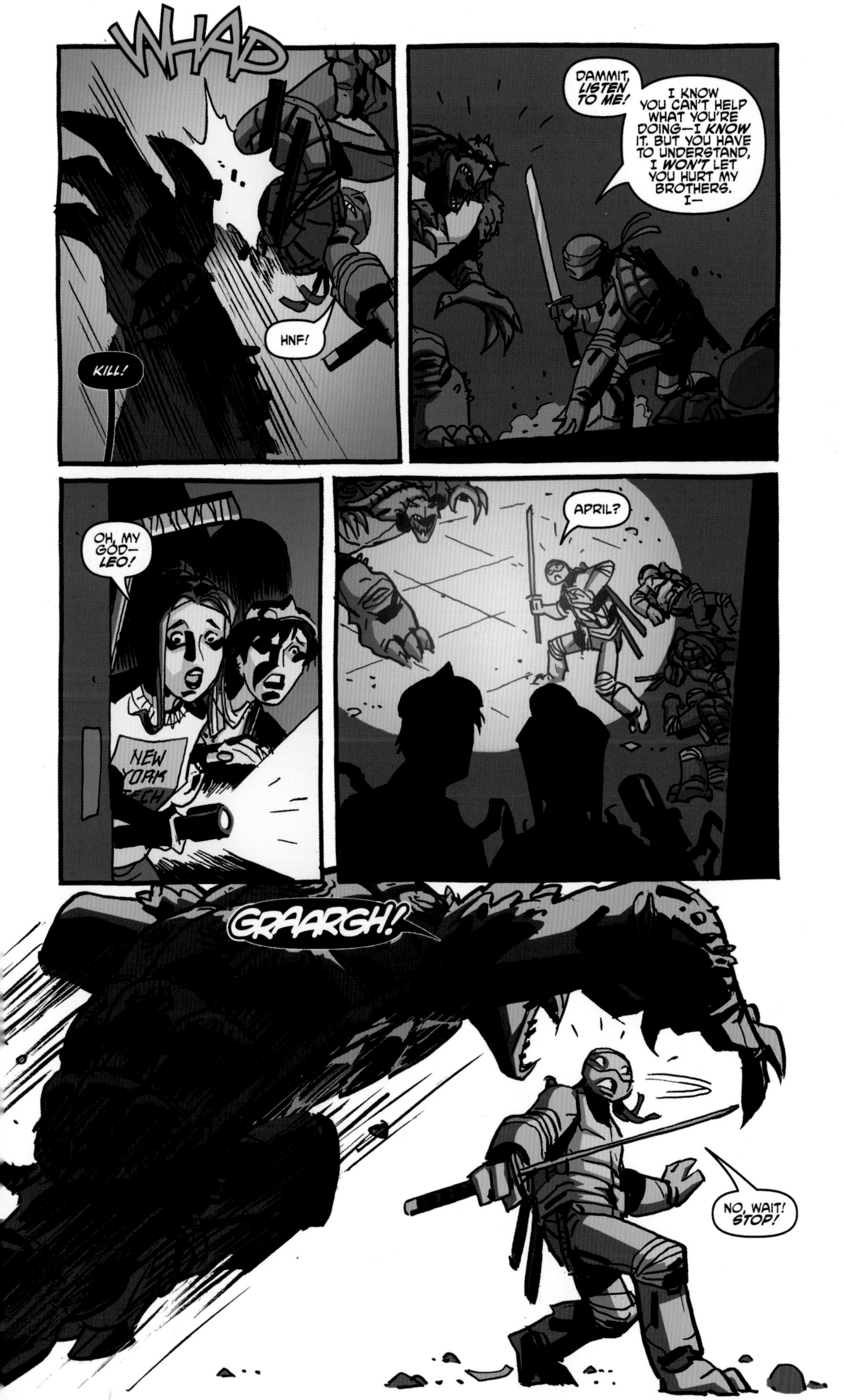
WHAD
HNF!
KILL!
DAMMIT, LISTEN TO ME!
I KNOW YOU CAN'T HELP WHAT YOU'RE DOING—I KNOW IT. BUT YOU HAVE TO UNDERSTAND, I WON'T LET YOU HURT MY BROTHERS. I—
OH, MY GOD— LEO!
NEW YORK TECH
APRIL?
GRAARGH!
NO, WAIT! STOP!

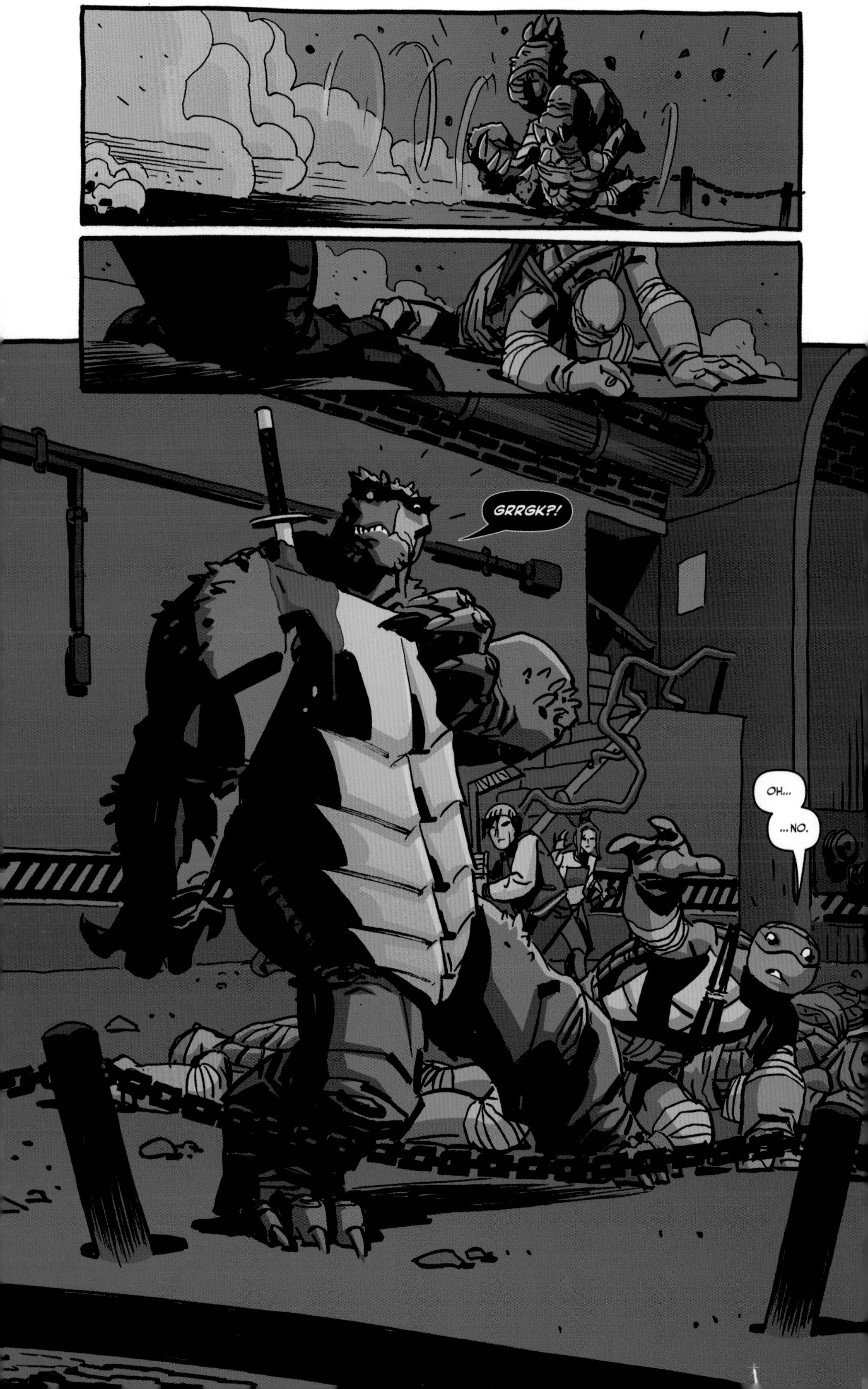
GRRGK?!
OH...
...NO.

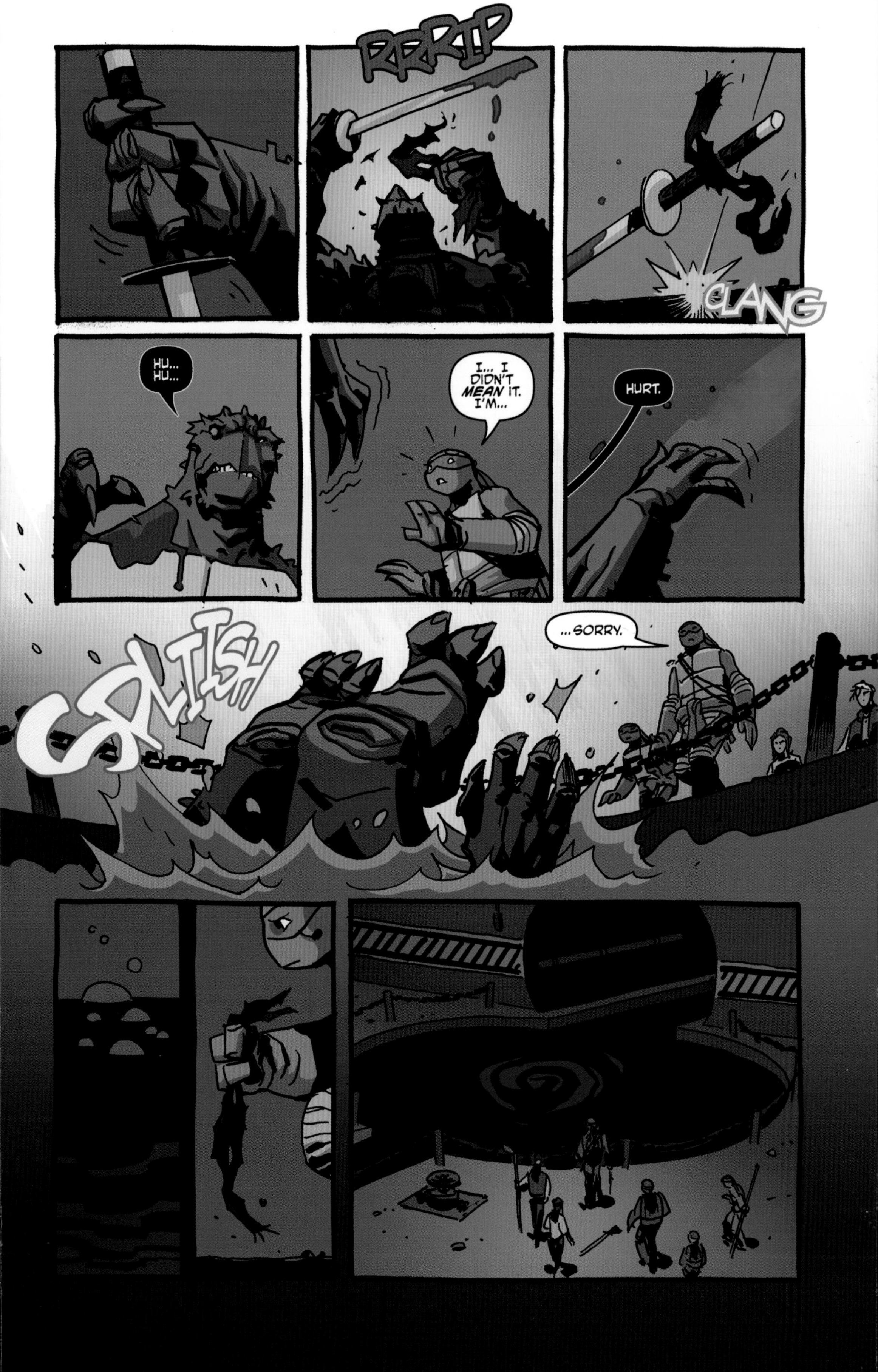
RRRIP
CLANG
HU... HU...
I... I DIDN'T MEAN IT. I'M...
HURT.
SPLISH
...SORRY.

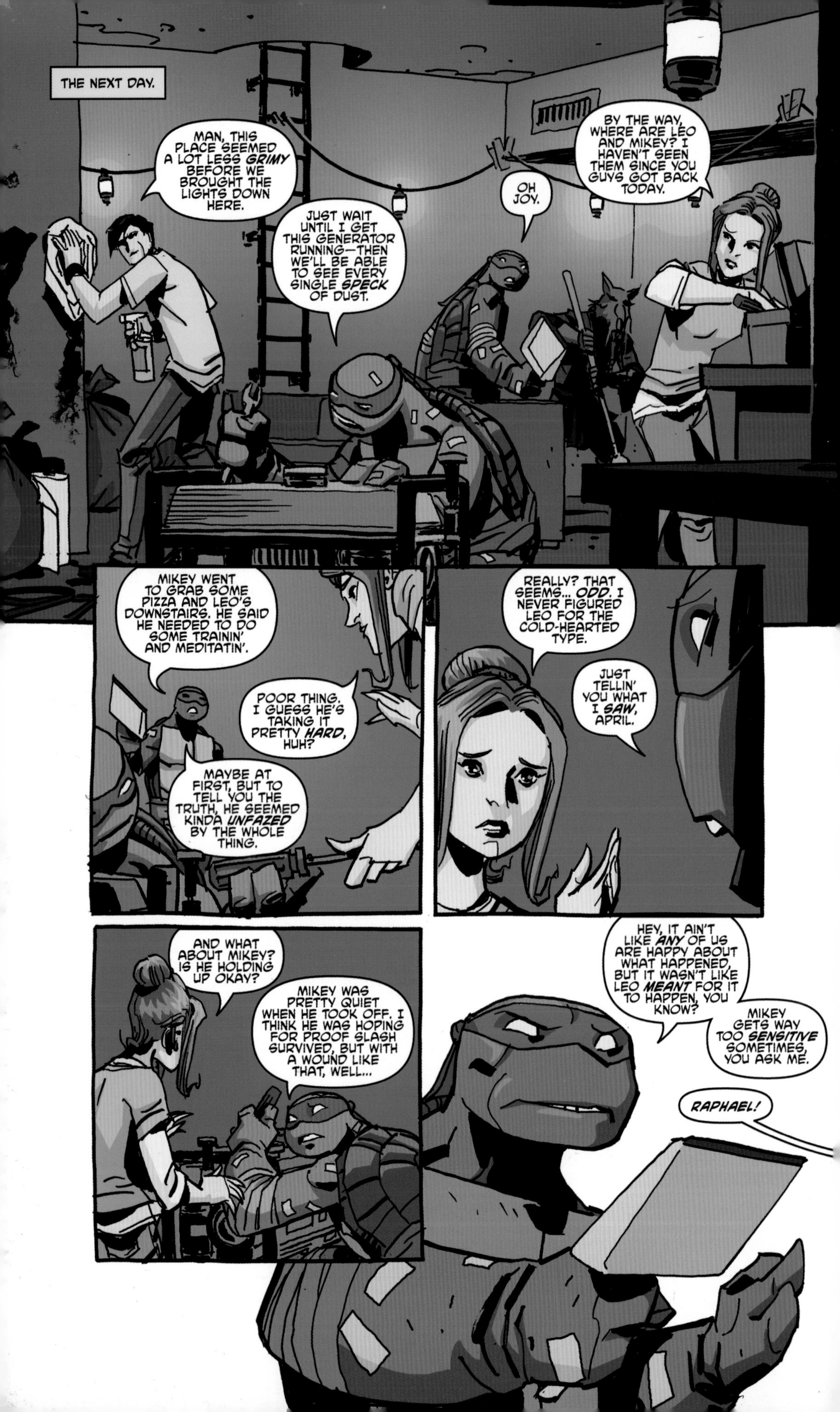
THE NEXT DAY.
MAN, THIS PLACE SEEMED A LOT LESS GRIMY BEFORE WE BROUGHT THE LIGHTS DOWN HERE.
JUST WAIT UNTIL I GET THIS GENERATOR RUNNING—THEN WE'LL BE ABLE TO SEE EVERY SINGLE SPECK OF DUST.
OH JOY.
BY THE WAY, WHERE ARE LEO AND MIKEY? I HAVEN'T SEEN THEM SINCE YOU GUYS GOT BACK TODAY.
MIKEY WENT TO GRAB SOME PIZZA AND LEO'S DOWNSTAIRS. HE SAID HE NEEDED TO DO SOME TRAININ' AND MEDITATIN'.
POOR THING. I GUESS HE'S TAKING IT PRETTY HARD, HUH?
MAYBE AT FIRST, BUT TO TELL YOU THE TRUTH, HE SEEMED KINDA UNFAZED BY THE WHOLE THING.
REALLY? THAT SEEMS... ODD. I NEVER FIGURED LEO FOR THE COLD-HEARTED TYPE.
JUST TELLIN' YOU WHAT I SAW, APRIL.
AND WHAT ABOUT MIKEY? IS HE HOLDING UP OKAY?
MIKEY WAS PRETTY QUIET WHEN HE TOOK OFF. I THINK HE WAS HOPING FOR PROOF SLASH SURVIVED, BUT WITH A WOUND LIKE THAT, WELL...
HEY, IT AIN'T LIKE ANY OF US ARE HAPPY ABOUT WHAT HAPPENED, BUT IT WASN'T LIKE LEO MEANT FOR IT TO HAPPEN, YOU KNOW?
MIKEY GETS WAY TOO SENSITIVE SOMETIMES, YOU ASK ME.
RAPHAEL!

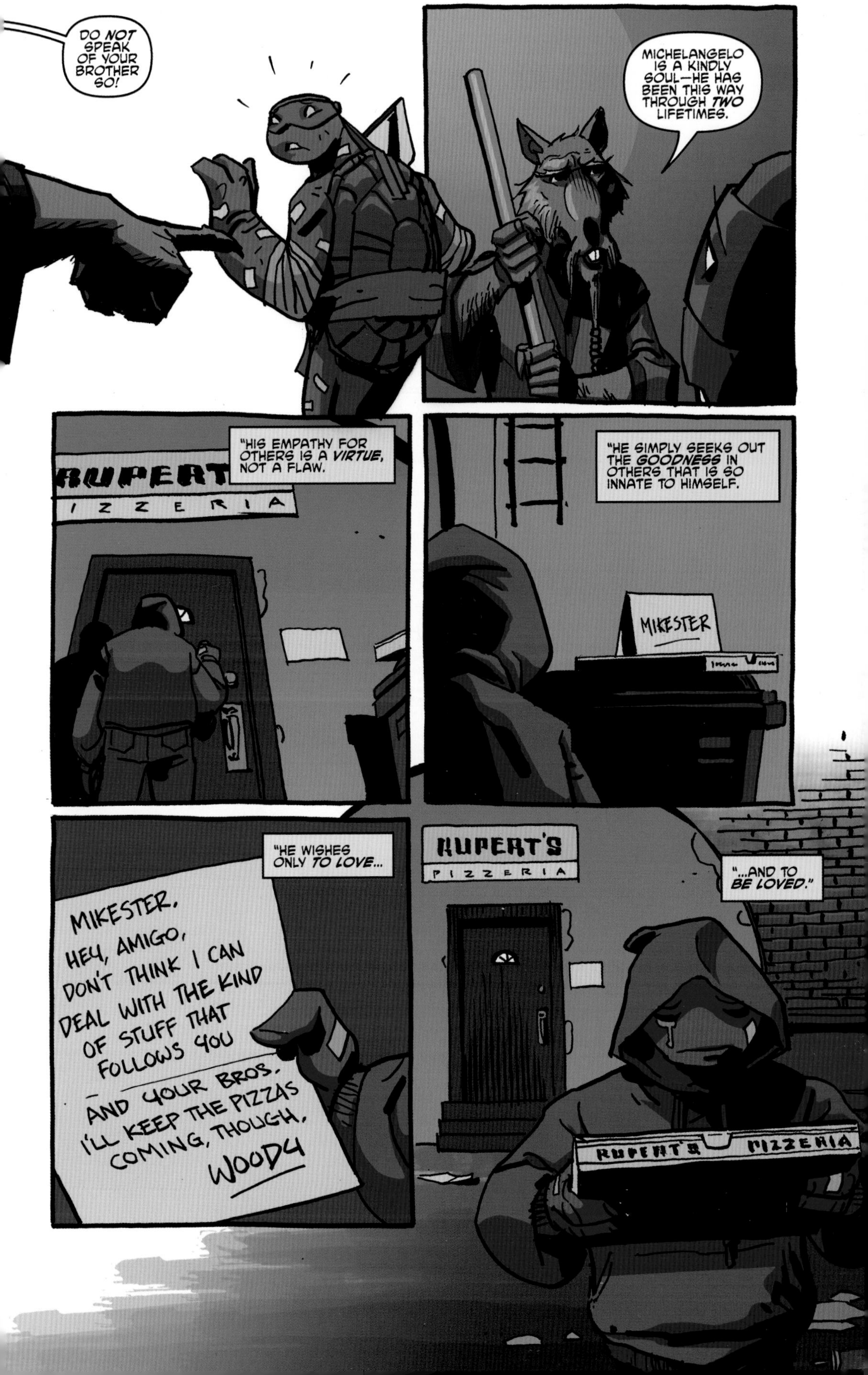
DO NOT SPEAK OF YOUR BROTHER SO!
MICHELANGELO IS A KINDLY SOUL—HE HAS BEEN THIS WAY THROUGH TWO LIFETIMES.
"HIS EMPATHY FOR OTHERS IS A VIRTUE, NOT A FLAW.
RUPERT
PIZZERIA
"HE SIMPLY SEEKS OUT THE GOODNESS IN OTHERS THAT IS SO INNATE TO HIMSELF.
MIKESTER
"HE WISHES ONLY TO LOVE...
MIKESTER.
HEY, AMIGO,
DON'T THINK I CAN DEAL WITH THE KIND OF STUFF THAT FOLLOWS YOU
—AND YOUR BROS.
I'LL KEEP THE PIZZAS COMING, THOUGH.
WOODY
RUPERT'S
PIZZERIA
"...AND TO BE LOVED."
RUPERT'S PIZZERIA

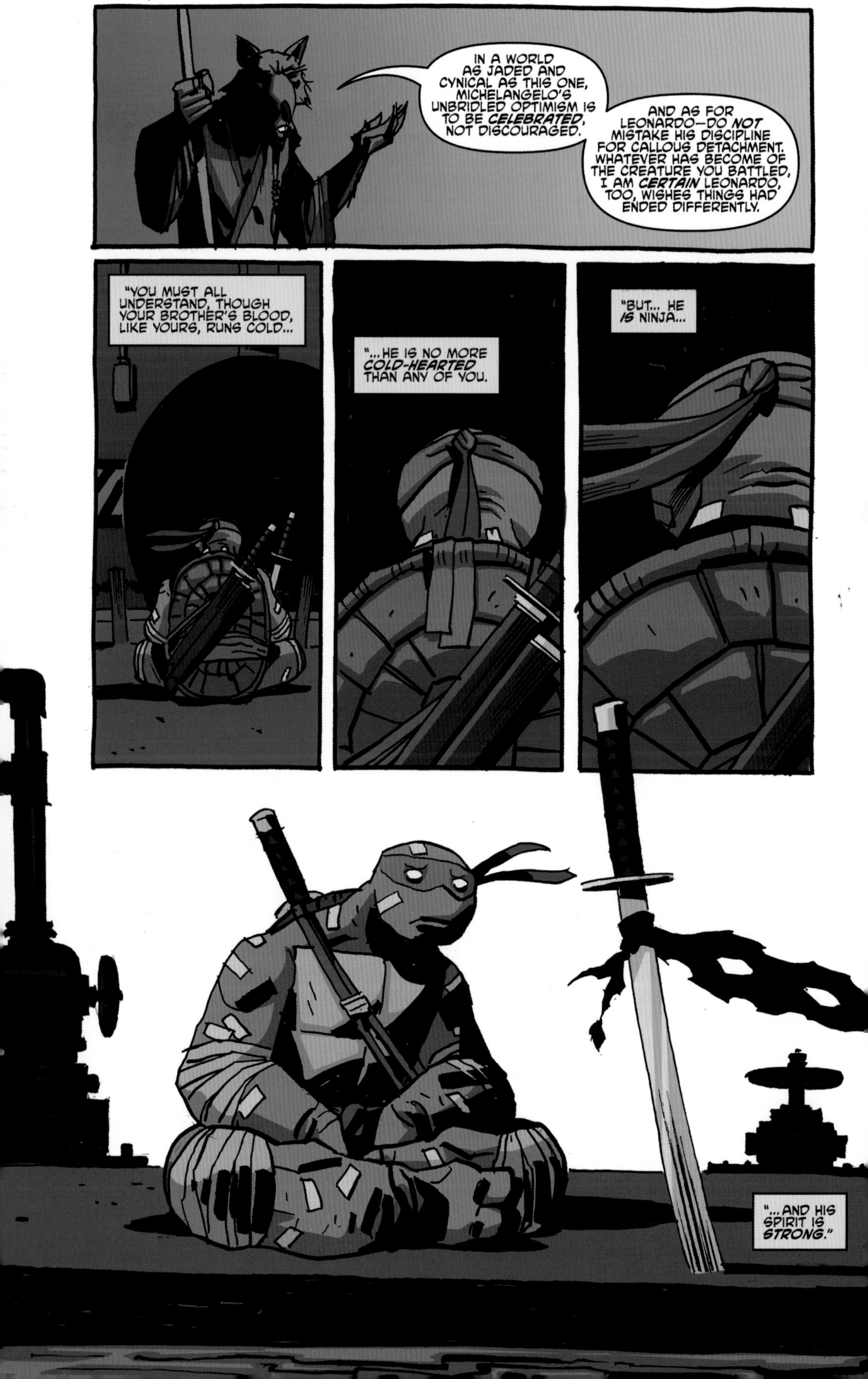

IN A WORLD AS JADED AND CYNICAL AS THIS ONE, MICHELANGELO'S UNBRIDLED OPTIMISM IS TO BE *CELEBRATED*, NOT DISCOURAGED.
AND AS FOR LEONARDO—DO *NOT* MISTAKE HIS DISCIPLINE FOR CALLOUS DETACHMENT. WHATEVER HAS BECOME OF THE CREATURE YOU BATTLED, I AM *CERTAIN* LEONARDO, TOO, WISHES THINGS HAD ENDED DIFFERENTLY.
"YOU MUST ALL UNDERSTAND, THOUGH YOUR BROTHER'S BLOOD, LIKE YOURS, RUNS COLD...
"...HE IS NO MORE *COLD-HEARTED* THAN ANY OF YOU.
"BUT... HE *IS* NINJA...
"...AND HIS SPIRIT IS *STRONG*."

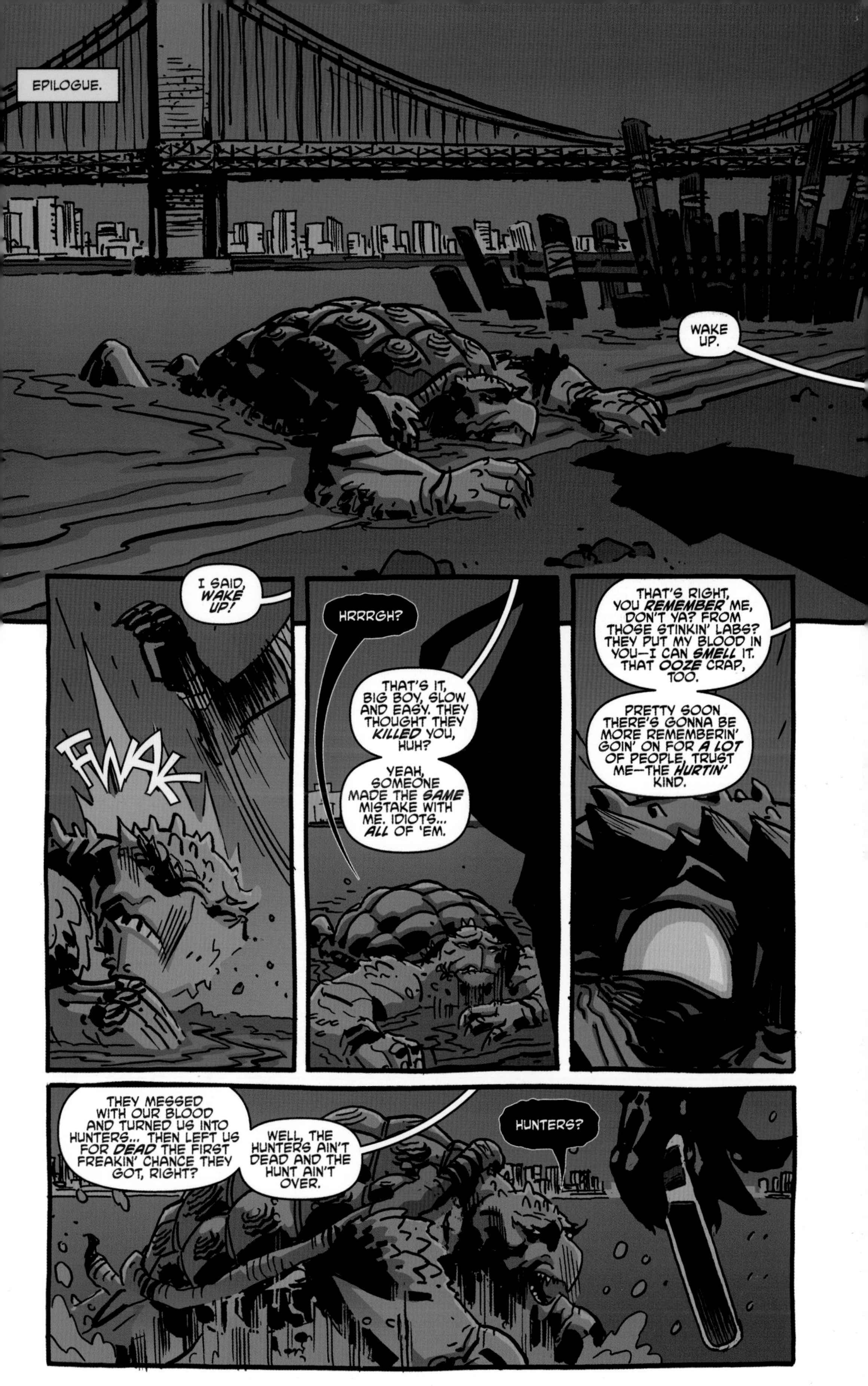
EPILOGUE.
WAKE UP.
I SAID, WAKE UP!
FWAK
HRRRGH?
THAT'S IT, BIG BOY, SLOW AND EASY. THEY THOUGHT THEY KILLED YOU, HUH?
YEAH, SOMEONE MADE THE SAME MISTAKE WITH ME. IDIOTS... ALL OF 'EM.
THAT'S RIGHT, YOU REMEMBER ME, DON'T YA? FROM THOSE STINKIN' LABS? THEY PUT MY BLOOD IN YOU—I CAN SMELL IT. THAT OOZE CRAP, TOO.
PRETTY SOON THERE'S GONNA BE MORE REMEMBERIN' GOIN' ON FOR A LOT OF PEOPLE, TRUST ME—THE HURTIN' KIND.
THEY MESSED WITH OUR BLOOD AND TURNED US INTO HUNTERS... THEN LEFT US FOR DEAD THE FIRST FREAKIN' CHANCE THEY GOT, RIGHT?
HUNTERS?
WELL, THE HUNTERS AIN'T DEAD AND THE HUNT AIN'T OVER.

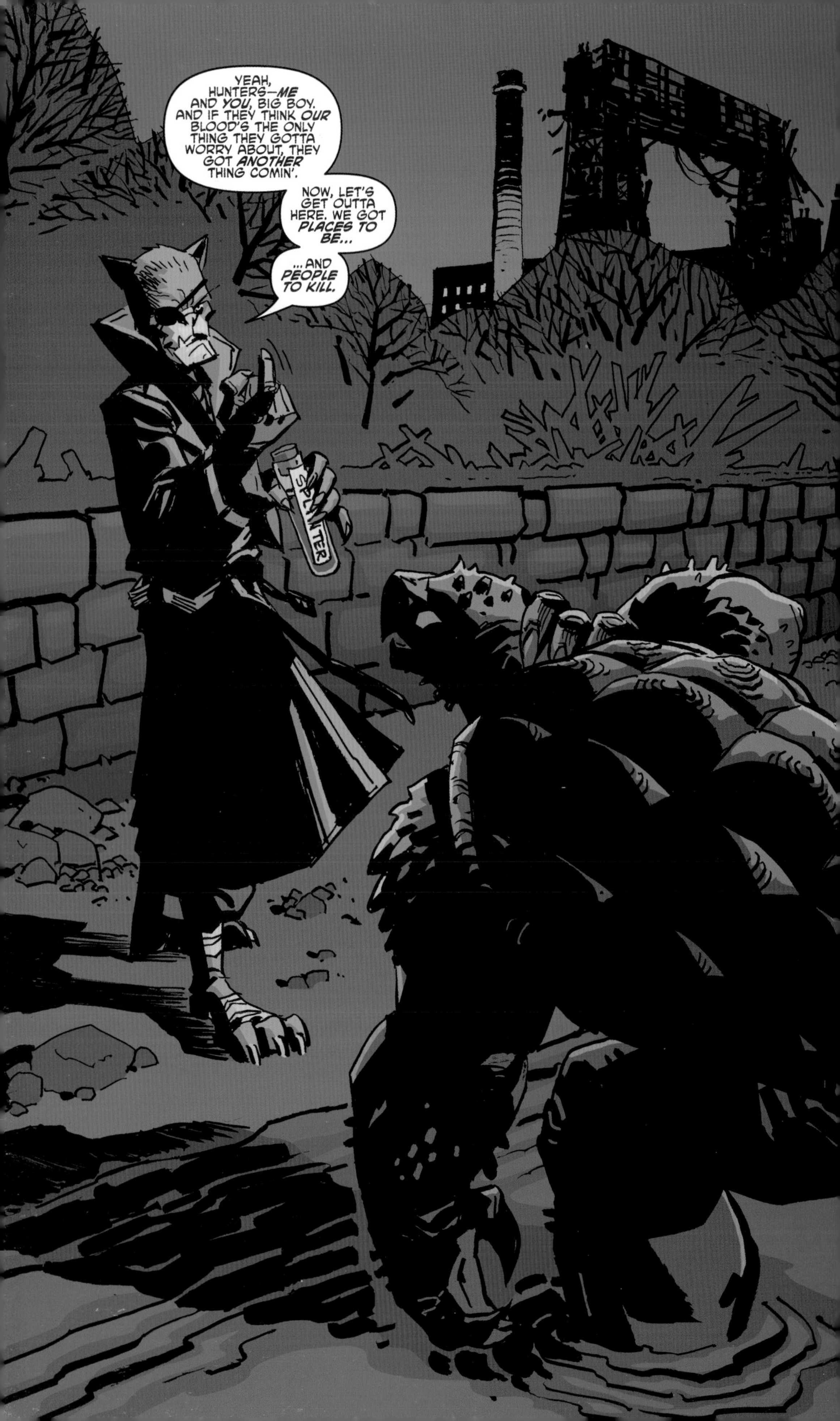
YEAH, HUNTERS—ME AND YOU, BIG BOY. AND IF THEY THINK OUR BLOOD'S THE ONLY THING THEY GOTTA WORRY ABOUT, THEY GOT ANOTHER THING COMIN'.
NOW, LET'S GET OUTTA HERE. WE GOT PLACES TO BE...
...AND PEOPLE TO KILL.
SPLINTER

ART GALLERY

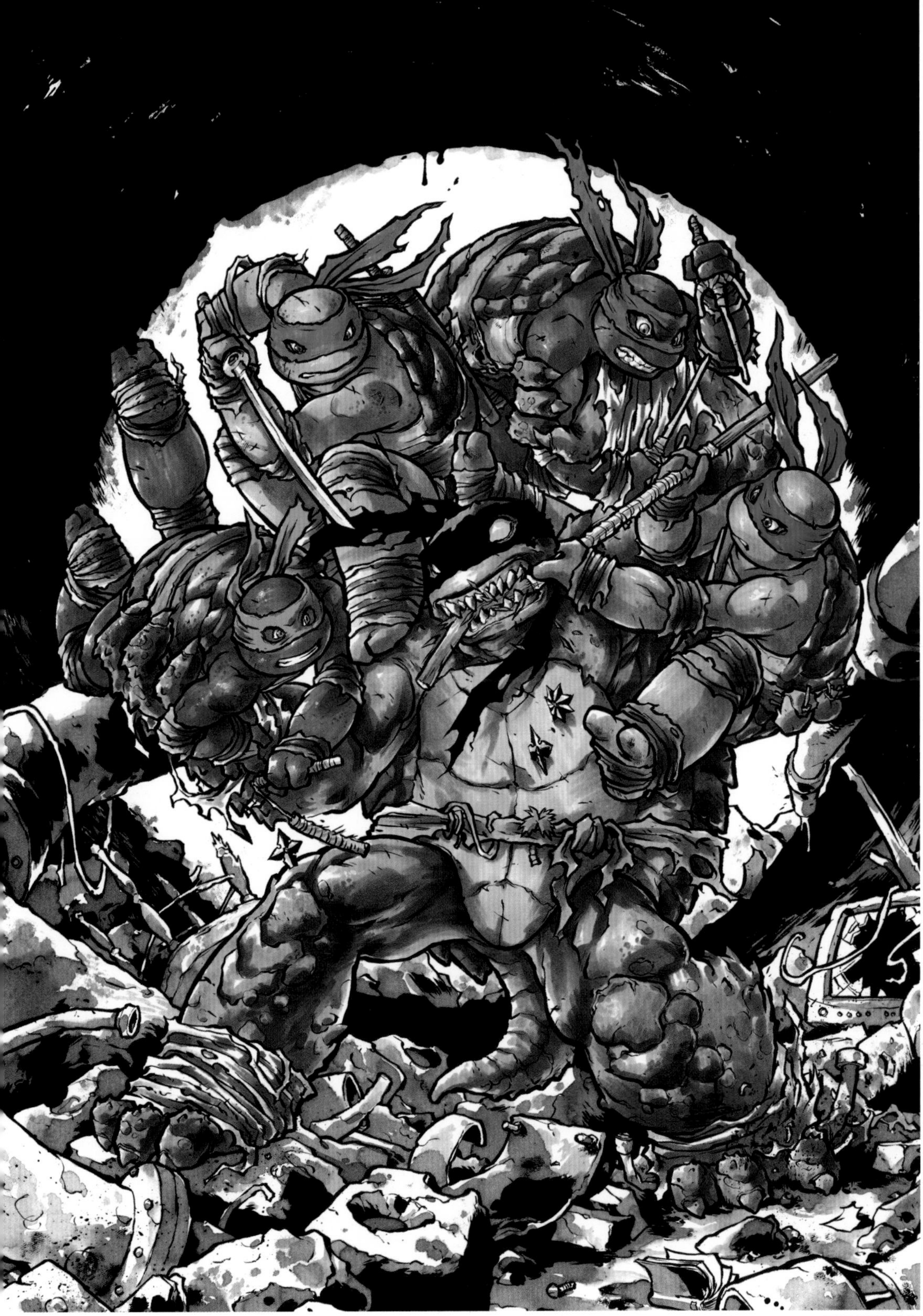

ART BY ROSS CAMPBELL

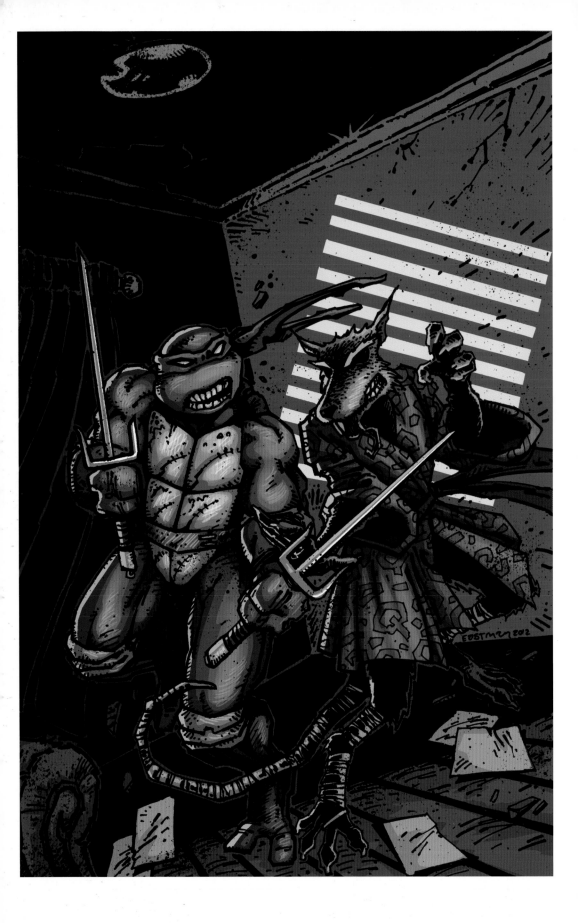

THIS PAGE AND OPPOSITE PAGE: ART BY KEVIN EASTMAN · COLORS BY RONDA PATTISON

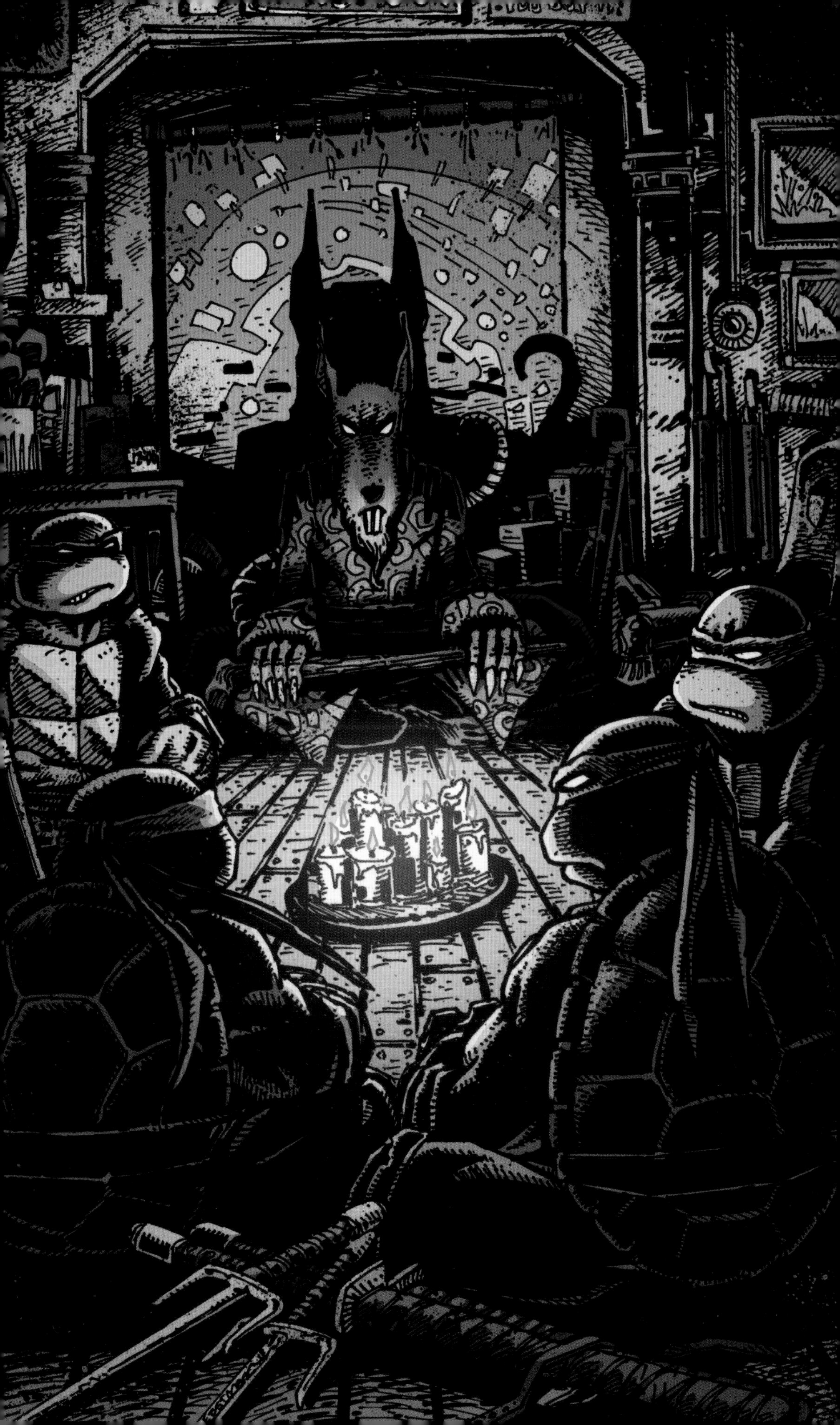

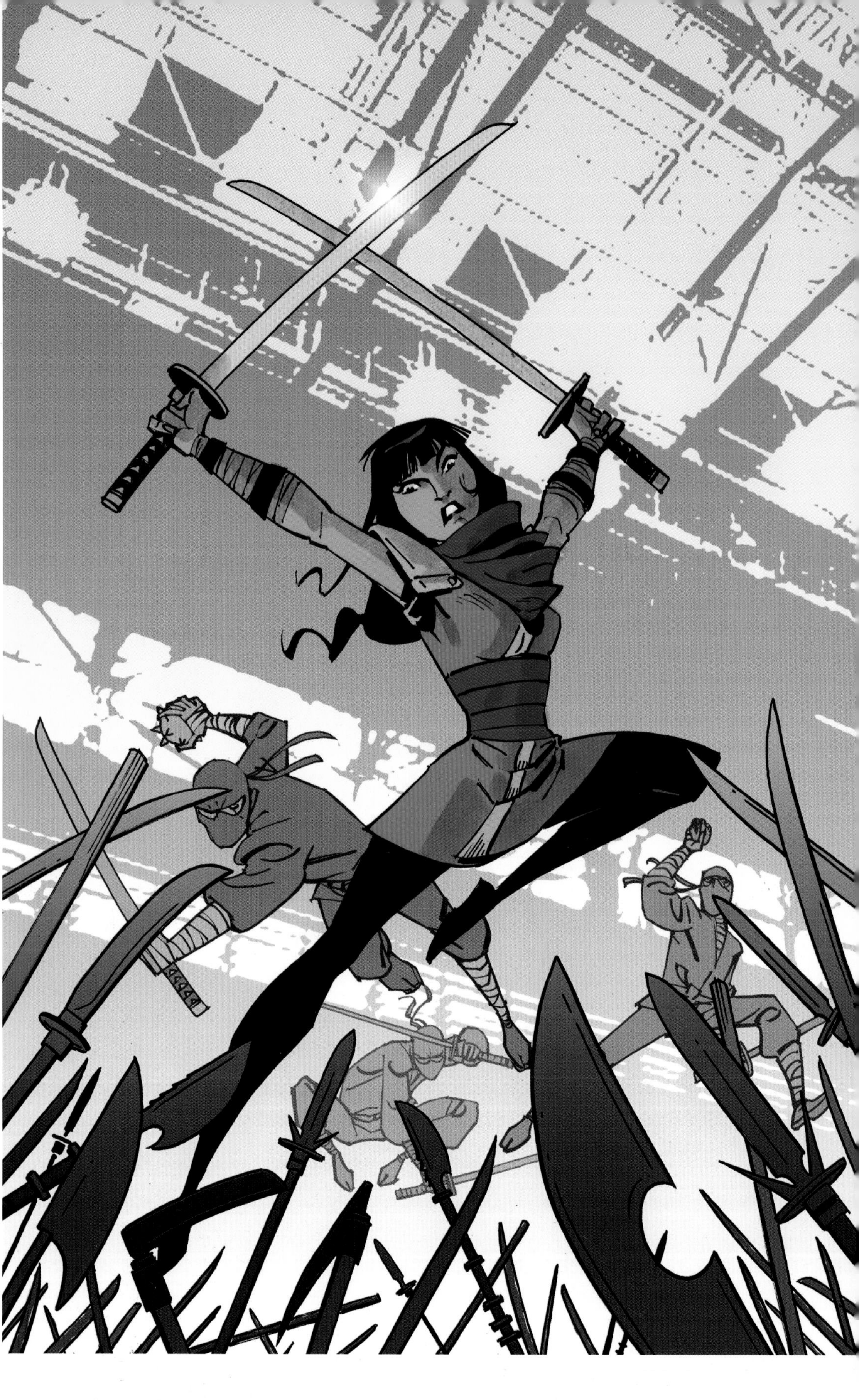

THIS PAGE AND OPPOSITE PAGE: ART BY ANDY KUHN

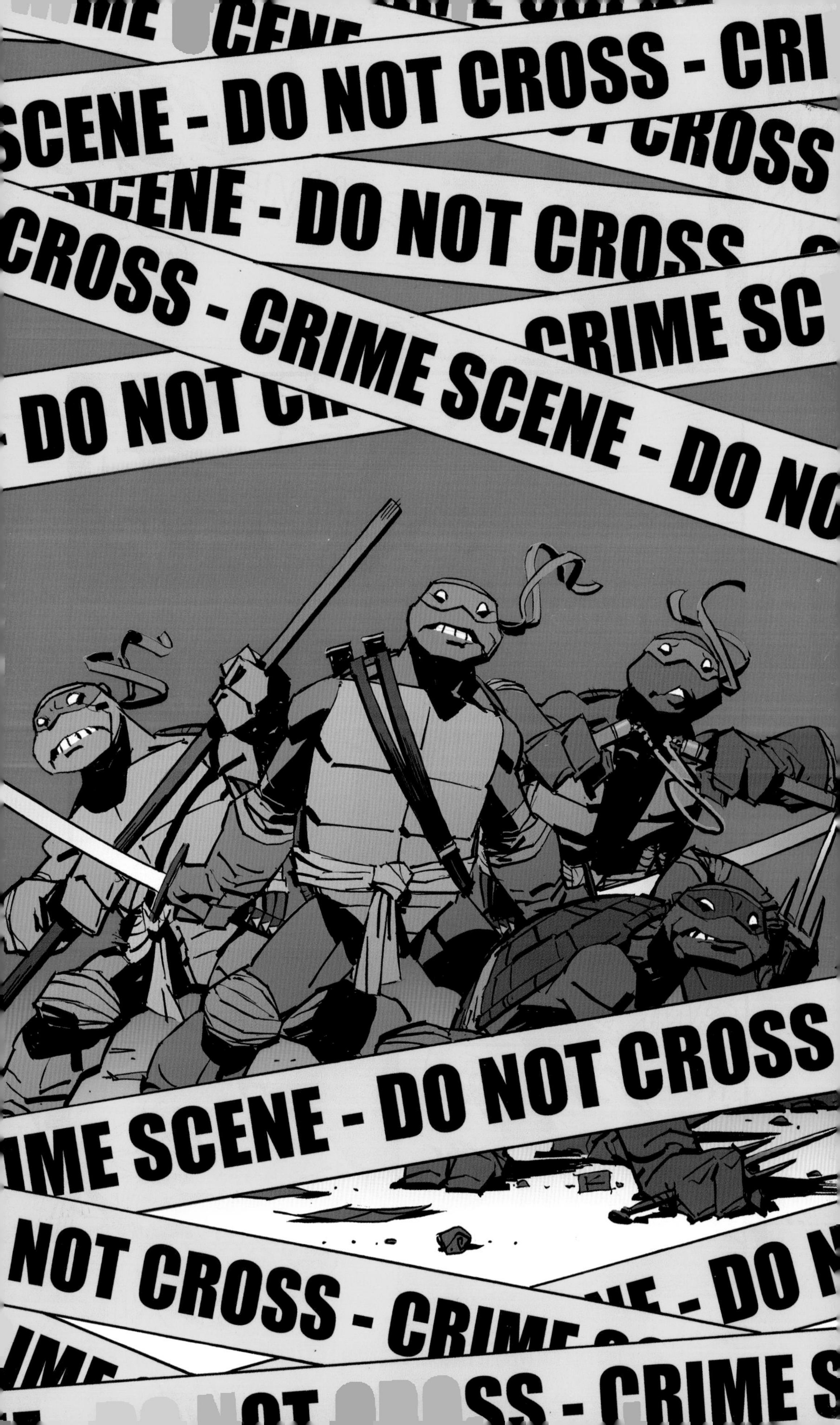
SCENE - DO NOT CROSS - CRI
CENE - DO NOT CROSS
CROSS - CRIME SCENE - DO NO
CRIME SC
- DO NOT
IME SCENE - DO NOT CROSS
NOT CROSS - CRIME
- DO
SS - CRIME

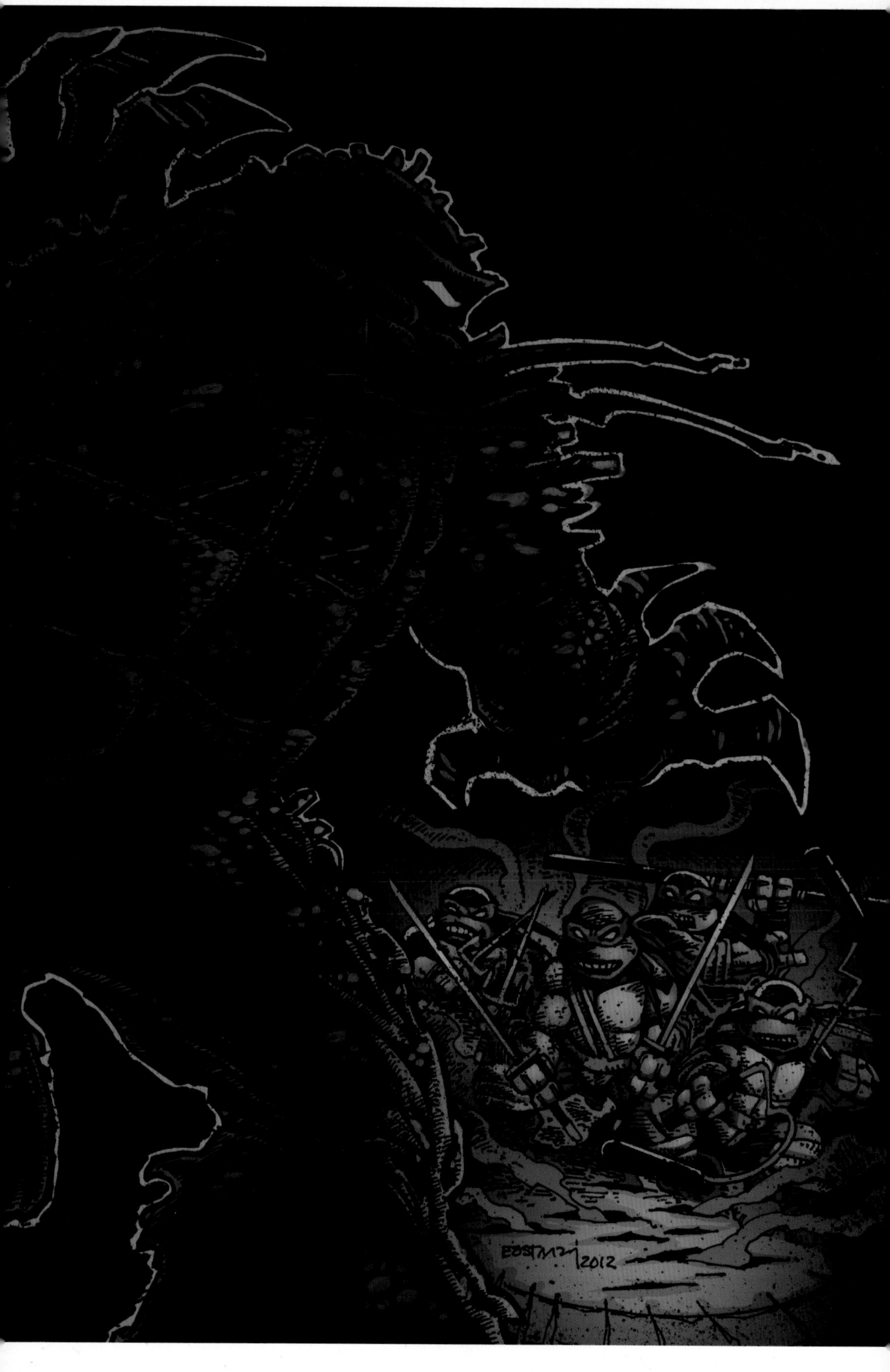
EASTMAN 2012

THIS PAGE AND OPPOSITE PAGE: ART BY KEVIN EASTMAN · COLORS BY RONDA PATTISON

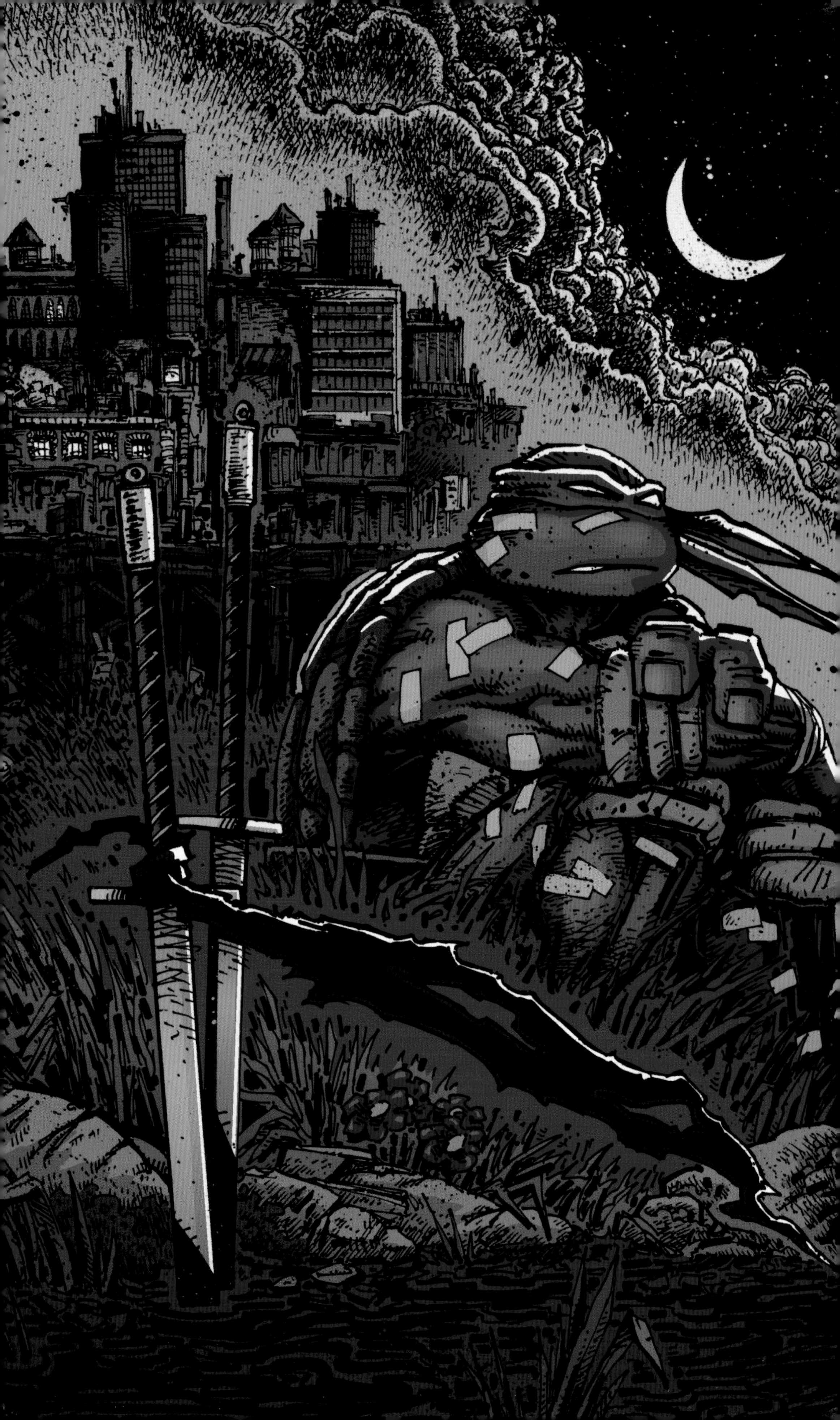

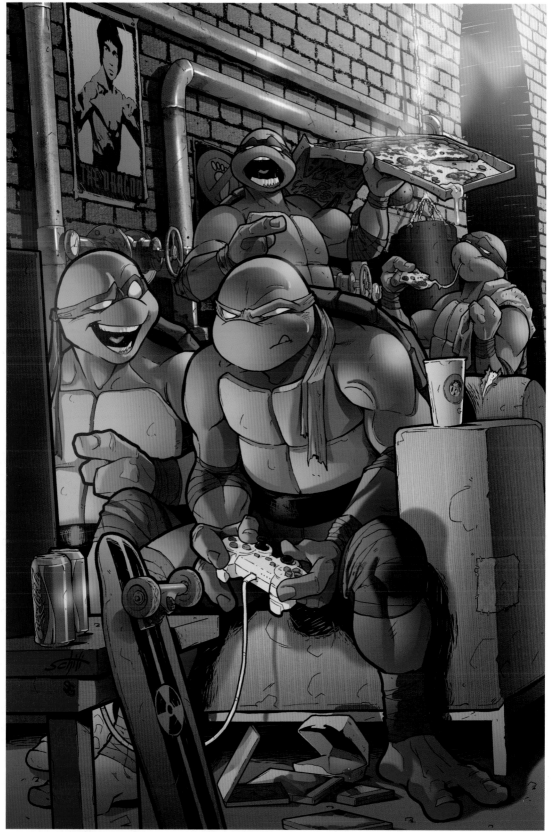

ART BY VALERIO SCHITI · COLORS BY CLAUDIA SGC

OPPOSITE PAGE: ART BY RAMÓN PÉREZ · COLORS BY IAN HERRING

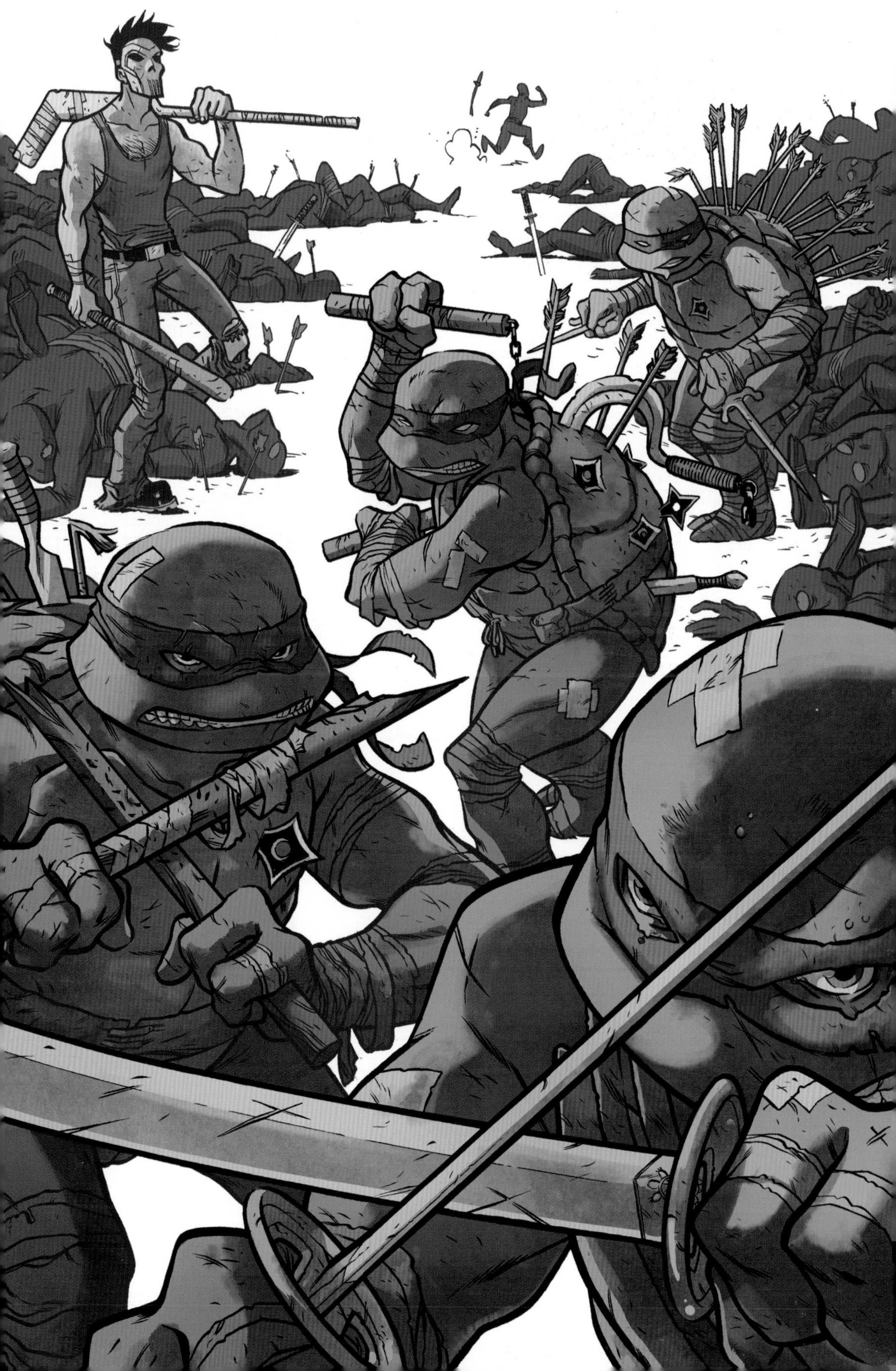

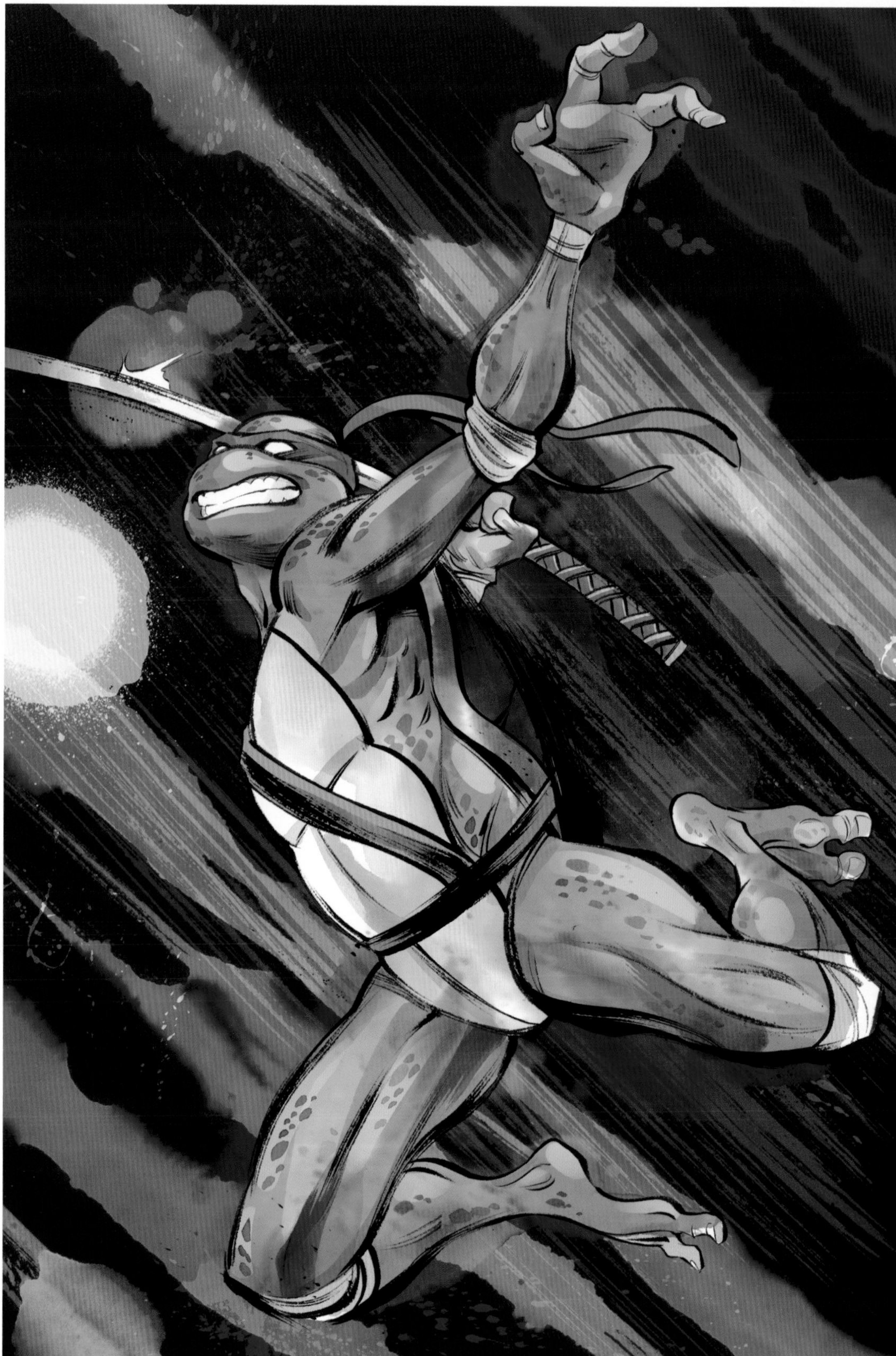

ART BY KAGAN MCLEOD

OPPOSITE PAGE: ART BY ANDY KUHN

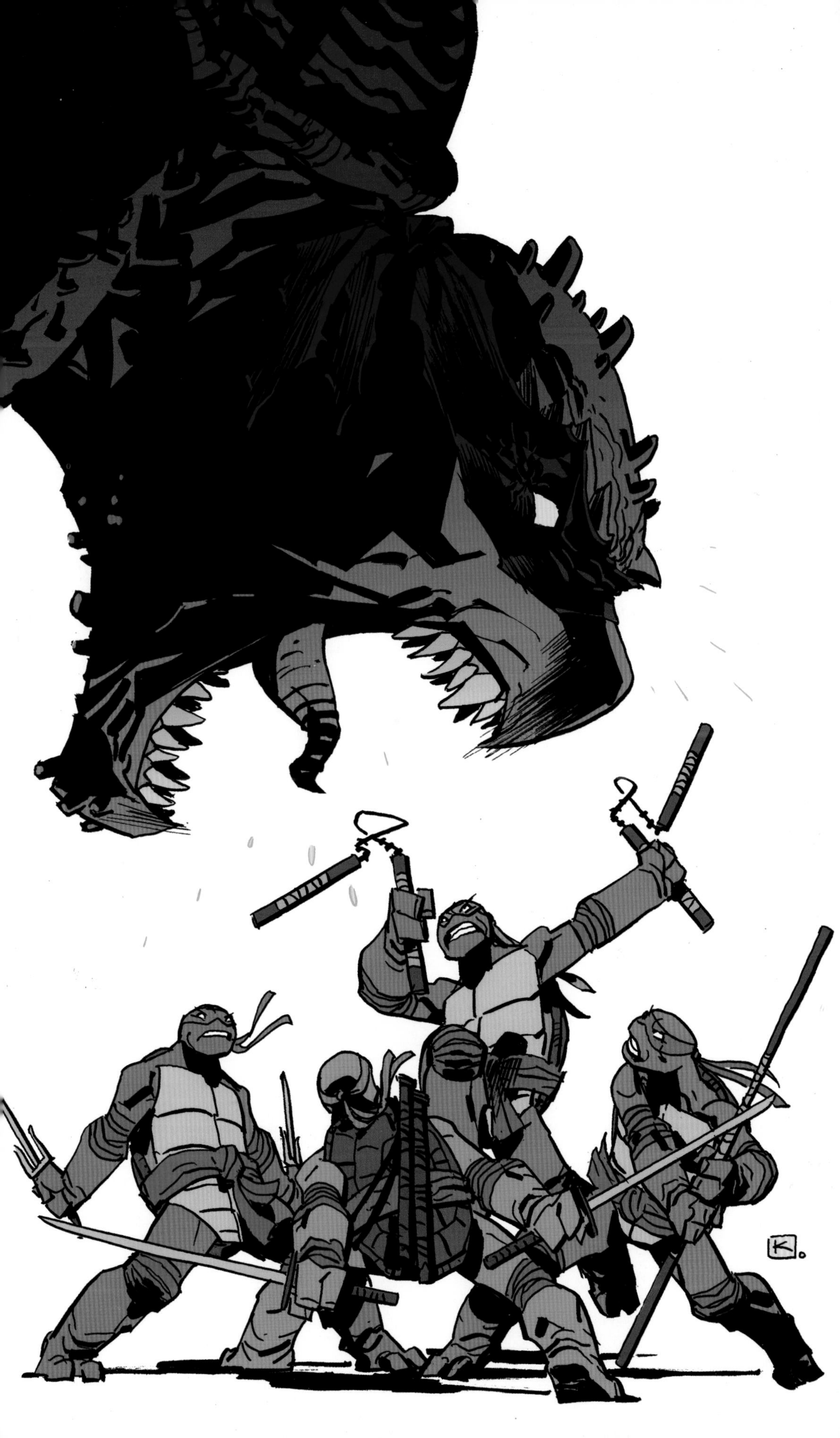

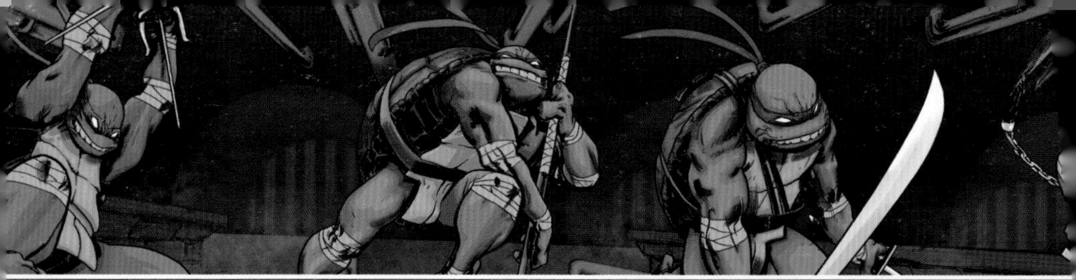

TEENAGE MUTANT NINJA TURTLES

MORE TURTLE ACTION

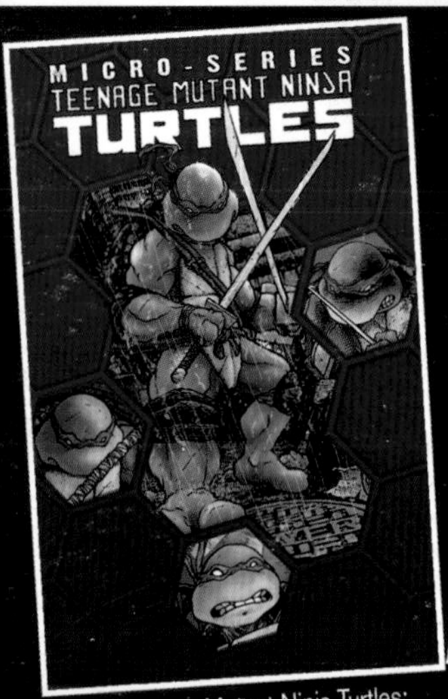
MICRO-SERIES
TEENAGE MUTANT NINJA
TURTLES

Teenage Mutant Ninja Turtles:
Micro-Series, Vol. 1
ISBN: 978-1-61377-232-4

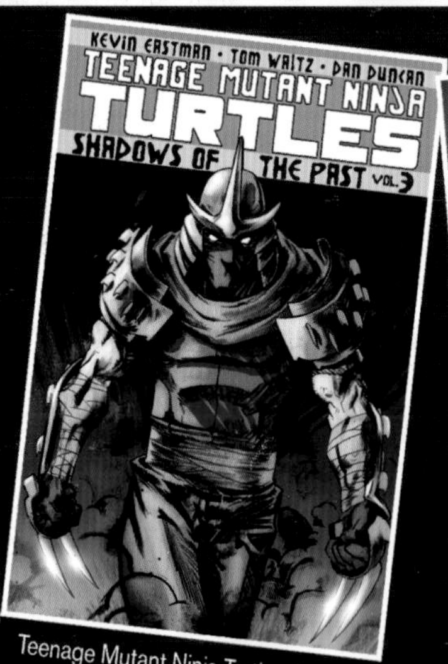
KEVIN EASTMAN • TOM WAITZ • DAN DUNCAN
TEENAGE MUTANT NINJA
TURTLES
SHADOWS OF THE PAST VOL.3

Teenage Mutant Ninja Turtles, Vol. 3:
Shadows of the Past
ISBN: 978-1-61377-405-2

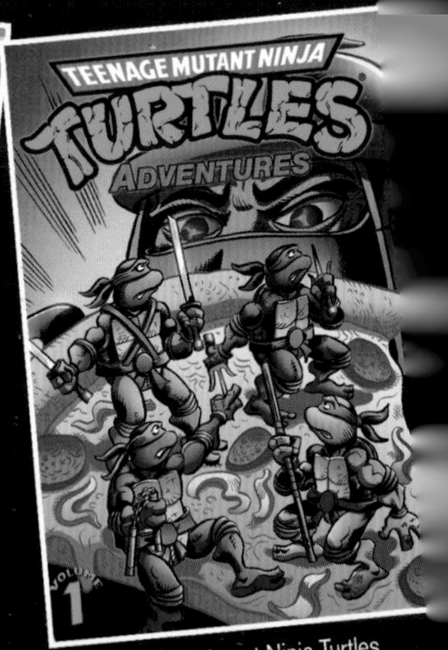
TEENAGE MUTANT NINJA
TURTLES
ADVENTURES

Teenage Mutant Ninja Turtles
Adventures, Vol. 1
ISBN: 978-161377-289-8

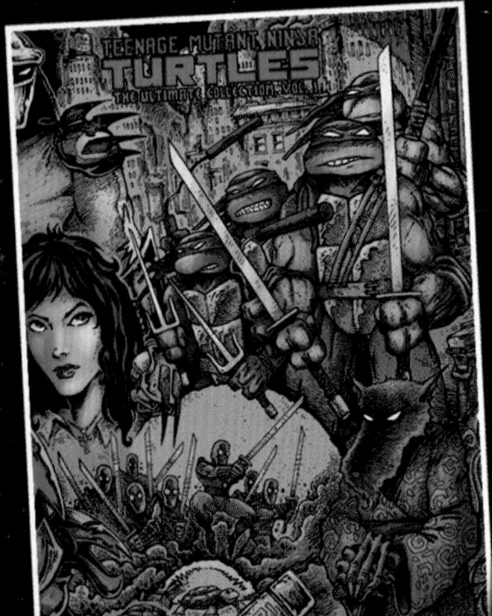
TEENAGE MUTANT NINJA
TURTLES

Teenage Mutant Ninja Turtles:
The Ultimate Collection, Vol. 1
ISBN: 978-1-61377-007-8

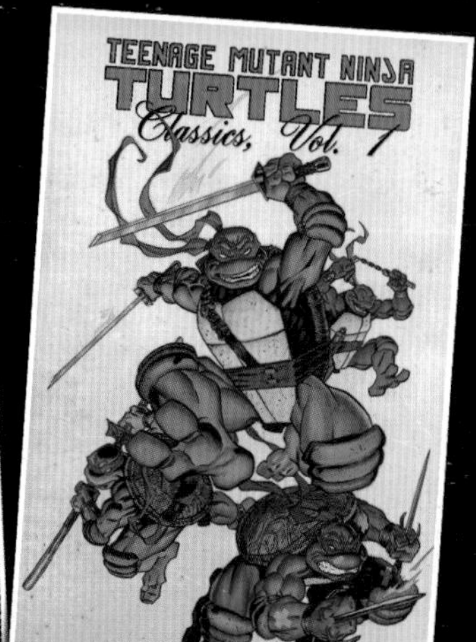
TEENAGE MUTANT NINJA
TURTLES
Classics, Vol. 1

Teenage Mutant Ninja Turtles
Classics, Vol. 1
ISBN: 978-1-61377-234-8

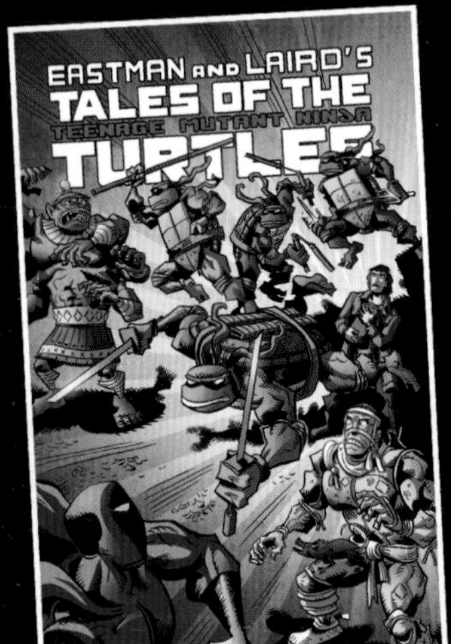
EASTMAN AND LAIRD'S
TALES OF THE
TEENAGE MUTANT NINJA
TURTLES

Tales of the Teenage Mutant
Ninja Turtles, Vol. 1
ISBN: 978-1-61377-416-8

ON SALE NOW

www.idwpublishing.com

IDW